GOD'S HEALING HANDS
VOLUME 1

Allow God to "Reshape your Soul"

Michael Barbarulo

O LORD, you are our Father.
We are the clay, and you are the potter.
We all are formed by your hand. (Isaiah 64:8)

Devotional Workbook

A Resource for Individuals, Groups and Discipleship Programs

Second Edition

W & B Publishers

For information:
W & B Publishers
Post Office Box 193
Colfax, NC 27235
www.a-argusbooks.com

ISBN: 978-0-6156012-0-5

Edited by Elizabeth Chamberlain
HarmonyEditors@gmail.com

Book Cover Design by Maria Marotta

Introduction

My experience in God's Reshaping Process

As a Christian, and a therapist, I became curious as to why so many Christians live in bondage and stop growing spiritually and emotionally. I didn't understand why they weren't living victorious Christian lives. A big part of my curiosity and passion to answer this question was due to the fact that I too, had found myself stuck in my walk and relationship with God. I wasn't growing in character or conforming to the image of Christ as I was supposed to, and I definitely wasn't living a victorious Christian life. Although I felt forgiven and an inner sense of peace, I also still felt anger, abandonment, shame and detachment. I was still shattered inside. As I examined my own walk with Christ I began to realize that I was stuck in the sanctification process because I wasn't going deep with God. As a result, my spiritual and emotional growth came to a halt about ten months into it. I wasn't changing internally because I was only seeking surface level truth about God and myself.

As I started to dig into God's Word and other resources, God showed me that at the time of my salvation He started in me the process of restoration, redemption, reconciliation and transformation, and through the Holy Spirit I will be molded into the image of His Son [and share inwardly His likeness] (Rom. 8:29, AMP). This is when it became clear to me that I needed to do more than confess my sin. I needed to repent and surrender my character (flaws and defects), personality, brokenness, immaturities, and bad habits to God. I needed to submit to the Holy Spirit and get on, or stay on, the 'potter's wheel'. (Isaiah 64:8) One of the biggest reasons I wasn't experiencing any change is that I kept getting off the potter's wheel. I didn't like what the Holy Spirit wanted to do within my soul. I fell into Satan's lies and deception, thinking I wasn't ready. The Holy Spirit was convicting me to confess and renounce certain sins and bad habits, and I ignored Him. Because of my fears about change, as well as my rebellion, I wasn't receiving the healing and growth God wanted for me. It was at this point that I realized the only way out, was through. I had to allow God to reshape my soul and take me through the mess had I made of my life.

Bind up the brokenhearted

Our Father wants us to grow spiritually and heal emotionally. He wants to strengthen our character, refine our personalities, meet our unmet needs, help us with the unfinished business of the past, and heal the hurts that occurred before we received His Son, so that we can become oaks of righteousness. (Isaiah 61:1-4)

As believers, we need to realize that when we accepted Jesus into our life, our spirit became united with God but our old nature (the soul: mind, will, emotions) remains. I've come to realize that this is where the pruning - or healing - process begins. (Isaiah 64:8, John 15:1-8) God, our Father, will fill and heal any voids we experienced in our childhood; with His love, grace and truth, He will remove the need for any sin or idol we used to feel loved, needed, accepted, significant, secure and in control (Hebrews 10:14). As I grow in Christ I'm realizing more and more that "Abba Father" not only wants me to "…go and sin no more…" (John 8:1-8) but He also wants to meet my spiritual, emotional and relational needs. (1 Peter 4:10) We need to remind ourselves that the process of sanctification requires us to have a collaborative relationship with God. (Phil 1:6; Matt 6:9-13; Matt 5:3-12; Rom. 12:1-3)

Designed for Dependency: The Sanctification Process

Our Father designed us to be dependent on Him. He created us to love only Him, to serve Him, to glorify Him, and to be blessed with an abundant, satisfying life. When I received Jesus as my Savior, God became my Father and I became His child. As God's child I needed, and need, to be re-parented (daily). I'm not saying my parents failed me, what I am saying is that I had, and have, to take redemptive time to line up what I was taught (my beliefs about the world, others, myself and my values) with God's Word. I needed God's help to identify and expose the root causes of my dysfunctional attitudes and behaviors, because I was just trying to fix my symptoms. I was looking for quick fixes for my sin, pain and bad habits. Through God's spirit I realized that my issues and immaturities stemmed from unmet developmental needs in my childhood.

I believe children are Satan's main focus of destruction and lies. (John 10:10) They are innocent and lack the ability to defend themselves, especially in the formative years. Children don't know right from wrong. They depend on their parents or caretakers to teach them about themselves, the world and people.

Satan attacks children through their parents, and the weapons that are formed against them are abuse, neglect, poor values, ungodly belief systems and unhealthy views of God. Many parents are completely separated from God.

Children that are abused physically, sexually, verbally and emotionally are *severely wounded and damaged* both spiritually and psychologically. Even after the abuse stops, the haunting memories linger on. When a person is neglected or abused early in life they become emotionally stuck at the age they were abused or mistreated. Satan's goal is to create generational havoc in families. (Exodus 34:7) He hates God so he attacks His children. (John 10:1-14)

Children don't have the maturity or ability to process the abuse (especially at a young age) so they blame themselves for it. This is exactly what Satan wants – deception – and to shackle them in shame. Satan wants to distort God's truth so that each generation will be affected and ruined.

I believe that "Abba Father" is continuing to heal me spiritually and emotionally by taking me through the developmental stages while pruning my character. Paul said, *"When I was a child, I spoke and felt like a child, thought like a child, and reasoned like a child. When I became an adult, I no longer used childish ways. [12]Now we see a blurred image in a mirror. Then we will see very clearly. Now my knowledge is incomplete. Then I will have complete knowledge as God has complete knowledge of me."* (1 Cor. 13:11-12 God's Word translation, PH). Paul is describing the sanctification process. I can totally relate to Paul because when I received Christ I was chronologically twenty six years old, but still acting like a child in so many ways and areas in my life. To be honest with you, I still do (at times) at age forty three. Here's a confession for you:

Childlike attitudes and behaviors that God had to change in my soul:

- I feared commitment and intimacy
- I was detached and isolated from people because I didn't allow myself to rely and depend on people. I was very self-sufficient. I had push-pull relationships
- I had, and at times still have, problems with trust
- I had trouble acknowledging my needs
- I had trouble expressing my feelings (both negative and positive) and ideas
- I feared rejection and disapproval
- I was very punitive
- I struggled with failure
- I had, and still have, a hard time setting limits with myself and others
- I feared social settings and gatherings because I was very self-conscious about my physical appearance. I felt socially inadequate
- I ran away from loss and struggled with facing reality. I used alcohol and self-destructive behaviors to avoid my pain and fears
- I lacked conviction and morals
- I had trouble setting goals for my life and had a hard time finishing things
- I was very rebellious. Some people have a problem being assertive, but I had a problem with aggression and rage
- I lacked character and still do in some ways. **For example**: I couldn't admit that I was wrong; I had a hard time forgiving others (I still struggle at times); I had, and still sometimes have, an inability to receive constructive criticism or deal with reality when confronted with it; managing particular emotions like anger and sensuality; I lacked empathy for others
- I felt like a victim of life's circumstances

- •I didn't like the word "No" (I still don't-but God's grace helps me)
- •Some people have trouble taking responsibility for someone else's life; I could care less because it was all about me.
- •Honesty was optional
- •Others are easily manipulated, I was the controller
- •Fear being controlled

God is re-parenting us, or should I say <u>sanctifying</u> us

I think the development of my character and knowing who I am in Christ determines my success in my relationship with God, relationships with others, (Matt. 22:37-39) and my future (professionally). I believe God uses the sanctification process to develop our character, to heal childhood wounds (that can cause us to get stuck in the developmental stages) and losses we incurred along the way. We can connect a lot of our immaturities, habitual sins, bad habits, character issues and brokenness to generational habits, generational curses and family upbringing.

Based on my personal and professional experience, I believe God re-parents (sanctifies) us by healing our mind, will and emotions. He does this by restoring and reconciling the voids we experienced in our childhood development, adolescent development and adult development. (Isaiah 61:1-4; Jeremiah 29:11-14) As I said before, a lot of my adulthood problems and issues were connected to sin, family of origin issues, and my lack of character, as well as being under-developed both emotionally and spiritually. As I grew closer to God He gave me the wisdom and skills I needed to grow up. When I invited the Holy Spirit into the secrets of my soul, I finally started to become whole.

God is your Daddy (Abba) and He will:

1. Show you your true purpose and potential
2. Teach you how to learn from your mistakes and how to fail forward
3. Teach you to receive love instead of hiding from it
4. Teach you how to work through your negative emotions and, most importantly, be aware of them
5. Teach you how to communicate in love, grace and truth
6. Teach you how to work through temptation and how to delay self-gratification
7. Teach you how to make healthy choices and decisions
8. Teach you how to love Him, others and yourself
9. Teach you how to build strong emotional attachments
10. Teach you how to develop an identity based on who you are in Christ which allows you to establish autonomy and separateness.

The Purpose of this book

This book was born out of my passion to help people grow in Christ, my 17 year relationship with Jesus, my 12 years of experience with overseeing a men's discipleship program at a homeless shelter, my 12 years of being in Christian counseling private practice, and my 19 years of clinical experience working with adults and adolescents who struggle with addictions, depression, anxiety disorders, personality disorders, anger and rage issues, developmental issues, and those who have been abused sexually, spiritually, physically, verbally and emotionally.

In my experience working with Christians, many of those that see me for discipleship counseling struggle to apply the truth of who they are in Christ to their lives and relationships, and forget the fact that their minds aren't automatically renewed when they are born again. (John 3:1-3; Eph. 4:20-24) Many of us come from broken homes and dysfunctional families (substance abuse, neglect, emotional issues and compulsive behaviors). I've written this book to help you heal from your past by showing you who God the Father is, to clear away any distorted images you might have of Him, and show you how to walk in the victory that has already been won for you by Jesus.

Despite this victory we have in Christ, we still need to go through the sanctification process. Many of us have to deal with the by-product of our childhoods. Many of us lack the internal abilities and tools we need to manage our emotions, to delay gratification, and to handle loss and adversity. We come to Christ with self-defeating behaviors, immaturities, habitual sin, experiences, memories, wrong patterns of thinking and brokenness, and we've learned unhealthy ways of relating to people. Because of this it's hard to behave like a mature, Christ-like adult.

The Bible says that Jesus went through a growth process and that He grew in stature and wisdom (Luke 2:39-52). One of the main goals of this book is to help you become an adult, child of God. Like Jesus said, "*I tell you the truth, anyone who will not receive the kingdom of God like a little child will never enter it.*" (Mark 10:15) We need to have childlike faith, yet at the same time be spiritually and emotionally mature. This is all part of the sanctification process, or should I say the "pruning process." (John 15:1-9)

My aim is to show you how to "put away childish things" and help you to understand why you think, feel and act like a child at certain times and in certain relationships. (1 Cor. 13:1) Childlike behaviors can be triggered by unmet needs from your childhood, unresolved issues of the past, unhealthy belief and values systems, and the lies of Satan. David Seamands once said, *"Childish things don't simply fall away by themselves as dead leaves fall from a tree. We have to put them away and be finished with childish things."*

Sanctification and Spiritual Warfare

Satan's main goal once we become believers is to distract us from God's truth by finding a way to get us off God's potter's wheel. He doesn't want you or me to get to the root of our sin and dysfunction, because once we see and receive the truth about our self or the situation we will be set free. A key truth to always remember is to *"put on all of God's armor so that you will be able to stand firm against all strategies of the devil. [12] for we are not fighting against flesh-and-blood enemies, but against evil rulers and authorities of the unseen world, against mighty powers in this dark world, and against evil spirits in the heavenly places."* (Eph. 6:11- 12) It's amazing how quickly I grew up once I accepted the truth about myself and Christ.

If Satan is able to deceive us, our sanctification stops and we stop growing in Christ. The Bible says, "For as he thinketh in his heart, so he is." (Prov. 23:7 KJV) Satan's goal is to convince you that you're not free in Christ. This is why we need to confess our sins and believe that our past doesn't determine our future. See, what we need to do is remind Satan of *his* future by rebuking him and claiming the power and authority of Christ in our lives. Our chains of sin and pain are broken and we no longer have to be deprived or robbed of our freedom in Christ because of Satan's temptations, accusations, control or influences. The good news is that when we receive Jesus as our Lord and Savior we are set free from the sins of our forefathers and we can stop the sin and curse(s) from ruining our lives. (Rom. 6:6; Isaiah 61:1-4, Lev. 26:40-42)

God's Healing Hands will:

1. Help you to grow into the image and likeness of Christ (Gal. 4:6)
2. Help you identify and work through any distortions of God you might have as a result of your childhood and/or poor teaching
3. Renew your mind to God's truth
4. Help you sort through faulty beliefs that keep you stuck in habitual sin and immature behaviors and attitudes:
    - Don't talk
    - Don't trust
    - Don't feel
    - I must meet certain standards to feel good about myself
    - Sex is dirty
    - I must make everybody happy to feel good about myself
    - If I fail I'm a failure
    - Performance based love and acceptance
2. Teach you how to love others and yourself unconditionally (Rom. 15:7)
3. Work through the effects of living in a dysfunctional family
    - Parental neglect
    - Abuse
    - Lack of father figure

●Lack of mother figure

5. Teach you how to surrender to the true counselor which is the indwelling Holy Spirit so that you can live according to God's will and purpose

6. Show you how to put away childish things (1 Cor. 13:11)

7. Help you identify your obstacles to spiritual and emotional maturity (sanctification)

   ●Identify your inner conflicts that prevent you from becoming the person God has designed you to be

   ●Identify the lies you believe that keep you stuck (John 10:10, James 4:7; Eph. 6; 1 Peter 5:8) and replace them with God's truth so you don't take your eyes off Jesus and sink like Peter did (John 6:15-21; Matt 14:22-33; Mark 6:45-52)

   ●Clarify your identity in Christ

   ●Understand your position in Christ

   ●Delay instant gratification and fight temptation (1 Cor. 10:13)

8. Help you identify areas where you're not trusting God

9. Help you understand God's grace and truth and how they relate to spiritual maturity and the sanctification process

10. Help you to see your childlike behaviors and attitudes that are keeping you from having mature relationship(s), and that result in sin and separation from God

11. Teach you how to take responsibility and ownership of your soul: thoughts (beliefs), choices, feelings, values, behaviors, desires, attitudes and limits

    For example:

             ●Feelings of not belonging and feeling abandoned
             ●Shame and guilt of the past
             ●Isolation and detachment
             ●Un-forgiveness, resentment and bitterness toward self and others
             ●Approval-seeking behaviors
             ●Fear of rejection
             ●Inability to fail forward
             ●Fear of conflict
             ●Not knowing where you end and the other person begins
             ●Perfectionism
             ●Selfishness
             ●Over-responsible or irresponsible
             ●Rage, anger, hostility
             ●Pent-up anger
             ●Passive aggressiveness
             ●Pessimistic toward life and people
             ●Lack of purpose and goals

How the book is set up:

To illustrate how the sanctification process works, we are going to spend time studying and exploring key concepts, principles and lessons from the following stories, Bible characters and parables:

1. The Lost son
2. The Lost son's brother
3. The Lost son's Father
4. The adulterous woman
5. The Lost sheep
6. Peter walking on the water
7. The Garden of Gethsemane

Some days you will have just a devotion to read, and on other days you'll have a devotion to read and questions to answer that are designed to help you explore the depths of scripture and your soul. Some devotions are designed to take more than just one day to complete.

I want to mention that at some points along your journey it might seem like the devotions are repetitious. I did this intentionally because, based on my experience, we learn best from repetition and practice. I want *God's Healing Hands* to stand out from other conventional devotionals. *God's Healing Hands will* "Equip you, Encourage you and Empower you" to live a *Victorious Christian Life*.

Journaling....

My hope is that you will record all your work in a journal or note book. I purposely didn't leave space for you to write in the book because I think it's important to record your answers in a separate book so you can expand on your thoughts.

Take action...

In this section you will be asked to look up passages and paraphrase them. The passages relate to the topic being discussed and/or provide you with a background so you can understand the principle being studied. It's important that you take the time to look up each passage and put it in your own words so that you can understand and apply God's principles and truth to your life. Make sure you use a good commentary and cross-reference for each passage so you can get a deeper understanding. Don't worry about the number of passages I listed for you. Take your time. You can't rush spiritual growth. ☺

Reshaping: Review and Repair

Every 30 plus days you will have *review and repair* questions to answer. These questions will help you to review your work for the month and to see how God is working in your life to make the needed *Holy Spirit adjustments* within your soul.

Letters

I created letters that are written from God's, Jesus's, the Holy Spirit's, Satan's and Peter's perspective on certain issues pertaining to sanctification, identity in Christ, lies and deception, the healing process, relationships etc.

Foundational Truths I use in this book are:

Philippians 1:6; Ephesians 3:16-19; John 8:32; Isaiah 61:1-4; Romans 8:17-18; Romans 8:28; Philippians 3:8-11; Philippians 2:12-13; Hebrews 5:8-9; Philippians 3:12-14; John 14:6; Ephesians 4:21-24; Mathew 22:36-40

In Closing…

My hope and prayer is that you will allow the Holy Spirit to free you from a broken heart and an under-developed character so that you will receive a deep healing from the inside out, enabling you to live a Victorious Christian Life. Stay on the "Potter's Wheel" no matter how hard life gets and, always remember, God is *reshaping you.*

Biography

Michael Barbarulo is an author, mental health and addiction life coach/consultant and educator, addiction specialist, motivational speaker, and certified life coach with an office in Albany, NY. He is a well credentialed and trained professional in the field of addictions, mental health, wellness, anger management, stress management and conflict resolution for the last 19 years. He has been in private practice for 13 years.

Michael also has over 15 years experience in Christian Ministry/shelter operations and discipleship. He is well trained and experienced in Creating, Directing and Leading discipleship programs for men and women who struggle with addictions and mental health issues. He specializes in Leadership Development as well as addictions and mental health issues.

He's also receiving his PhD in Counseling and Advanced Human Behavior. He is currently in the dissertation phase.

Dedication

To my children Michael and Alyssa

Thank you for giving me the time, support and love to write this book, and to pursue my dream of becoming an author. I Love You.

TABLE OF CONTENTS

SANCTIFICATION & FAITH

SANCTIFICATION & TRUTH

SACTIFICATION & RELATIONSHIPS

SANCTIFICATION & HEALTHY SELF-IMAGE

SANCTIFICATION & ADVERSITY

SACTIFICATION & SPIRITUAL WARFARE

REVIEW & REPAIR

WORKING OUT YOUR SALVATION

Therefore, my dear ones, as you have always obeyed [my suggestions], so now, not only [with the enthusiasm you would show] in my presence but much more because I am absent, work out (cultivate, carry out to the goal, and fully complete) your own salvation with reverence and awe and trembling (self-distrust, [a]with serious caution, tenderness of conscience, watchfulness against temptation, timidly shrinking from whatever might offend God and discredit the name of Christ) (Phil 2:12)

PREFACE

HEART OF THE FATHER

*M*y guess is, that if you're reading this devotional it's because you have received Jesus as your Lord and Savior and you want to learn more about sanctification and God "Our Father", or you're exploring what it means to be a child of God; or maybe you're stuck in your walk with God and you're not quite sure why.

1 Corinthians 1:2 tells us… that God the Father has chosen you and has given you a personal invitation to be reconciled back to Him through His Son. Our Father is offering you forgiveness for your sins, bad habits, hang ups and your independence. He's offering you a new life and He wants to repair you from the inside out. He wants to heal you spiritually, emotionally and relationally.

Think about it, God loves you and chose you before He ever made the world. He chose you through Christ to be without fault in His eyes. This was His plan for you all along. God's plan was always to adopt you into His family through the Lamb of God. He wants to be your Daddy. God will teach you how to come under the authority of Jesus (Ephesians 1:4-5,10). You had a life before Christ. You had, or have, parents and caretakers that fell short of the glory of God (Rom. 3:23). Many of us were taught beliefs and values that went against God's way of doing things. Before we received God's invitation you and I were dead in our transgressions and sins. We used to follow the ways of the world, the ruler of the kingdom, the spirit who is now at work in those who are disobedient and refuse to obey God (Ephesians 2:1– 2).

Before Christ we used to live a certain way; we followed our own passions and the desires of our evil nature. Why? Because we were born with an evil nature. (Ephesians 2:3) Our father was Satan (John 8:44). The thing about this is, you don't ever know or realize how your living is wrong (Proverbs 14:12). It becomes a way of life. Sure you get these little tugs at your heart saying 'this is wrong' but you ignore them and your heart gets hard and calloused over time.

Our Father, God, wants us to live in a way that's pleasing to Him (1Thess. 1:12). So therefore, He will teach you how to do that (Phil. 2:13). He knows that you're not perfect and that you came with baggage. Your Father wants to refine you, restore you, renew you, and rebuild you. In other words your Father wants to ***sanctify you.***

DAY 1

HEART OF STONE

Create in me a clean heart, O God. Renew a right spirit within me.

Psalm 51:10

The best day of my life was when I surrendered to Christ. It was February 1993. I said the sinner's prayer and for hours after that I felt this overwhelming sense of peace. I was told to buy a Bible and go to church. That was the best advice I have ever received. It was life changing.

I remember reading the gospel of John. I couldn't stop crying. I was so grateful for what Jesus did for me. I felt forgiven. I felt washed clean. A few days later I went to my priest to talk to him about what had happened to me. I remember having this empty feeling in my heart. I mean, it felt like I had a hole there. My priest told me that God had taken my heart of stone and replaced it with a heart of flesh. Ezekiel 36:26 says *"And I will give you a new heart, and I will put a new spirit in you. I will take out your stony, stubborn heart and give you a tender, responsive heart."*

I was as stubborn as they come. It amazed me how God's spirit just softened me. It was spooky! I felt free. I couldn't stop talking about Jesus. I went from listening to Ozzy Osborne to Kathy Troccoli. All I desired was to know who Christ was, and what he did for me. I was on a pink cloud for about 10 months. My prayers were being answered. I was receiving favor and grace. It was like God just made this clear path for me.

Then one day it was like I hit a brick wall. Everything became a challenge for me. My prayers weren't being answered as fast as they were in the beginning of my walk. My faith was being tested and I started to feel discouraged so I gave up. I stopped reading the Bible; I stopped praying, going to church and attending Bible studies. And then I went right back to my old life style.

God was showing me that I had rocky soil in my heart. This represents those who hear the message and immediately receive it with joy, instantly responding with enthusiasm but there is no depth, so it doesn't last. I had no soil of character. So when *my* emotions wore off and some difficulties arrived, I had nothing to show for it (Matt 13:20-21 The Message and NLT).

It was at this time that God was telling me the honeymoon period was over and He wanted to prune off my dead branches (John 15:2). In other words, He was going to deal with my character defects, bad habits and old hurts, damaged emotions, negative attitudes and behaviors, as well as refine my personality.

I thought that when I received Christ it was a new beginning and that I started fresh from that point on. Nobody told me that I had to deal with my past or even my defects of character. I thought the past was the past and that's where it stayed. I guess I thought that salvation was enough. I was wrong. I was entering the *sanctification process*. Max Lucado said it best: "God loves me just the way I am, but he refuses to leave me that way." God wanted to cut off every branch (character defect, bad habit, hurt and immaturity) in me that wasn't bearing fruit, while every branch that did bear fruit he was pruning so I can be even more fruitful (John 15:2-5).

Ask yourself…

1. What do you expect from Christ now that you have invited Him into your life?
2. Describe your first experience with Jesus.
3. What does sanctification mean to you? What's the difference between sanctification and salvation?
4. If I back slide what would be the reasons why?
    a. If I were to pick a soil in Matt 13:1-23 that best represents my first year with Christ what soil would I pick? Why?
    b. What soil best describes where you are today? Why?

Take Action…

Look up the following passages and paraphrase each one.

☐Phil. 2:12-13; Matt.18:3; 1 John 2:3-6; John 14:21; Eph. 4:22-24; 2 Cor. 5:17; Isaiah 55:8-9; Prov. 14:12; 1 Cor. 10:13

Reflection

1. After reading today's devotion, I realize…
2. The key statements I need to remember and work on are…
3. The positive consequences of remembering and working on these statements will be…

DAY 2

FIRST THINGS FIRST

I have read in Plato and Cicero sayings that are very wise and very beautiful; but I never read in either of them: "Come unto me all ye that labour and are heavy laden." ~St Augustine

Therefore, accept each other just as Christ has accepted you so that God will be given glory (Rom. 15:7)

Get to know Him and line your beliefs and values up with His

What does it mean now that you have accepted Christ? It means that you have made peace with God (Rom. 5:1). You made a decision to give account to Him now rather than later. It means you chose heaven instead of hell. You're forgiven for all your transgressions and you're starting life over with a clean slate.

What you're going to do now is line your life up with God and see where you fall short. God's will is important to you now. You will develop a desire that gets stronger and stronger to follow and obey God's way of doing things. This will occur as you build your relationship with Him. You will grow to trust him more and more, so be patient in this process. Augustine once said, *"To fall in love with*

God is the greatest of all romances; to seek Him, the greatest adventure; to find him, the greatest human achievement."

Spiritual Development...

Spiritual development is your goal. You're going back home in your spirit and getting reacquainted with your real Father. You're looking for purpose, freedom, serenity and healing. Cyril Brookes said, "*There are so many different ways of being healed. The best way, and by far the commonest, is to be loved. To be loved by God, and to know it and live it, is to be healed indeed. The Good News first of all is that you and I are accepted and loved by God. From all eternity you and I have been in the mind of God. God's love for us is utterly reliable and has no conditions whatsoever.*"

Settling your Accounts...

Now you want to settle your account with God (Romans 8). You want to stop feeling guilty, depressed, angry, anxious, ashamed, and broken. You want to get to the bottom of why you're here on this earth. Daily, you're going to try to sin less. The Holy Spirit will help you to fight your temptation to go back to Egypt (Exodus 19:4, 2 Cor. 6:17). Your values and beliefs will change as you draw near to God through prayer, worship, connecting with fellow believers, and reading and APPLYING God's word. Your attitude and outlook on life will change daily. You will start to see the **big picture**.

The main focus at this point is to get to know your Father and build your faith and trust in Him. Your heart will desire to spend time getting to who He is, who Jesus is, and who the Holy Spirit is.

As you gain an understanding of your true purpose here on earth, you will gradually use this new insight to guide your actions on a daily basis.

Take Action...

Look up the following passages and paraphrase each one.

> □Eph. 4:25-32; Col. 3:5-17; Rom. 12:9-21; 1 Pet. 2; 1 Pet. 3; Gen. 4:7; John 14:21; John 15:10-11; 2 Cor. 4:7-10; 2 Cor. 4:16-17; Matt.6:33; Matt. 7:5; Eph. 4:29; Matt. 5:16

Reflection

1. After reading today's devotion, I realize…
2. The key statements I need to remember and work on are…
3. The positive consequences of remembering and working on these statements will be…

DAY 3

"SURRENDER TO GOD"

Submit yourselves therefore to God. Resist the devil, and he will flee from you. (James 4:7)

Today I want you to think about what it means to surrender to God so I made a list of 10 signs of surrender. Read through them and see what applies to you. Feel free to add your own.

10 Signs of Surrender…

You know that you're surrendering to God when:

1. You let go and let God. You allow God to do with you as He wills. You desire His perfect will.
2. You accept that God knows best and that His way is the best way
3. You stop fighting and being stubborn and you try to do things His way despite how you feel or what you believe should happen
4. You start to trust that God has your best interests at heart, and you allow Him to take care of you
5. You confidently trust Him
6. You allow God to show you what you really need
7. You stay close to God and remain content during both good and bad times.
8. You accept that God is the one who is in control and the only one who can judge; you also accept that He's the source of all things and therefore He's the one who created the rules for life.
9. You decrease so He can increase in your life. You start to consider His will and His way because you care about your relationship with Him

10. You take the time to line up your attitudes and behaviors with God's word. You seek Him for guidance and direction regardless of the situation.

God's Grace...

Paul's Memoir

A.D 56: 2 Cor. 12:7-10

I ***know*** God made me for heaven. I learned how to accept that, whatever happens to me, it came from heaven and God approves of it. I don't sweat it anymore. I used to but now I rely on God's grace because I've learned that it's always enough. I do the best I can each day. I take the time to think and act like Christ regardless of my mood, opinion or situation. I know that it's God that works in me to help me to do His will regardless of how I feel about it (Phil 2:13). I must be honest, I don't always agree with it but I go with it anyway. It's a struggle some days but He works through me. I do my best each day to role model Christ. That's all I can do.

God's Control...

Life becomes easier when you accept that God made all things and that He's in control. I'm learning to say 'thank you' for whatever He sends me. I need His help to keep me from sin and help me to keep from reacting to people, places and things. I can say this, God gives me the grace I need so I can see and accept His will each day of my life, even when I don't understand it.

Take Action...

1. Look up the following passages and paraphrase each one.

   ☐Col. 1:10; I John 1:7; Luke 17:10; John 14:5; 2 Cor. 5:15;   2 Cor. 10:5; Col. 3:1-7; 1 John 1:9; Matt. 3:8; 2 Cor. 7:9-11; James 4:8-10; Eph. 4:31-32; 1 Thess. 5:17; John 5:30; John 17:23

Reflection

1. After reading today's devotion, I realize...
2. The key statements I need to remember and work on are...
3. The positive consequences of remembering and working on these statements will be...

DAY 4

RECONNECTING TO YOUR TRUE PURPOSE

And all of this is a gift from God, who brought us back to himself through Christ. And God has given us this task of reconciling people to him For God was in Christ, reconciling the world to himself, no longer counting people's sins against them. And he gave us this wonderful message of reconciliation
(2 Corinthians 5:18-19)

God's Plan...

God wants you to discover His will, His way of handling day to day life. He wants you to be more focused on Him and less on yourself. He wants to be involved in your life, your decisions, and choices. He wants to help you work through your brokenness and to restore your life and relationships. He wants to disciple you. He wants you to become a servant of Him.

God will help you to discover the truth about who He is and the truth about who you are because of Him. You've been living lies for a while so He will help you to break free from anything that goes against His truth (2 Cor. 10:5).

Refocus...

When you take your eyes off yourself, you will begin to see who God really is. You're here to serve God not yourself. When you serve him and keep him first you become a very rich and successful person. This is the pursuit of happiness. Serving God, not man, will give you the peace that surpasses all understanding.

God wants your faithfulness, loyalty and obedience. He wants your devotion. He wants to use you to help Him gather His children so they can return to Him. Hell wasn't designed for God's children; it was designed for Satan and his crew.

Take Action...

Look up the following passages and paraphrase each one.

☐Rom. 7:18,25; Rom. 8:10; Phil. 2:12-13; Gen. 1:26; Eph. 3:3-4; Phil. 3:13-14; 2 Tim. 1:9-10; Gal. 2:20

Reflection

1. After reading today's devotion, I realize…
2. The key statements I need to remember and work on are…
3. The positive consequences of remembering and working on these statements will be…

DAY 5

"GIFTS AND TALENTS"

For God's gifts and His call are irrevocable. [He never withdraws them when once they are given, and He does not change His mind about those to whom He gives His grace or to whom He sends His call.] (Romans 11:29)

Now there are distinctive varieties and distributions of endowments (gift[1] extraordinary powers distinguishing certain Christians, due to the power of divine grace operating in their souls by the Holy Spirit) and they vary, but the [Holy] Spirit remains the same. (1 Corinthians 12:4)

Gifts, Talents & Abilities…

God has given each one of His children specific gifts, talents and abilities. He wants you to use them to advance his kingdom. They were given to you to honor Him and to help fellow believers.

Peter would tell you that God gave him gifts and he had to learn how to use and manage them so that they would bring honor and glory to God (1 Peter 4:10). God wants you to use your gifts every day. This is how you serve the Lord and His people.

Prior Occupations…

Think for a minute about the disciples. Before they knew Jesus they had their occupations: some were fishermen; there was a tax collector, a doctor, and others were farmers. Then, when they came to know Jesus, their purpose and desires changed. This also happened to me. I was going to college for criminal justice because I wanted to be a State Trooper. But when I received Jesus as my Savior, my desire changed. I changed my major to psychology and went on to become a therapist and Life Coach.

Now, this doesn't mean that this will happen for you. God may intend to keep you in your occupation or degree of study. Just know that He will use the gifts He gave you to advance His kingdom by serving others. Focus on using your talents and skills and don't bury them. The more you use them, the more you show your love for Jesus. People need what you have. When you operate in your gifts and calling, you're allowing Jesus to live His life through you.

Purpose...

God has given everyone a purpose for their life. We all have talents and abilities to make an impact on this world. I think it's important for all of us to take time to discover our passions and dreams. We all want to know why we exist.

Obstacles...

For those who are already living their passions and dreams, don't expect everything to go your way. It's not unusual to hit speed bumps now and then, just don't quit. Push through and fight even harder. Always trust God to give you the strength and direction you need, and always **keep the faith**.

Discover your Passions...

The first thing you need to do to find and discover your passions and dreams is to stop and think about the kind of legacy you want to leave. What kind of impact do you want to make? What do you want people to think and feel when they hear your name? What makes you excited and jazzed every day?

Responsibility is the key to creating the life you desire. You have the ability to respond in any way you want to. In order to take responsibility for your life and situation, make sure you eliminate any excuses you might have. If you're having a pity party, stop. If you continue to blame people, places and things for your life, nothing will change. This leads to failure and heartbreak. Washington Irving said it best, "The easiest thing to do whenever you fail, is to put yourself down by blaming your lack of ability for your misfortunes."

Take Action...

Look up the following passages and paraphrase each one.

☐Ezek. 18:20; Jer. 17:10; Ezek. 18:2-3; Eph. 5:18; John 14:21-22; Ps. 119:11; Acts 2:1-4; Prov. 19:21; Matt. 25:14-30; Rom. 12:6; 1 Cor. 11:1-2; Matt. 6:33; Psalm 37:4; Psalm 21:2

Reflection

Ask yourself:

1. My personal definition of responsibility is…
2. I'm removing the following excuses…
3. I'm afraid of…
4. Reasons why my life can change are…
5. How will my life change if I take responsibility?
6. What will my life be like one year from now if I **don't** take responsibility?

DAY 6

PURPOSE FOR LIVING

*For ye know what commandments we gave you by the Lord Jesus. ³For this is the will of God, **even your sanctification**, that ye should abstain from fornication: ⁴That every one of you should know how to possess his vessel in sanctification and honor; ⁵Not in the lust of concupiscence, even as the Gentiles which know not God: ⁶That no man go beyond and defraud his brother in any matter: because that the Lord is the avenger of all such, as we also have forewarned you and testified.*
(1 Thessalonians 4:2-6)

Introduction…

Please open your Bible and take a few minutes to read 1 Thessalonians 4 -*Live to Please God.* I want you to think about why God saved you.

I believe God saved us for two reasons: 1) eternal life and 2) service to Him-pleasing Him (loving, honoring Him), loving others and sharing the good news of the salvation found in Jesus Christ.

Intentions...

When you come to Christ your intentions change. You start to see life differently because you're seeing things through God's eyes. You want to live according to your Father's principles. God has given you supernatural powers for supernatural living. Jesus said, "I tell you the truth, anyone who believes in me will do the same works I have done, and even greater works, because I am going to be with the Father." (John 14:12) Think about that for a minute.

Dark Times...

The more you draw near to God, the more you're going to want to please Him, lean on Him, and trust Him. You're going to want to do your best each day to follow His will. When dark times come - and they will - lean on Him, find your refuge in Him. Don't separate yourself from Him because you're angry or hurt. Don't go back to your old ways of coping. The dark times are there for you to grow and to create a dependency on God. This is all part of your sanctification process. You can't escape tough times. Don't forget that in Jesus, you have already overcome them (John 16:33).

Big Picture...

Paul's Memoir

A.D 57: Romans

I know that in the beginning of my walk I didn't see things clearly. God had to make me blind so I could see. I realize that God originally made me for heaven. I wasn't made to be here on earth without my Father. I've come to realize that I can't control everything, and that I need God's grace to live out His will and principles. I do the best I can each day to live out God's will for my life even if I have to be in prison to do it. God does send me to strange places, but I guess I was built for it. I really trust that God knows what's best for me. I must admit that, at times, I can see a different way of going about it, but then again I don't see the big picture.

Advice from: Paul

Dear Brothers and Sisters:

1. Let go and Let God. Let Him work through you. Don't try to control everything; God knows what He's doing.
2. Learn to receive what God gives you to do and handle each day, don't try to change it. If you fail or fall short, don't condemn yourself (Rom. 8:1). Let it go and learn from it.

3. Ask God to help you to stay clear from sin and temptation from your impulses and sinful desires. The more you're honest with Him, the stronger you become because of His grace and strength.

Take Action…

1. Look up the following passages and paraphrase each one.

   ☐Luke 9:62; Eph. 1:8-9; Isaiah 46:10-11; 1 Thess. 2:13; Eph. 3:20-21; Col. 1:25-29; 1 John 2:20; Eph. 2:10; Rom. 1:20-32; Phil. 3:13; 1 John 2:3-6; John 14:21; Galatians 5:17

Reflection

1. After reading today's devotion, I realize…
2. The key statements I need to remember and work on are…
3. The positive consequences of remembering and working on these statements will be…

DAY 7

ACCEPT PERSONAL RESPONSIBILTY

Accept responsibility for your life and your relationship with God and others.
(Acts 17:30)

Designed to follow…

You are responsible, and accountable, to God for your actions and how you choose to live your life. You are called to repent and believe in God. You were designed to follow him. Paul was sending a message in Acts 17:30…. TURN AWAY from idols and turn to Him. Why? Because you weren't designed to follow anything else.

So what does this mean? It means that for you to live the life God designed for you, you need to know that God is giving you the control and the power to change things.

Today, right now as you read this, God has empowered you take responsibility for your life. He designed you and equipped you to live a successful life. But in order to do that you need to accept responsibility for your actions, your thoughts, and your feelings. You will feel empowered when you start to ask God for the help you need to achieve success in any areas you may be struggling with.

Empowered...

The exciting thing is, that God has given you the responsibility to exercise dominion over the animal kingdom and creation. God is giving you a purpose and a plan in which He empowers and equips you, and encourages you to take responsibility over your very own particular space in this world. For example, Noah had the responsibility to build the ark. Joseph was given the responsibility to oversee Potiphar's household, to oversee the whole of Egypt, and to oversee the other prisoners; and of course Jesus had the responsibility for dying on the cross. They all had a responsibility to God, they each had a calling and they obeyed despite how hard it was. What is your calling, and are you taking responsibility for it or are you stuck in being distracted by idols and selfishness? Take up your cross today.

You're not responsible for others...

Let me ease your mind about something. You are not responsible for other people's actions and responsibilities. You're only called to be responsible for the duties and calling that God has assigned you... that's it. You are called, however, to support those whom God has placed in your life. You are responsible to share the burdens of others – but again, only those that God has placed in your path.

Consider this...

1. God will reshape your soul by showing you the areas you need to tend to.
   For example:
   - Your emotions- Negative- places of hurt, bitterness, sadness etc.
   - Relationships
   - Your body
   - Renewing you mind
   - Beliefs and values
   - Baggage from the past
   - Your future
   - Talents and skills
   - Personality
   - Attitudes about people, places and things

•Your character and morals

2. To produce spiritual fruit we need to build an intimate relationship with Jesus, stay committed to studying God's Word, and put to death the ways we used to cope when we lived independently from Christ. Things we did to feel accepted, approved, validated, in control, significant, and to relieve stress, anger, worry, pain, fear, guilt and shame. (John 15:4-5; Psalm 1:1-3; John 12:24)

3. We have the responsibility to repent, and to live and behave like God's children.

4. We need to find solutions to our problems. We need to take ownership of our brokenness and shortcomings. If we have hurt people we need to make amends.

5. We need to take a personal inventory on a daily basis (2 Corinthians 13:5).

Take Action...

1. Look up the following passages and paraphrase each one.
   ☐Rom. 7:8,24; 2 Cor. 8:12; Matt. 7:1-5; Rom. 12:1-2; 1 Cor. 3:21-23; Eph. 4:22-24; Psalm 31

Reflection

1. After reading today's devotion, I realize…

2. The key statements I need to remember and work on are…

3. The positive consequences of remembering and working on these statements will be…

DAY 8-9

VALUES ARE LIKE A COMPASS

"But seek ye first the kingdom of God, and his righteousness; and all these things shall be added unto you." (Matthew 6:33)

A man who dares to waste one hour of life has not discovered the value of life.
~ Charles Darwin

Today I want you to look at the values that drive you. Defining your values is an essential part of working out your salvation.

You need to know that finding your purpose, and/or living out your purpose, takes a lot of prayer, mental sweat and undisturbed thinking.

Values...

In this section I want to help you explore your most important values. Values are a road map to life. They are things that are important to you like principles and morals. They are based on your beliefs. Values help you set priorities and point your life in a certain direction. For example, if getting along with people is important to you, then you will make sure you practice good communication skills and assertiveness. You value honesty, openness and integrity.

Barbara De Angelis once said, "Living with integrity means: Not settling for less than what you know you deserve in your relationships; asking for what you want and need from others; speaking your truth, even though it might create conflict or tension; behaving in ways that are in harmony with your personal values, and making choices based on what you believe, not what others believe."

Live by your values...

I've come to realize that one of the main reasons people stop working out their salvation, and don't live lives of purpose, is that they stop listening to God and don't live by God's principles and values which will lead them to success, peace and joy. Oftentimes, Christians spend too much time reacting and listening to man instead of God. We need to listen to God, not what people say.

Peace and joy come when you live your life according to God's values and principles.

Read through the list of values and check off what's important to you. Add to this list if you want to.

Achievement	Friendships	Physical challenge
Advancement and promotion	Growth	Pleasure
Adventure	Having a family	Power and authority
Affection (love and caring)	Helping other people	Privacy
Arts	Helping society	Public service
Challenging problems	Honesty	Purity
Change and variety	Independence	Quality of what I take part in
Close relationships	Influencing others	Quality relationships
Community	Inner harmony	Recognition (respect from others, status)
Competence	Integrity	Resourcefulness

		Religion
		Reputation
Competition	Intellectual status	Respect
Cooperation	Involvement	Responsibility and accountability
Country	Job tranquility	Security
Creativity	Knowledge	Self-respect
Decisiveness	Leadership	Serenity
Democracy	Location	Sophistication
Ecological awareness	Loyalty	Stability
Economic security	Market position	Status
Effectiveness	Meaningful work	Supervising others
Efficiency	Merit	Time freedom
Ethical practice	Money	Truth
Excellence	Nature	Wealth
Excitement	Being around people who are open and honest	Wisdom
Fame	Order (tranqulity, stability, conformity)	Work under pressure
Fast living	Personal development	Work with others
Financial gain	Freedom	Working alone

Resource: (www.selfcounseling.com/personalvalues)

I also suggest that you visit websites like these for more lists of values.

　　1.www.stevepavlina.com
　　2.www.selfcounseling.com/personalvalues

Reflection

　　1. After reading today's devotion, I realize…
　　2. The key statements I need to remember and work on are…
　　3. The positive consequences of remembering and working on these
　　　　statements will be…

DAY 10-11

TRANSITIONS

"Nobody can go back and start a new beginning, but anyone can start today and make a new ending."

~*Maria Robinson*

Don't copy the behavior and customs of this world, but let God transform you into a new person by changing the way you think. Then you will learn to know God's will for you, which is good and pleasing and perfect. (Rom. 12:2)

When God called me to Himself and I received my salvation, it was only a matter of time until He made me aware that I was on His potter's wheel. I quickly learned that I had a lot of rough edges that needed to be smoothed out. In other words, I was about to make some serious lifestyle changes and transitions.

In order to go through our transitions, we have to change our attitude and thinking about the situation, or our life. (Rom. 12:1-2) Here are some ideas and practices that will help you go through your new beginning.

1. Develop proactive thinking habits.

A. **Proactive Thinking:** "There's an opportunity in this somewhere, God will show me."

1. **Do:** Look for opportunities and go through the process.

B. **Proactive Thinking:** "These feelings of anxiety, stress, worry, fear, disappointment and anger will pass; it's all part of the process."

1. **Do:** Always work through your emotions. Journal, pray. Talk with a counselor, Life Coach and trusted friends. Develop a support network. Don't go through transitions alone.

C. **Proactive Thinking:** "Keep my focus."

1. **Do:** Stay focused on what you can do or change. Continue to remind yourself of your life's purpose, as well as the type of person you want to be in any given situation.

a)*Inspiration*: Anthony Robbins nailed it when he said, "It's not what's happening to you now, or what has happened in your past, that determines who you become. Rather, it's your decisions about what to *focus on*, what things mean to you, and what you're going to do about them, that will determine your ultimate destiny."

D. **Proactive Thinking:** "This seems overwhelming, but I can break down what I have to do into manageable steps."

    1. **Do:** Each new beginning can be broken down into steps and tasks. Again, new beginnings require process. I know you want the outcome, but growth occurs during the process.

        a)*Inspiration:* Leonardo da Vinci would say, "I have been impressed with the urgency of doing. Knowing is not enough; we must apply. Being willing is not enough; we must do."

E. **Proactive Thinking:** "Change is part of life; everything will work out in the end."

    a) **Do:** Expect change to occur. Work through it. Try not to panic or jump to conclusions. Life isn't predictable, nor are people, even you.

F. **Let go of the past.** If you find yourself being more nostalgic then you want to be, you might have an issue in your past that needs to be processed, accepted and let go.

    L= Let yourself feel and acknowledge your loss

    E= Explore your losses

    T= Talk to someone

    G= God will comfort you as you mourn your losses

    O= Opportunity for new beginning. I know at first it might not feel that way, but in time you will see what I'm talking about.

Take Action…

1. Look up the following passages and paraphrase each one.
    ☐John 15:1-17; Isaiah 55:8-9; Eph. 4:22-24; Rom. 6:6; Heb. 4:14-16; 2 Cor. 5:21; Heb. 9:14; Eph. 2:4-10

Reflection

1. After reading today's devotion, I realize…
2. The key statements I need to remember and work on are…
3. The positive consequences of remembering and working on these statements will be…

DAY 12-13

NEW BEGINNINGS

"Every end is a New Beginning"

~ An Old Proverb

"Have I not commanded you? Be strong and courageous. Do not be frightened, and do not be dismayed, for the Lord your God is with you wherever you go."
(Joshua 1:9)

Life is full of transitions and new beginnings. Transition is another word that describes working out your salvation.

Sometimes we have unexpected situations in our lives that cause us to change our focus. We always have to welcome change, but we don't have to allow the change to dominate us to the point that we lose control of our lives.

A new beginning can be:

1. Getting married
2. Getting divorced
3. Break up
4. Affair(s)
5. Starting a business
6. New friends
7. New location
8. Death of a loved one
9. Broken dreams
10. Having children
11. Losing a job

12. Getting a new job
13. Starting a new career
14. Change in health
15. Aging
16. Going back to school
17. Personal failures
18. Demotion

Loss...

In every new beginning I experienced a sense of loss. In some situations I lost my independence and other situations I lost certainty, security, trust and a sense of self. On the other hand I gained a lot of positive life experiences, a strengthened character and a deeper faith. I had to push through the process. I had to keep moving forward and trust God with whatever he was doing. I found more peace in knowing that God is in control and has my best interests at heart. Change and new beginnings are all part of working out our salvation.

Chogyam Trungpa said, "There are times to cultivate and create, when you nurture your world and give birth to new ideas and ventures. There are times of flourishing and abundance, when life feels in full bloom, energized and expanding. And there are times of fruition, when things come to an end. They have reached their climax and must be harvested before they begin to fade. And finally of course, there are times that are cold, and cutting and empty, times when the spring of **new beginnings** seems like a distant dream. Those rhythms in life are natural events. They weave into one another as day follows night, bringing, not messages of hope and fear, but messages of how things are."

This devotion may take a few days to work through. Take your time. I created a list of attitudes and practices to help you work through changes. Read through the list and check off what you need to work on. (Pick 1or 2 attitudes and behaviors to work on throughout the week)

The best way to deal with changes (Isaiah 43:19):

☐Face change head on, don't avoid it. It can change your life for the best. In every change there's an opportunity to grow. Trust God with your life.

☐Don't try to keep your life so routine and predictable. This only creates stress and hyper vigilance.

☐Accept losses as they occur

☐Grieve your losses

☐Learn to accept feedback and constructive criticism when it comes, regarding your attitudes and behaviors.

☐If you find yourself starting to withdraw from something you need to change, call someone. Ask for help, support and prayer. Pray together. Use your faith.

☐Re-evaluate your patterns and routines

☐Live in reality, not fantasy. Accept your life as it is and make the needed improvements.

☐Express your feelings about the change. Don't stuff or hide them. Bad feelings are signals that something needs changing.

☐Lower your defenses and admit that you need help and guidance.

☐Seek out a mentor

☐Study successful people to see what system they followed to achieve success.

☐Hang out with people who want to grow and reach new levels in their lives. Try to avoid people who don't set goals or try to aspire to much. Mediocrity shouldn't be anyone's goal.

☐When change occurs, behave in a way that keeps your self- respect

☐No pity parties, they only prolong the pain and what needs to happen in your life.

☐See change as an opportunity to:
  o Grow closer to someone
  o Grow personally and professionally
  o Grow in character
  o Love yourself
  o Define your purpose
  o Put you back on course

☐Evaluate your beliefs and values about change.

☐Love yourself by:
  o Being honest with yourself and others.
  o Accepting that life will never stay the same.
  o Loving others
  o Problem solving. Find your own answers. You will always find a solution to your problems.

☐Focus on what you can change

☐Focus on your purpose in life

☐Brainstorm solutions and strategies

☐Remove negative people and self talk from your life

☐Practice reality based self talk

☐Focus on your strengths and resources

☐Spend time with people who have gone through what you're going through or attempting to change.

☐Give to others

☐Listen and seek to understand

☐Ask a lot of questions

☐Learn from your experiences, don't judge them

☐Take a stance but be adaptable and flexible

☐Turn situations into opportunities

Questions you can ask when going through transitions:

1. The transitions I'm currently going through are…

    a. What do I believe about these new beginnings?

    b. How is this transition affecting my life? For the good? For the worse?

    c. Am I placing any limitations on myself? My doubts are…

    d. How do I feel?

    e. What do I need? What do I want?

    f. What's within my control? What's out of my control?

    g. My plan is… My steps are…

    h. The people who are supporting me and holding me accountable at this time are…

Take Action…

1. Look up the following passages and paraphrase each one.

    ☐Isaiah 46:4; Heb. 6:11; Prov. 23:18; Heb. 6:19; Heb. 13:6; Psalm 118:6-7; Psalm 3:6; Psalm 46:1-3; Psalm 10:17; Psalm 27:3; Isaiah 12:2; Eph. 6:10 See also Jdg 16:3,6,18-20; Psalm 68:35; Psalm 27:1; Psalm 44:4-8; Psalm 118:6; Isaiah 40:29-31

Reflection

1. After reading today's devotion, I realize…

2. The key statements I need to remember and work on are…

3. The positive consequences of remembering and working on these statements will be…

DAY 14-15

THE REASON FOR YOUR SALVATION

For I know the thoughts and plans that I have for you, says the Lord, thoughts and plans for welfare and peace and not for evil, to give you hope in your final outcome. Then you will call upon Me, and you will come and pray to Me, and I will hear and heed you. Then you will seek Me, inquire for, and require Me [as a vital necessity] and find Me when you search for Me with all your heart.
~ Jer. 29: 11-13

Blessings...

God chose you because He wants to have a relationship with you. He wants you to dwell with Him forever in heaven. God wants to be your father. He has blessings for you and wants you to live the life He designed for you. He has emotional and spiritual healing for you. He wants to conduct surgery on your soul (mind, will and emotions). "You shall love the Lord your God with all your heart and with all your soul and with all your mind. This is the great and first commandment. And the second is like it: You shall love your neighbor as yourself. On these two commandments depend all the Law and the Prophets." (Matthew 22:37-40).

Sanctification...

When you received Christ your sanctification process started. So what does that mean? It means you consider Him before you make your decisions and choices. It means you take responsibility for your past, present and future. It means you seek to please Him with your attitudes and behaviors. You ask Him daily... "Search me [thoroughly], O God, and know my heart! Try me and know my thoughts! And see if there is any wicked or hurtful way in me, and lead me in the way everlasting (Psalm 139:23 AMP). Are you doing this? If not there's a good chance you're not changing into the person God wants you to be.

As I disciple people, I notice that some individuals separate their bad attitudes, negative habits and personality traits, aspects of their past, emotional pain and hang ups from Jesus. This is **not** what Jesus wants. He wants **all your baggage**. He saved you so you wouldn't have to drag your past around with you anymore. He saved you to spread the word, the good news! In order to do this, you need to personally experience His healing power and develop that personal connection with Him. How can you talk about someone you *don't really know?*

Here's what I want you to consider....

1. Ask God to show you any bad habits, selfishness, emotional pain, disobedience or sin that's affecting your relationship with Him.

2. Examine your daily motives, attitudes and behaviors. Look for anything that may be interfering with your relationship with the Trinity.
3. Make sure that you're putting God first each day, each hour, every minute and every second. If you wake up struggling, **pray**. Release your burdens and be anxious for nothing. Work it through but still keep moving forward.

Take action…

1. Look up the following passages and paraphrase each one.
   ☐Matt 28:16-20; Col. 1:13; 2 Tim. 4:17-18; 1 Cor. 6:16-20; Phil. 3:17-20; John 15:5-7; Matt. 16:24-25; Eph. 4:22-24; Rom. 12:1-2; Phil. 2:5; Phil. 3:10; 1 Pet. 2:23; 1 Pet. 3:13-18

Reflection

1. After reading today's devotion, I realize…
2. The key statements I need to remember and work on are…
3. The positive consequences of remembering and working on these statements will be…

DAY 16-17

NEW LIFE ~ NEW DESIGN ~ NEW SYSTEM

Sanctify them through thy truth: thy word is truth (John 17:17)

But now your sins have been washed away, and you have been set apart for God. You have been made right with God because of what the Lord Jesus Christ and the Spirit of our God have done for you. 1 Corinthians 6:11b (NRSV)

God expects you live by His design….

Surrender... The rules change when you do things God's way, in fact, the whole system changes. How you deal with life, yourself and others will change, if it doesn't line up with God's way of doing things. Expect a makeover in some areas of your life. Part of becoming a new creation is learning how to live again, and learning how to accept the following truths:

•God is boss

- God is the resource
- God is Judge
- God created the system and design for life and relationships
- God is the one who is in control

Exploration…Take some time to look at how Peter, Paul, Moses, David and Jesus lived by God's system and design. Study the Cloud of Witnesses in Hebrews 11.

- Start to explore your values system. Be sure to line up your values with God's values. (review days 8-9)
- Explore your beliefs about:
  - Forgiveness
  - Love
  - Reconciliation
  - God's will
  - Prayer
  - Confession
  - Repentance
  - Salvation
  - Suffering
  - Temptation
  - God's word
  - Purpose
  - Relationships
  - Truth
  - Grace
  - Brokenness
  - Sanctification
  - Regeneration
  - Justification and sin
  - Discipline and correction
  - God's theology
  - The role Christ plays in your life
  - Church and the body of Christ
  - The role of the Holy Spirit in your new life and old life
  - Support
  - Worship
  - Mentoring
  - Accountability
  - God's created order
  - The Trinity

oRedemption

oGod's way of healing and pruning our character and
hurts from the past

oEmotions: guilt, shame, fear, anger and pain

Trust... Our Father designed us to be dependent on Him, to love Him first, to serve Him, to glorify Him, and to be blessed with an abundant satisfying life in Him.

- List what you can't provide for yourself
- List the reasons why you're seeking God
- List times you received God's power, strength and insight, to help you work through a situation
- List what support and empowerment you need from God right now
- List the consequences of doing the same thing and expecting different results
- Noah is a great example of how God provides for us. It seemed impossible to build an ark and to fill it with every kind of animal and insect (Gen 6-9). As you read the story you can see how God provided for Noah and his family in the following ways:
  - oSupport
  - oWisdom
  - oStrength
  - oCourage
  - oDirection
  - oHope
  - oFaith
  - oSkill
  - oInsight
  - oResources

Take Action...

1. Look up the following passages and paraphrase each one.

   ☐Gen. 1:28; Matt. 28:18-20; Rom. 5:3-5; 2 Tim. 3:16-17;
   James 1:21-25; 2 Peter 1:2-4; John 15:10-11; John 16:33;
   Matt. 6:33; 1 Cor. 6:19-20; Heb. 4:12; Rom. 6:12-13

Reflection

1. After reading today's devotion, I realize...

2. The key statements I need to remember and work on are…

3. The positive consequences of remembering and working on these statements will be…

DAY 18-19

OVERCOMING YOUR HURT

God blesses those who mourn, for they will be comforted. (Matt. 5:4)

Jesus is giving us the go-ahead to feel our negative feelings. For you to mourn, you need to lower your defenses. Protecting your pain will not bring you change or healing. Jesus wants to renew your heart and strengthen your character. In order for Jesus to do that, you need to learn how to grieve your losses, pain, unfair treatment, etc.

Grief…

When you grieve it allows you to draw closer to God. Jesus was sent to preach the Gospel of good tidings to the meek, the poor, and the afflicted; He was sent to bind up and heal your broken heart, to proclaim liberty to the [physical and spiritual] captive, and to break open up the doors of whatever is holding you prisoner, allowing you to instead walk freely in the light of His love. (Is 61:1)

For us to heal our broken hearts we need to identify the source of our pain. God wants you to express it to him. Yes, He already knows. But He wants us to **express** our anger. When we don't, Satan gains a foothold on soul. If you don't identify your pain you start to feel bad, maybe guilty, and in some cases even shame.

Lamentations 3 tells us that God may bring us grief, but He also brings His unfailing love and comfort. Through your suffering comes growth and character. Let go, and let God have any pain you might be holding onto today. Life is full of lessons. Be open to learn. If you're unhappy, admit it. If you don't like how you feel, say it. Don't disown yourself -- **respect yourself**. Face the truth even if it hurts.

"Forget the former things; do not dwell on the past. See, I am doing a new thing!

Now it springs up; do you not perceive it? I am making a way in the desert and streams in the wasteland." Isaiah 43:18-19

I don't know about you, but it's hard for me to drive forward when I'm looking in my rear view mirror. I find the same to be true when I continuously live in the past ... I can't move forward because I'm looking backward.

It doesn't make sense for us to live in the past and relive our offenses, mistakes, failures, disappointments and discouragements. Our past doesn't determine our future.

"When the door of happiness closes, another opens. But often times we look so long at the closed door that we don't see the one which has been opened for us." (Unknown) So many people try to open a door that God closed. We need to trust God and go through the door that's open no matter how scary it is. God is in the unknown.

If a door closes, always remember that there's a reason for it. Alexander Graham Bell nailed it when he said, "When one door closes, another opens; but we often look so long and so regretfully upon the closed door that we do not see the one which has opened for us. Do your best to live in the present and take in what you have before you."

Ask Yourself:

1. Do I have a problem expressing my feelings?
2. Are there certain feelings I have a hard time expressing?
3. Do I need to grieve a loss, a bad decision, unfair treatment?
4. Do I have regrets I'm hanging onto?
5. Am I bitter, resentful?
6. Am I trying to open a door that's closed? If so, what's behind the door? What is it that I miss, want, or need?
7. When I think about moving on I feel....
8. What are my feelings telling me? My wants? Needs? Desires?
9. What's preventing me from moving forward with God?

Ask the Holy Spirit to:

1. Show you any unresolved hurt, pain or loss
2. Help you identify your feelings
3. Give you the strength and grace to face the truth

Take action...

1. Look up the following passages and paraphrase each one.

☐2 Sam. 13:9; Job 2:12-13; Lam. 3:32-33; 2 Cor. 1:3-4; Psalm 116:8;
Matt 5:4; Rev. 7:17; Luke 7:11-13; John 11:33

Reflection

1. After reading today's devotion, I realize…
2. The key statements I need to remember and work on are…
3. The positive consequences of remembering and working on these
statements will be…

DAY 20-21

SEPARATE FROM YOUR OLD LIFE

*Dear friends, God is good. So I beg you to offer your bodies to Him as a
living sacrifice, pure and pleasing. That's the most sensible way to serve
God.[2]Don't be like the people of this world, but let God change the way you
think. Then you will know how to do everything that is good and pleasing to
Him. (Rom. 12:1-2)*

Give God Control…

One of the first things you need to do is to let go of all the things you find
yourself trying to control. The things you obsess over, such as people, problems,
relationships, feelings, or your past. Allow God to help you sort through these
things.

1. Learn to love without controlling, fixing, rescuing, changing and enabling.
2. Focus on what God is calling you to change.
3. Ask God to help you to stop thinking about everybody else's behaviors,
problems and feelings. Let go of unhealthy attachments. Learn to solve
your own problems and let others be responsible for theirs (Gal 6:1,2,4)
4. Learn to release things you can't change and ask God to help you change
what he has called you to change about yourself. Focus on what you can

influence. This is where you will receive God's strength, grace, wisdom, truth, and mercy.

5. God wants us to take responsibility for ourselves and share the burdens with others. You need to pray and ask God before you start sharing burdens. Make sure that it's your Father's business and not your own.

Life... just doesn't work when you...

- Obsess and worry
- Overreact
- Personalize
- Accept responsibility for another person's life and problems
- Live in the future
- Create chaos in your mind
- Ignore reality
- Hold on to burdens and cares
- Tell yourself that you can be happy when all your problems are solved
- Believe you're responsible to make everyone else happy
- Think everybody should like you
- You don't allow yourself to be angry at the one you love and care about
- Live by other people's opinions and not your own
- Live life through others

Relationships...

Part of the old life is being anxious and acting out. We make problems bigger than they need to be. When you live God's way, He teaches you how to love without being enmeshed. He shows us how to make healthy choices based on our values and beliefs, not others. When you love others you're not supposed to hurt yourself in the process. Keep your identity; keep your opinions, values and limits. If you're not sure what healthy love looks like, read 1Cointhians 13, the love chapter. Study each verse and evaluate yourself and others against it.

- Apply this daily to your relationships ... Col 3:12-14 "Therefore, as God's chosen people, holy and dearly loved, clothe yourselves with compassion, kindness, humility, gentleness and patience. [13] Bear with each other and forgive one another if any of you has a grievance against someone. Forgive as the Lord forgave you. [14] And over all these virtues put on love, which binds them all together in perfect unity." Remember: others need to love you this way too. Love is a two-way street.

Old Life...

Part of separating from your old life is to learning how to separate yourself from others. Being your own person – the person God created you to be. In our old life we would find ourselves:

- Being preoccupied with someone or something
- Losing control of our emotions because of something or someone
- Sacrificing our values because life seems, or feels, out of control
- Changing ourselves to make someone else happy
- Trying to fix things, but only making them worse
- Saying things we don't mean
- Moving ahead of God
- Desperate – and as a result, sacrificing our values, choices, beliefs, and limits.

New Life...

The new life is the opposite of the list above. When we're in Christ we are to act like Christ and model Him for others. Jesus is the way, the truth, and the life. It's important to mention that Jesus:

- Gives us the responsibility to solve our own problems with His help, love, strength, truth, wisdom, grace, and time
- Gave us the fruit of His Spirit: **self**-control (not other-control)
- Wants us to let go of people that were trying to rescue, fix, change or enable. It's important that we don't interrupt the law of sowing and reaping (Gal. 6)
- Doesn't want us to worry or obsess about other people's shortcomings, hurts, burdens, hang-ups, and circumstances. In fact, He wants you to pray and ask Him how you can help. He will give you wisdom, insight and guidance (James 1:5-8)

Take action...

1. Look up the following passages and paraphrase each one.

    ☐ 1 John 5:4; Isaiah 40:30-31; Eph. 4:22-24; Col. 3:9-10; 2 Tim. 1:6; Titus 3:5; Eph. 2:1,5; Col. 2:13

Reflection:

1. The After reading today's devotion, I realize...
2. key statements I need to remember and work on are...
3. The positive consequences of remembering and working on these statements will be...

DAY 22-24

BE WILLING TO GO DEEPER

But I need something more! For if I know the law but still can't keep it, and if the power of sin within me keeps sabotaging my best intentions, I obviously need help! I realize that I don't have what it takes. I can will it, but I can't do it. I decide to do good, but I don't really do it; I decide not to do bad, but then I do it anyway. My decisions, such as they are, don't result in actions. Something has gone wrong deep within me and gets the better of me every time.

Romans 7:17-20 (The Message)

Feeling Stuck...

I reached a point in my relationship with Christ where I needed to make a decision as to how far I wanted to go, and how deep I wanted my relationship to be. I didn't know what I wanted from Him. All I knew was that I wasn't changing anymore.

I developed an understanding that Jesus died for me, and that I was forgiven for my sins, but I kept repeating the same ones. Sin became a burden. Sin lost its appeal but I couldn't stop. I knew God wanted to change something inside of me but I just didn't know what. I was broken and lost. How could this be? I had lost my peace again. I was miserable. Finally, I started take a look at what triggered my sinful behaviors. I discovered that my anger and lack of self worth was underneath my sin.

Inner Wounds...

We can't hide from our inner wounds. We need to face our hurts and brokenness. If we deny our past we are denying God. If you're trying to forget your past, stop. Let God into your soul so you can heal. Break away from denial-based forgiveness. Yes you're forgiven, but you need to know what for. I believe that we sin because of our sin nature, but I also believe that we sin because we are hurt and broken people.

Matthew 5:4 says, "Blessed are those who mourn, for they will be comforted." This verse is telling us that we need to face up to our pain and allow God to heal us. We need to release our tears and face our fears. If you have repressed emotions ask God to help you release them.

Grieving Process...

God created the grieving process. Grieving is a way to release your pain and to work through loss. God wants you to deal with your past so you can live in today. 'God will heal your broken heart, but He has to have all the pieces.' (Author Unknown) Don't harden your heart or disregard the possibility that you might need to grieve, because if you do, you run the risk of getting stuck spiritually and emotionally.

Stages of Grief...

I want you to take some time to read Elisabeth Kübler-Ross's 5 Stages of Grief. When we experience loss, transitions and change, our old man goes through these stages as we mourn and grieve.

Denial

Denial isn't always a bad thing. In fact, God uses it to help us grieve our losses. Denial helps us to slowly accept the truth about our situation. I believe God gives us His mercy, grace and compassion when we are in denial and are unwilling, or unable, to accept the loss or change. When we experience an unexpected loss or change, we might experience shock, numbness, and feel absolutely powerless, or helpless.

God will help us to eventually accept the reality of the loss. We need to go to Him and to others so we can start the healing process. Inviting God into the grieving and sanctification process prevents us from repressing our emotions and losing our purpose in life. It also keeps us growing in character, and keeps us connected to Him and others (John 15: 5). God calls us to mourn because if we don't, we only lengthen our pain and suffering. As you work through denial, feelings about the loss, transition or change will begin to surface.

Anger

Anger is a necessary stage of the healing process. Paul said, "Be angry and sin not. Don't let the sun go down upon your anger (Eph 4: 26). So we need to be willing to feel our anger until it subsides. Let yourself feel it, and talk to God and others about it. Keep in mind that anger has secondary emotions so don't be surprised when you go from anger to fear, guilt, or regret. You might be angry at yourself, God, family, friends, pastors, medical professionals, or the transition or change, itself.

Bargaining

Bargaining is when we start to make deals with God. We want a second chance, an opportunity to do it over. Sometimes we say, "God, if you will do this for me, I promise that I will _____(fill in the blank). Another part of working through the bargaining stage is dealing with the regrets and the 'if only's.' We need to make sure that we don't stay here to long because it leads to condemnation; or we end up getting stuck in the past because of our guilt and shame. This occurs because we are having a hard time accepting the truth and reality of our situation. The best thing to do is to embrace the truth and run to God for His strength and grace. When we do this, the nightmare won't last forever; God will use it for good (Rom. 8:28).

Depression

I want to remind you that we don't move through these stages in a linear fashion, so don't try to. If you find yourself feeling angry and depressed one day, and accepting the situation the next, that's normal.

Feeling sad about your loss is normal. Depression is sadness distorted. When you lose someone or something important to you, like a loved one or a job, you lose a part of your soul. Your heart has a void now. We need to feel our sadness and pain, and ask God to fill the emptiness. When we experience a change we might need some time alone to figure it out. We might need to withdraw for a while to pray and regroup. Just make sure that you're not doing this for long periods of time. Let your support team know where you're at emotionally and physically. Don't keep secrets, and be honest about your anger, frustration, resentment and bitterness. Let your breakdown become a breakthrough.

Acceptance

I want to share with you 14 signs of acceptance. Read through the list and see where you think you are.

1. You come to the point when you say, "Okay, this happened and I don't necessarily like it but I have to move on."
2. You're ready for a new chapter in your life and you seek God's will and purpose in your loss, change or transition.
3. You're ready to create a new identity. When we lose something important to us we lose a part of our identity because our soul was attached.
4. You're ready to readjust your plans and goals.
5. You're willing to enjoy life again without feeling guilt, shame or regret.
6. You start to rebuild, or build new relationships and make new connections.
7. You listen to your needs and wants. You feel your emotions and are able to talk about your loss. Your loss is part of your testimony.
8. You seek God's comfort. You ask God what to do.
9. You let go of self-pity.
10. You stop blaming.
11. You accept responsibility for your soul (actions, attitudes, commitments and promises)
12. You extend forgiveness. Let go of resentments and grudges.
13. You accept what happened to you and stop denying that it happened.
14. You make amends.

Consider this…

1. His favor lasts a lifetime. "Weeping may last for the night, but there is a song of joy in the morning." (Psalm 30:5)
2. Change the negative character traits and personality patterns in your life.
3. As you grieve, make sure you're connected to Godly people so they can offer you hope, comfort, grace, truth, support, validation, acceptance and love.
4. Keep your conscience clear. Then those who treat the good Christian life you live with contempt, will feel ashamed that they have ridiculed you (1 Peter 3:15-16)
5. Sit with God and ask Him to search your conscience. Ask Him to show you issues that need to be reconciled, healed, forgiven and let go.
6. Confess and repent: Do you have contempt for God, who is very kind to you, puts up with you, and deals patiently with you? Don't you realize that it is God's kindness that is leading you to him and trying to change the way you think and act? (Romans 2:4)

Ask yourself:

1. What changes does God want me to make in my life, character and personality? (John 15:2,5-8)

Keep in mind:

1. When Jeremiah wrote Lamentations he was heartbroken. As you read through Lamentations pay attention to how he expressed his emotions to God.
2. "Giving up doesn't always mean you are weak; sometimes it means that you are strong enough to let go." (Author Unknown) Read 2 Cor.12:8-10.

Take action...

1. Look up the following passages and paraphrase each one.
   ☐Psalm 34:18; Isaiah 53:4-6; Ecc.7:2-4; Luke 17:32-33;   2
   Cor. 6:11-13; Eph. 5:11,13; Col 1:19-20

Reflection

1. After reading today's devotion, I realize...
2. The key statements I need to remember and work on are...
3. The positive consequences of remembering and working on these statements will be...

DAY 25

IT'S HARD

Even when I walk, through the darkest valley (Psalm 23:4)

When you are sorrowful look again in your heart, and you shall see that in truth you are weeping for that which has been your delight ~Kahlil Gibran

Broken Hearts...

I'm guessing that by this time in your life you've experienced a broken heart. Maybe you experienced a break up recently, your partner died, a family member passed away, or you might be in a bad relationship and want to get out of it but you can't, or you made some bad choices and it cost you your relationship.

Whatever the case may be, you need to grieve and let go.

Don't Ignore your Pain…

We can't ignore our pain or numb out. We have to feel it and let it go. I felt physically and emotionally sick, but I got through it one day and one tear at a time. Do your best to work through your loss and truly heal. Adjusting takes time but you can do it. When I was going through my grieving process and allowing the pain to surface, I was able to clarify what I needed and wanted. Working my way through my losses, God was able to fill my voids and replace what I needed in my life (Psalm 23).

Letting Go…

Is there anything that you're hanging onto today that you need to grieve and let go of? Are you living in the past? Do you need to accept that the relationship you're in needs to end? Is your rear view mirror getting clearer? Take time today to see if you're living in the past.

Consider this…

1. When you look to resolve your issues of the past, make sure you're doing it as a child of God, a new creation. Remember, you're free now. All you need to do is learn how to walk in it.
2. Use the past to grow and move forward (Phil 3:13-14).

Take action…

1. Look up the following passages and paraphrase each one.
   ☐Heb. 4:12,15-16; Jer. 23:29; 1 Peter 2:3-4; John 15:3;
   2 Tim. 2:15; Gen. 4:5-7; Matt. 15:18-20; Eph. 4:22-24;
   Col. 3:9-10; Acts 17:27; Deut. 4:29; Isaiah 55:6; Jer. 29:13;
   Luke 9:23; John 1:12; Prov. 11:30

Reflection

1. After reading today's devotion, I realize…
2. The key statements I need to remember and work on are…
3. The positive consequences of remembering and working on these statements will be…

DAY 26-27

CHANGE IS A CHOICE

But I will be merciful only if you stop your evil thoughts and deeds and start treating each other with justice; [6] only if you stop exploiting foreigners, orphans, and widows; only if you stop your murdering; and only if you stop harming yourselves by worshiping idols. [7] Then I will let you stay in this land that I gave to your ancestors to keep forever. Jeremiah 7:5-7

Childlike Faith...

To live our new life in Christ we need to go to God with childlike faith, and with a childlike attitude (Col. 3, Matt 18:3).

Change occurs when we are humble and childlike before God.

"No one pours new wine into old wineskins. If they did, the wineskins would burst, the wine would spill, and the wineskins would be ruined. Instead, people pour new wine into new wineskins so that both are kept safe." (Matt 9:17)

This is true about our rebirth. You're a new person now so your old ways of doing things needs to change. Old behaviors in new wine skins will burst; the old ways of coping must come to an end. Living independently from God does not work, nor does it bring love, peace or joy. God has a new start for you.

Change...

There are five stages of change: pre-contemplation, contemplation, preparation, action, and maintenance.

- •Pre-contemplation is the stage at which there is no intention to change behavior in the foreseeable future. Many individuals in this stage are unaware, or under-aware, of their problems.

- •Contemplation is the stage in which people are aware that a problem exists, and are seriously thinking about overcoming it, but have not yet made a commitment to take action.

- •Preparation is a stage that combines intention and behavioral criteria. Individuals in this stage are intending to take action in the next month and have unsuccessfully taken action in the past year.

- Action is the stage in which individuals modify their behavior, experiences, or environment in order to overcome their problems. Action involves the most overt behavioral changes and requires considerable commitment of time and energy.

- Maintenance is the stage in which people work to prevent relapse and consolidate the gains attained during action. For addictive behaviors, this stage extends from six months to an indeterminate period past the initial action.

Prayer...

Take time to think and pray about the things you want to change (behaviors, attitudes, defects, hang-ups, habits, reactions, automatic responses). Make a list.

- Review the stages of change and identify where you're at on the stages of change

- List (on paper) the advantages to what you want to change, and then list the disadvantages.

- Identify if the behavior that you want to change brought you security, protection, escape, approval, validation, significance, relief, acceptance, or control.

- How can you meet these needs in a healthier way?

- Develop a support team: "Two are better than one because they have a good return for their hard work. [10] If either should fall, one can pick up the other. But how miserable are those who fall and don't have a companion to help them up! [11] Also, if two lie down together, they can stay warm. But how can anyone stay warm alone? [12] Also, one can be overpowered, but two together can put up resistance. A three-ply cord doesn't easily snap." (Ecc.4:9-12)

Persistence...

Making changes requires persistence...

• If you feel stuck, bring your whole self to Christ, not just the problem. Ask God to change your heart. Commit yourself to pray to that end. It's God's heart to give good gifts to His children. ~ Sheila Walsh

• Everyone wants to change, but change demands desire and discipline before it becomes delightful. There is always the agony of choice before the promise of change. ~ Larry Lea

• Change is one of the seven basic needs of human happiness! -- And variety is the spice of life! (Word of love.com)

• Because they have no changes, therefore they fear not God. (Ps. 55:19)

New Perspective on Change…

See Change as:

• Christ challenging you to grow stronger and wiser as a person

• Hope for the future. Take an honest look at your life and ask yourself, what needs to change?

• Action: Attitude adjustment. Faith without works is dead

• No more nonsense: it's time to grow, mature and heal

• God has a plan and purpose for every change

• Equipped: God will provide the resources, strength, courage and support you need to make the changes He's calling you to make

Take Action…

1. Look up the following passages and paraphrase each one.
   ☐ Eph. 1:18-19; 1 Peter 2:9-10; Rom. 8:28-29; Col. 1:9;
   2 Cor. 10:5; Psalm 143:10; Prov. 2:1-2; Acts 20:32; 27:7-16;
   Eph. 1:17; John 1:5; Eph. 4:22-24; Rom. 6:6

TODAY'S RESOLUTIONS

1. Father, help me to stay committed to change.

Reflection

1. After reading today's devotion, I realize…
2. The key statements I need to remember and work on are…
3. The positive consequences of remembering and working on these statements will be…

Source:

Prochaska JO, DiClemente CC, Norcross JC. In search of how people change. *Am Psychol*. 1992; 47:1102–4.

DAY 28-30

CREATE A PLAN TO DEAL WITH YOUR OBSTACLES TO CHANGE

And as he sowed, some seed fell along the path, and the birds came and devoured it. [5] Other seed fell on rocky ground, where it did not have much soil, and immediately it sprang up, since it had no depth of soil.[6] And when the sun rose, it was scorched, and since it had no root, it withered away.[7] Other seed fell among thorns, and the thorns grew up and choked it, and it yielded no grain (Mark 4:4-7)

Obstacles…

It's not uncommon to encounter obstacles when we're trying to change something about ourselves. We just need to be prepared for them and to create a plan to deal with them.

1. What are common obstacles to life change? **Check off** what applies to you:
    o **People:** your change will affect the people in your life. You want to come out of the dark, yet the light of your change can be blinding to some.

o **Lack of support from your family or friends**: if this occurs, seek support elsewhere. God will provide it. You can trust in that. (Eph. 4; Ecc. 4:9-12)

o **Fear**: we often wonder what will happen when we face our ashes, our issues, and the people that hurt us.

    a. Take time to list your fears on paper. Name them and then surrender them.

    b. Face each fear one by one

    c. Common fears are: vulnerability, intimacy, setting new boundaries, failure, success, dealing with real emotions, re-defining yourself, risking, facing reality, taking responsibility and ownership.

o **Lack of commitment**

o **Lack of motivation**

o **Negative self-talk**

o **Lack of courage, hope, and faith in God's promises**

o **Being enabled, rescued, or fixed by others**

o **Too many choices**

o **Defense mechanisms**

o **Unhealthy and irrational values and belief systems**

o **Procrastination**

o **Doubt**

o **Feeling overwhelmed**

o **Denial**

o **Self-pity**

o **Victim mentality**

o **Martyrdom**

o **Inability to manage stress**

o **Excuses**

o **Pessimism and negativity**

o **Worst case scenario thinking**

o **Lack of trust in God and others**

o **Habitual ways of reacting to stress**

o **Lack of patience**

o **Lack of faith based self-talk**

o **Lack of vision and purpose**

o **No plans and goals**

o **Not connecting pain to lack of change**

o **Prosperity from the negative habit or sin**

o **Too many choices**

o **Depression**

2. ***Fear***...Don't let your fears stop you. Keep moving forward and remember: God didn't give you a spirit fear (2 Tim. 1:7)

    ☐Jesus faced His purpose and mission afraid

    ☐Remember, it's possible that you built a lifestyle and image around your fears, so your mind will have automatic responses. When your fears are triggered, be aware of your automatic coping mechanisms. Subconsciously, you have formed habits of response to survive and to manage your feelings.

    ☐Remain obedient to God's word

    ☐Listen to your accountability partners

    ☐Practice humility and honesty

    ☐Ask for help and advice

    ☐Pray

    ☐Admit and accept where you are right now so you can get to where you want to be

Take Action...

1. Look up the following passages and paraphrase each one.
    ☐Matt 5:13; John 15:6; 2 Cor. 12:20-21; 1Tim. 1:18-19
       Heb. 4:14-16; 2 Cor. 5:21; Heb. 9:14; Eph. 2:4-10
       Eph. 6:10-12; Col. 1:10; 1 John 1:7; 2 Cor. 5:17-21

Reflection

1. After reading today's devotion, I realize...
2. The key statements I need to remember and work on are...
3. The positive consequences of remembering and working on these statements will be...

REVIEW & REPAIR

Reshaping Your Soul

1. What did I learn this past month about myself, God and others?

2. What concepts or ideas stood out to me in the devotions? Why?

3. What adjustments do I need to make in my life?

4. What needs to change (if anything) about how I think, feel, and act?

5. What changes have I made so far? What actions have I taken?

6. How are people reacting to my changes?

7. Steps I will continue to take are…

8. I'm committed to…

9. My victories this week were…

10. God please help me with…

DAY 31-32

SATAN WILL TRY TO KEEP YOU FROM WORKING OUT YOUR SALVATION

The thief comes only to steal and kill and destroy; I have come that they may have life, and have it to the full. (John 10:10)

Put to death, therefore, whatever belongs to your earthly nature: sexual immorality, impurity, lust, evil desires and greed, which is idolatry. [6] Because of these, the wrath of God is coming.[b] [7] You used to walk in these ways, in the life you once lived. [8] But now you must also rid yourselves of all such things as these: anger, rage, malice, slander, and filthy language from your lips. [9] Do not lie to each other, since you have taken off your old self with its practices [10] and have put on the new self, which is being renewed in knowledge in the image of its Creator. (Col. 3:5-10)

Sin, Bad Habits, Brokenness & Addiction…

Satan will try to:

oKeep you worrying, preoccupied and obsessing about your problems, past, circumstances, loss, hardships, unfair treatments, offenses, and the people in your life.

oGet you to take life personally so he can get you to be impulsive and react in ways that resemble your old life. If Satan can get you to react then he tricked you to move ahead of God. His goal is to isolate you from God. He tries to make you a Lost Sheep or a Prodigal Son or Daughter.

oMake you more emotionally dependent on others than on God. So make sure that you seek first the kingdom of God and love Him first because He first loved you.

oFill you with pride so you can get people in your life overly dependent on you, instead of on God.

oConvince you that only you can solve the issues or problems in your life.

oConvince you that life should go your way.

oGet you angry if people don't follow your advice.

oGet you to focus on your imperfections and try to fix them in your own strength.

oGet you to be idealistic instead of realistic.

oGet you to lose your autonomy by staying in unhealthy relationships. He does this by lying to you. He makes you think that you will fall apart without this person.

oGet you to base your image on how others act or treat you.

oBuild your worth on fixing, rescuing or enabling others.

oGet you to personalize your failures and to make them your identity.

oGet you to be driven by shame and guilt. He will try to get you to make decisions and choices based on fear and/or guilt.

oGet your thoughts tangled and twisted. He attacks your mind. Be sure to take your thoughts captive (2 Cor. 10:5). His goal is to get you to detach from your values, beliefs, support, and from God. If you lose touch with yourself then you become powerless to take responsibility for your thoughts, feelings, and actions. Satan's goal is to get you to lose control.

Thoughts… Be aware of what you're thinking about. Make sure that you're not allowing your mind to be preoccupied with a person or a problem so much so that it's all you think about, talk about, dream about or feel about. If you're connecting your problems and issues to everything that other people are saying and doing, you're obsessing and you are disconnected from God.

A note to Fixers/Caretakers/Rescuers...

*Make sure that you're **not** trying to ...*

> o Change things that you can't change
> o Take responsibility for problems that aren't yours
> o Fix things that aren't yours to fix
> o Change people
> o Give advice without being asked
> o Control others
> o Protect people from the consequences of their behaviors
> o Manage other people's feelings
> o Avoid your feelings, needs and wants
> o Disconnect from God's wisdom
> o Get overly involved in other people's problems
> o Be perfect to be loved and needed

Take Action...

1. Look up the following passages and paraphrase each one.

> ☐ Gal. 5:22-23; Titus 2:12; Eph. 4:22-24; 2 Peter 1:6-9; Rom. 5:3-5;
> 1 Kings 22:22; 2 Chron. 18:20-22; Acts 5:3; John 10:10;   1
> Peter 5:8; Dan. 10:12, 13; Mark 4:15; 1 Thess. 2:18

Reflection

1. After reading today's devotion, I realize...
2. The key statements I need to remember and work on are...
3. The positive consequences of remembering and working on these
   statements will be...

DAY 33

LOOK AT THE BIG PICTURE

"The trick to forgetting the big picture is to look at everything close up"
~ Chuck Palahniuk

"For I know the plans I have for you," says the LORD. "They are plans for good and not for disaster, to give you a future and a hope." (Jer. 29:11)

Stay Focused...

I want to encourage you to stay focused on the big picture. The big picture is the story of your life, the reason why God saved you. Even though pursuing our dreams and passions can leave us feeling sideways, we can't give up – we need to stay determined.

Dale Carnegie once said, "Most of the important things in the world have been accomplished by people who have kept on trying when there seemed to be no help at all."

Persistence...

Whenever you think you can't do any more and you are feeling defeated, think about Beethoven's **perseverance and determination**. It was said that he handled the violin awkwardly and preferred playing his own compositions instead of improving his technique. His teacher called him "hopeless as a composer." And, of course, you know that he wrote five of his greatest symphonies while completely deaf.

It's amazing what you can do when you allow your passions to overtake you. You have God given potential; don't let anything or anyone stop you. Remember, God doesn't want you to stop using your gifts and talents just because you hit a roadblock. Maybe the roadblocks are there because you're not paying attention. Live your life **every day.** Put your hand to the plow (Luke 9:62).

Ask yourself the following questions:

1. Am I still focused on my goals?
2. Am I feeling stuck?
3. Am I motivated?
4. Do I need to let go of a failure or be more assertive?
5. I want...
6. I need...

Take Action...

1. Look up the following passages and paraphrase each one.

☐Matt. 22:37-39; John 6:63; John 5:19; John 15:5; James 1:2-4
 2 Peter 1:3-10; 1 John 1:7; Psalm 32:5; Luke 11:2-4; Isaiah 61:1-4

Reflection

1. After reading today's devotion, I realize…
2. The key statements I need to remember and work on are…
3. The positive consequences of remembering and working on these statements will be…

DAY 34

GRACE AND FORGIVENESS

Forgiveness does not change the past, but it does enlarge the future.

~Paul Boese

For while the Law was given through Moses, grace (unearned, undeserved favor and spiritual blessing) and truth came through Jesus Christ. (John 1:17)

We need to rely on God's grace if we want to change and become the person God called us to be. Today I want you to explore your own definition of, and experience with, God's grace.

1. Grace is…
2. How do I connect to the grace of God?
3. How have people in my life helped me understand God's grace?
4. For me to open my heart to someone they need to…
5. How has the application of James 5:16 help me to grow, change, heal and become whole?

 a."Confess to one another therefore your faults (your slips, your false steps, your offenses, your sins) and pray [also] for one another, that you may be healed and restored [to a spiritual tone of mind and heart]. The earnest (heartfelt, continued) prayer of a righteous man makes tremendous power available [dynamic in its working]." James 5:16 (AMP)

    b.Describe the situation and your feelings about being forgiven both before and after your confession
6. What keeps me from opening up my heart? What has this cost me relationally, emotionally, spiritually?
7. I need to confess… I will confess to ……

Support and Strength…

Change is hard without support from others. We need help and strength on those days our cross gets heavy. Take a few minutes and do an inventory of the support systems you have in your life.

1. How has the support from others change my life?
2. What has been my experience with 1 Thess 5:14:

    a.[14] Brothers and sisters, we urge you to warn those who are lazy. Encourage those who are timid. Take tender care of those who are weak. Be patient with everyone.
3. What has been my experience with Gal. 6:2:
    a.Bear (endure, carry) one another's burdens and [a]troublesome moral faults, and in this way fulfill and observe perfectly the law of Christ (the Messiah) and complete [b]what is lacking [in your obedience to it].
4. How did the strength from someone else change or save my life?
5. What current set of circumstances in my life might be easier to deal with if I let myself be vulnerable and turn to God's people for support? What kind of support do I need? How will I structure the support?

Consider this…

1. Because of God's grace you can:
    ☐Face the truth without feeling condemned or ashamed
    ☐You can be real instead of ideal
    ☐Face your fears with confidence
    ☐Risk failing
    ☐Love others and yourself unconditionally
    ☐Admit to your flaws, defects, hang ups and hurts
    ☐Stop lying
    ☐Put your defenses or fig leaves down
    ☐See truth as a friend and as a way to be more Christ like
    ☐Face challenges, hardships, persecutions, unfair treatment and adversity
    ☐Be bold and assertive

Take Action…

1. Look up the following passages and paraphrase each one.
   ☐2 Cor. 12:9; Eph. 2:8-9; Rom. 11:6; Job 22:21-22; 2 Cor. 5:18-19; 1 John 4:20; 2 Cor. 3:18; Rom. 3:31; 1 Cor. 3:15: Eph. 4:30

Reflection

1. After reading today's devotion, I realize…
2. The key statements I need to remember and work on are…
3. The positive consequences of remembering and working on these statements will be…

DAY 35-36

LEARN HOW TO ASK FOR HELP

For by grace you have been saved through faith. And this is not your own doing; it is the gift of God. (Ephesians 2:8)

Asking for help sounds like an easy thing to do, but in reality it isn't. God has taught me that I can't fix myself because I need His grace. Grace allows us to do things our personality and will power can't do.

I wrote a note describing how grace will help you heal and go through God's sanctification process.

A note from Grace

I'm here to help you. I know you try to fix everything yourself. You've been doing it for years. I get that. But if you want to change from the inside out you need to rely on me. When you read the Word you think, "I need to change that." You try to apply God's principles on your own, but this doesn't work. You try to change everybody but yourself. This doesn't work either.

Following the law doesn't change you inside out. It only frustrates you, discourages you, causes you to feel fatigue, and heightens your fears, which leads to repeated failures in your healing process.

I'm here to help you grow and heal. Without my help there's a good chance that you might become anxious, worried, angry, depressed, and disconnected from God's Spirit. Some people slip back into addiction. God designed me to help you. It won't work any other way. Look at the lives of Jesus, the Apostle Paul, King David, Job, Moses, Joshua, and Peter. The list goes on and on. You need me to go from glory to glory.

To apply today's teaching to your life:

Let go of:

1. "Your need to rely on yourself."

Ask yourself:

2. Am I relying on grace to heal and grow?

3. Am I trying to solve my own problems alone? (Rom. 7:14-25)

4. What stops me from relying on God's grace?

Consider this…

1. Make a list of the issues and problems you're trying to fix on your own.

2. Start asking for help from God and others with the problems you're trying to fix by yourself.

3. Give grace a voice and create your own note.

Keep in mind

1. We all need a power greater than ourselves. God designed life in a way that we need Him. When you trust God and put your faith in Him, you will be able to do what you thought was never possible.

Take Action…

1. Look up the following passages and paraphrase each one.

   ☐Matt. 5:48; Rom. 12:1-2; Rom. 8:1-2; 2 Cor. 5:17,21; Eph. 4:22-24; John 5:37-40; Psalm 119:123-125; Phil. 3:7-9; Psalm 18:6

Reflection

1. After reading today's devotion, I realize…
2. The key statements I need to remember and work on are…
3. The positive consequences of remembering and working on these statements will be…

DAY 37

ADMIT TO YOUR MISTAKES

Confess your sins to each other and pray for each other so that you may be healed. The earnest prayer of a righteous person has great power and produces wonderful results. (James 5:16)

"Don't argue for other people's weaknesses. Don't argue for your own. When you make a mistake, admit it, correct it, and learn from it immediately."
~ **Steven Covey**

Working out your salvation is learning how to admit you're wrong.

Isolation...

Have you ever felt left out because you made a mistake or failed at something? Have you ever felt like everyone's in and you're left out? I know I have, plenty of times in my life.

We have a tendency to isolate from people when we make a mistake instead of admitting our wrongs and saying "I'm sorry, I was wrong", or "I made a mistake." For some people, those words are very hard to say. I want to encourage you not to separate yourself from God when you make a mistake. He doesn't stop loving you, in fact, He embraces you. He won't leave you discouraged. If everybody in your life turns against you, He won't. His love is unfailing and never ending. In some situations we just need to hang on to God until the storm passes (Rom. 8:28).

Confess…

If you screwed up, admit it. Be sure to settle your accounts, so this way you don't feel left out. Hugh White said, "When you make a mistake, don't look back at it long. Take the reason of the thing into your mind and then look forward. Mistakes are lessons of wisdom. The past cannot be changed. The future is yet in your power."

Take Action...

1. Look up the following passages and paraphrase each one.

        ☐Luke 5:32; James 5:19-20; Lev. 5:5-6; Ezr. 10:10-11; Neh. 9:1-3;
            Luke 19:8; Acts 19:18-19; Psalm 51:1-5; Luke 15:17-24;   2
            Chr. 7:13-14; Isaiah 55:7; Jer. 31:18-20

Reflection

1. After reading today's devotion, I realize...
2. The key statements I need to remember and work on are...
3. The positive consequences of remembering and working on these
    statements will be...

DAY 38

DECREASE SO JESUS MAY INCREASE

He must increase, but I must decrease. [He must grow more prominent; I must grow less so.] John 3:30

Self-Will...

I was working with a client name Tommy. He came for counseling because he felt like he had come to the end of his rope and couldn't hang on any more. The stress was getting to him. The more he tried to control his life the more out of control things became. He knew Christ but he didn't ask Him for help or guidance. He kept relying on his own resources, his own strength. He couldn't, and wouldn't, admit that he was failing. It was like he had something to prove. He wasn't surrendering to God. He wasn't admitting he was powerless and that his life was unmanageable. I was trying to teach him that nobody can really change or heal without surrendering to God and his Holy Spirit.

Surrender...

How are you doing at managing your life and soul? Have you given God permission to come into your life to help you manage it? When you accepted Christ you essentially said "I quit" or, "I surrender." Jawaharlal Nehru said, "The wheel of change moves on, and those who were down go up and those who were up go down." Think about this for a minute. We need to let go, and let God do His work in us to make us whole.

Take a few minutes and read what I think it takes to become a whole person: (Eph. 4:17-24)

10 ways to become a whole person

1. Admit that you need help
2. Be honest with yourself
3. Feel your feelings
4. Look at reality
5. Humble yourself
6. Build trust in God
7. Admit that you're lost and you don't know what to do
8. Confess your faults and sins, and repent
9. Accept that it's okay to need help
10. Stop pretending...lose the "I have it all together" image.

Take action...

1. Look up the following passages and paraphrase each one.

   ☐Phil. 2:12-13; Psalm 1:1; John 15:5; 1 John 2:3-5

Reflection

1. After reading today's devotion, I realize...
2. The key statements I need to remember and work on are...
3. The positive consequences of remembering and working on these statements will be...

DAY 39

SANCTIFICATION

It is because of him that you are in Christ Jesus, who has become for us wisdom from God—that is, our righteousness, holiness and redemption. (1 Cor. 1:30)

Today were going to define 'sanctification'. Let's look at some definitions together, shall we?

Sanctification is…

1. The process of being made holy through the work of the Holy Spirit
2. The process of renewal, redemption, reconciliation and restoration
3. A state of separation unto God; all believers enter into this state when they are born of God: "But of Him you are in Christ Jesus, who became for us wisdom from God—and righteousness and sanctification and redemption" (1 Corinthians 1:30). This is a once-for-ever separation, eternally unto God. It is an intricate part of our salvation, our connection with Christ (Hebrews 10:10).
4. A practical, progressive holiness in a believer's life, while awaiting the return of Christ.
5. The process of being changed into His perfect likeness—holy, sanctified, and completely separated from the presence of evil.
6. To make holy; purify. Lifestyle change.
7. Progressive: Sanctification refers to the process in our daily lives by which we are being conformed to the image of Christ.
    a. It is the process of becoming what we are in Christ. This involves the putting off of the old habits of lying, stealing, backbiting, etc., and putting on the Christ-like qualities of honesty, mercy, and love (cf. Colossians 3:1-10)
8. The putting off of the old man, and the putting on of the righteousness of Christ, is three dimensional: positional, progressive, and ultimate.
    a. The argument of the apostle Paul in Romans 6 is that we are obligated to experience *progressive sanctification* because of our positional sanctification accomplished on the cross of Calvary.

Take action…

1. Look up the following passages and paraphrase each one.
   ☐Ezek. 18:20; Rom. 8:28-29; James 1:2-4; John 16:13; Matt. 7:5
   ☐Rom. 2:2; Eph. 4:22-24; Heb. 12:15; Psalm 1:1-3; Josh. 1:8   2
      Cor. 3:18

Reflection

1. After reading today's devotion, I realize…
2. The key statements I need to remember and work on are…
3. The positive consequences of remembering and working on these statements are…

DAY 40-41

PLAYING A PART IN YOUR SANCTIFICATION

For I am confident of this very thing, that He who began a good work in you will perfect it until the day of Christ Jesus. (Philippians 1:6)

Growing in Christ…

If you want to grow in Christ, you need keep your heart open to seeing the truth that God wants to show you about Him, and about yourself. You need to be open to the truth, for Jesus is both grace and truth, and the way, the truth and the life (John 1:17; John 14:6)

He wants to show you about you. When you keep your heart open our Father will show you, in His loving and graceful way, why you lose your peace and joy; why you hurt, why you act and behave the way you do.

He helps you to accept what is real. God wants you to face the reasons why you separate yourself from Him. He will show you what you fear, what you need, and what you desire. He will inventory your beliefs and values, and help you line them up with His truth. Remember, when we were children we were raised by imperfect people. Like Paul said, we **all** fall short of God's glory. (Romans 3:23)

Parents and caretakers…

Parents, or caretakers, taught us our beliefs and values either through direct teaching or modeling. For me personally, God did an overhaul of my belief and values systems. I was so far-off from the truth. I had so many fearful reactions that caused me to separate from God. But He gave me grace to be open to seeing them, and allow Him to change them.

Faith…

The key for me was to have faith and trust in God to transform me. This was scary because the foundation that once kept me safe and secure was being taken from me! But I have to say, God sustained me. God was showing me why my way wasn't working. He was helping me to remove my old identity and, at the same time, revealing to me my true identity in Christ.

If you're open to the truth, then God will give you the resources you need to turn your life around. The question is, are you open and willing to stay on the potter's wheel?

16 Signs of Playing Your Part in the Sanctification Process

1. You're ready to leave your old life because you know it's not working and you want to know what God's will is for your life (Matt. 6:33)
2. You're ready to make some changes in your character and personality
3. You crave truth
4. You're willing to learn God's ways of doing things
5. You admit you're powerless and you need a power greater than yourself
6. You're ready to work on unresolved pain and loss
7. You're repentant
8. You're ready to stop rebelling and submit to God's authority
9. You want God to be your "Abba" (Daddy)
10. You take responsibility for your soul
11. You practice letting go and letting God
12. You're open to feedback
13. You connect to others for accountability, support, feedback and love
14. You're ready to face your shortcomings, mistakes and failures
15. You want to see God's truths so you can change your beliefs and build your life on what God values
16. You're ready to forgive, make amends, and want to keep short accounts

Take action…

1. Look up the following passages and paraphrase each one.
   ☐Eph. 5:14-16; Rom. 12:1-2; Eph. 4:25-32; Rom. 12:9-21

☐Col. 3:5-17; 1 John 3:8; 2 Cor. 3:18; Matt. 7:5; Phil. 2:12;
James 4:2

Reflection

1. After reading today's devotion, I realize…
2. The key statements I need to remember and work on are…
3. The positive consequences of remembering and working on these
   statements are…

DAY 42-44

OBSTACLES TO SANCTIFICATION

*Like newborn babies you should crave (thirst for, earnestly desire) the pure
(unadulterated) spiritual milk, that by it you may be nurtured and grow unto
[completed] salvation. (1Peter 2:2)*

Today we are going to look at common reasons why believers get stuck in the
sanctification process. Take your time working through the questions.

Obstacle #1: Lack of Sound Teaching

[1] I solemnly urge you in the presence of God and Christ Jesus, who will someday
judge the living and the dead when he appears to set up his Kingdom: [2] Preach
the word of God. Be prepared, whether the time is favorable or not. Patiently
correct, rebuke, and encourage your people with good teaching. [3] For a time is
coming when people will no longer listen to sound and wholesome teaching.
They will follow their own desires and will look for teachers who will tell them
whatever their itching ears want to hear (2 Tim. 4:1-3).

Keep in mind:

1. For faith to grow you need to be in God's Word. You need to take time
   to study and understand God's character, ways and promises.
2. Applying and living out God's word is essential. Just having knowledge
   and not applying it will not increase faith. Whatever truth God has
   revealed to you, you are now accountable to it.
3. Going to a church that preaches sound doctrine is very important. Make
   sure you're being fed sound doctrine and learning how to apply it to your
   everyday life in practical ways.

4. God uses the Bible to speak to you so he can build a relationship with you. (Psalm 119:27)
5. Try not to get hung up on doctrine to the point you where you forget the author....

Ask yourself:

1. How often do I study God's Word?
2. What doctrines have I studied?
3. Do I memorize scripture? Do I pray scripture?
4. Does my pastor teach me how to apply the doctrines being taught?
5. Do I need to meet with my pastor to talk about things that confuse me in God's Word?
6. Do I have a set devotional time?
7. Do I share God's Word with others?

Obstacle # 2: **Failure to progress beyond basic teachings**

In fact, though by this time you ought to be teachers, you need someone to teach you the elementary truths of God's word all over again. You need milk, not solid food! (Heb. 12:5)

Like newborn babies you should crave (thirst for, earnestly desire) the pure (unadulterated) spiritual milk, that by it you may be nurtured and grow unto [completed] salvation (1Peter 2:2).

How to Grow beyond the Basics

Keep in mind:

1. **The word of God:** rightly used, does not leave a man as it finds him, but improves and makes him better. (M.Henry)
2. **No Pain no Gain:** We need to be receptive to the pains of growth (letting go of our temptations, character defects, old ways of coping, defenses, hurts, and hang ups).
3. **We need to grow beyond the basics:** As a Christian you should be consistently practicing confession, repentance, surrender, prayer, Bible study, honesty, forgiveness, grieving, and obedience, to name a few.
4. **We need to allow God's Spirit to discipline us:** a) Be aware of your issues (hurts, sin, bad habits, defects of character, brokenness, immaturity, etc. b) Develop structure in your life so you can stay focused on your goals and grow in your character and personality traits, c) Confront unhealthy character patterns d) Learn how to receive God's grace along with living out the truth God is trying to teach you.

5. ***Learn from mistakes:*** If you keep making the same mistake then you're not allowing God to sanctify you.
6. ***Discipline:*** Don't take God's discipline personally.

Obstacle # 3: Not receiving God's forgiveness and mercy

Seeing their faith, Jesus said to the paralyzed man, "My child, your sins are forgiven." (Mark 2:5)

In order for you and I to ***change from the inside out*** we need to accept God's forgiveness. It's not a feeling, it's a fact that God's forgives me for my past, present and future sins. It doesn't make sense for me to now wallow in guilt and condemnation.

In the past I didn't want to be forgiven. In fact, I enjoyed the pity party more than the freedom that God's forgiveness brings. I wanted to stay stuck in my guilt because I truly didn't want to change. At the time it felt easier to stay angry at life, myself and others. My condemnation gave me the excuse to sin and do what I wanted to do because I was lost, wounded and broken.

Forgiveness connects us to God. Guilt separates us from God. When I feel guilt I act in a different way. When I know and want to be forgiven I act in a different way. In other words, if I want to do my own thing and not take responsibility for my life, I stay stuck in my guilt.

When I feel guilt it's because I have violated a value or belief that I hold. Sometimes I'm just not ready to live out a certain value or belief, so if I ask for forgiveness, I'm demonstrating that I'm ready to give up a particular sin or immaturity. For me, when I ask for God's mercy and forgiveness I'm ready to change from the inside out.

Ask yourself:

1. Do you accept God's forgiveness? Do you use your guilt and self-condemnation as an excuse not to change from the inside out?
2. Why wouldn't you receive God's forgiveness? Make a list of the reasons that come to mind.
3. Are you stuck in habitual sin? Are you not confessing because it would mean you would have to change your ways?
4. What do you feel guilty about? What beliefs or values do you consistently violate? What do you gain? What do you lose?

Take action...

1. Look up the following passages and paraphrase each one.

☐Matt. 5:13; John 15:6; 2 Cor. 12:20-21; 1 Tim 1:18-19; Eze. 18:24
Deut. 32:15-18; Job 34:26; 1 Peter 5:8-9; Acts 5:3; 2 Cor. 2:8-11
James 4:7; 1 Peter 1:14; Mark 4:18-19; 1 Cor. 10:6-8

Reflection

1. After reading today's devotion, I realize…
2. The key statements I need to remember and work on are…
3. The positive consequences of remembering and working on these statements will be…

DAY 45

SELF-CONTROL & SANCTIFICATION

I am the vine; you are the branches. Whoever abides in me and I in him, he it is that bears much fruit, for apart from me you can do nothing. (John 15:5)

Today I want you to read Romans 7:14-25 and focus on verses 14-24. What word, or words, comes to mind when you read through these verses?

Will power & control…

Along with those words you just listed I want you to focus on the word "control." Paul wasn't willing to admit defeat nor was he willing to give up control. He believed in God's laws and he was determined to see them through, although, the more he tried to gain control of himself or his life, the more it seems he lost control of it. He wasn't depending on God's Spirit for help. He relied more on the principles. What do you think?

When I counsel people I talk to them about the need to give up control to God and the need to surrender to him. I try to help them to develop the perspective of John the Baptist, *"I must decrease so that He may increase."* (John 3:30) …I think this is one of those kingdom paradoxes.

Ask yourself:

1. What are some things in my life that I need to let go of and admit defeat? If I do how might my life change?

2. What scares you about surrendering these issues to God? Explain

3. Who, or what, am I trying to control? Explain why?

4. What happens to me when I try to control something greater than myself or capabilities? Explain

Keep in mind:

1. The Serenity Prayer

> God grant me the serenity
> to accept the things I cannot change;
> courage to change the things I can;
> and wisdom to know the difference.
>
> Living one day at a time;
> Enjoying one moment at a time;
> Accepting hardships as the pathway to peace;
> Taking, as He did, this sinful world
> as it is, not as I would have it;
> Trusting that He will make all things right
> if I surrender to His Will;
> That I may be reasonably happy in this life
> and supremely happy with Him
> Forever in the next.
> Amen.

--Reinhold Niebuhr

Take action...

1. Look up the following passages and paraphrase each one.
   1 Cor. 2:14; Rom. 7:14; Jude 19; Rom. 8:5-9; Rom. 8:12-13
   Gal. 5:16-17; Eph. 5:18

Reflection

1. After reading today's devotion, I realize...

2. The key statements I need to remember and work on are...

3. The positive consequences of remembering and working on these statements will be...

DAY 46

SELF-DISCIPLINE

*A man without self-control
is like a city broken into and left without walls. (Prov. 25:28)*

Today we are going to discuss the importance of developing self-control and self-discipline. Without the fruit of self-control we really can't make progress in our sanctification. We need to be connected to Jesus because apart from him we can do nothing. We need to abide in Christ so the Holy Spirit can help us behave like God's children.

Self-Discipline…

God wants to teach us how to be disciplined. Self-discipline is the mark of a wise person, and it is also an aspect of Christian character. Winners and champions are made through self-discipline and self-control.

In his early days, the apostle Peter was known to be impulsive and impetuous, which means he lacked self-discipline and self-control. In 2 Peter 1:5-9 he gives us the formula for developing self-control and self-discipline:

"In view of all this, make every effort to respond to God's promises. Supplement your faith with a generous provision of moral excellence, and moral excellence with knowledge, [6] and knowledge with self-control, and self-control with patient endurance, and patient endurance with godliness, [7] and godliness with brotherly affection, and brotherly affection with love for everyone. [8] The more you grow like this, the more productive and useful you will be in your knowledge of our Lord Jesus Christ. [9] But those who fail to develop in this way are shortsighted or blind, forgetting that they have been cleansed from their old sins."

Focus on the words productive and useful. When you develop self-discipline and self-control you are able to achieve your goals and live your life according to God's purpose and plan.

Peter was able to keep his behavior on track because he taught himself how to control his thoughts, emotions and actions by getting to know God personally, and applying God's word to his life and situations.

Part of the reshaping process is asking God to help you be more self-disciplined so you can best serve Him and others with excellence. A sign of self-discipline is demonstrating the fruit of the Spirit. Review the list in Gal. 5:22-24 and see where you might be coming up short. Mediate on verse 24.

Take action…

> 1. Look up the following passages and paraphrase each one.
>   ☐Prov. 25:28; 1 Cor. 10:13; Titus 1:8; Gal. 5:23

Reflection

> 1. After reading today's devotion, I realize…
> 2. The key statements I need to remember and work on are…
> 3. The positive consequences of remembering and working on these statements will be…

DAY 47

LEARN HOW TO MAKE RIGHT CHOICES

"See, I have set before you today life and good, death and evil." (Deut. 30:15)

Self-Control…

The prodigal son lacked self-control and discipline. But when he made it right with God and took responsibility for his choices he started to develop discipline and self-control. He saw things as they were, not as he wanted them to be. Once he faced the truth he was able to control his actions and take responsibility for his life, and his relationship with his father.

There's no doubt that he felt out of control and that he couldn't control the situation nor make a change. Once he realized that he can change his mind and stop the lifestyle he was living, he was able to regain a sense of self-control.

Part of working out your salvation is repentance. When you repent you're actually doing the opposite of your old behaviors or defects of character. For instance, if you tended to lie before, now you practice honesty.

Ask yourself:

1. Am I currently making bad choices? Why?
2. What can I do to make right ones? What do I need to let go of?
3. How can God help me? Father, help me to....

Take Action...

1. Look up the following passages and paraphrase each one.
   □Deut. 30:15; Luke 13:3; Acts 3:9; James 4:8-10; Prov. 28:13;
     Psalm 38:18

Reflection

1. After reading today's devotion, I realize...
2. The key statements I need to remember and work on are...
3. The positive consequences of remembering and working on these
   statements will be...

DAY 48

CONFRONT YOUR BAD HABITS

Submit yourselves therefore to God. Resist the devil, and he will flee from you.
(James 4:7)

Walking away from insanity...

God has given you the ability to control, and walk away from, your bad habits.
The best way to break a bad habit is to keep trying to make better choices.

Paul tells us to "...throw off your old sinful nature and your former way of life,
which is corrupted by lust and deception. [23] Instead, let the Spirit renew your
thoughts and attitudes. [24] Put on your new nature, created to be like God—truly
righteous and holy." (Eph. 4:22) Unfortunately, this doesn't happen
automatically. Habits are patterns of behavior and, in some cases, sin. Habits
can be positive or negative.

God knows that your bad habits are hard to break. He wants to expose the
flawed belief that's causing the behavior. The answer to overcoming our bad
habits can be found in 2 Cor. 12:8-10. Paul said, "Three different times I begged

the Lord to take it away. Each time he said, "My grace is all you need. My power works best in weakness." So now I am glad to boast about my weaknesses, so that the power of Christ can work through me. That's why I take pleasure in my weaknesses and in the insults, hardships, persecutions, and troubles that I suffer for Christ. For when I am weak, then I am strong." God wants us to rely on His strength. He says we can do all things through Him who strengthens us.

The Holy Spirit will help you to identify the negative habits which are holding you back. Like any bad habit there's a desire that can only be met by God. In most cases, the bad habit is our way of living independent from God which only leads to frustration, guilt and shame. Underneath a bad habit is usually the need for acceptance, approval, control, significance, stress relief, and validation.

I also want to remind you that Satan knows if he can keep you in the bad habit or habitual sin, it separates you from God and you can't accomplish God's will for your life.

Jesus said "It is written" (Matt. 4:1-11)

Something that helps to break bad habits is our self-talk. Self-talk is your sword of truth (Eph. 6:17). We need to learn how to rebuke Satan when he lies to us. Remember, there are lies that fuel your bad habits. The key to breaking the bad habit is to fix your thoughts on what is true, honorable, right, pure, lovely, and admirable (Phil. 4:8). Think about things that are excellent and worthy of praise and you can shatter those bad habits. Jesus spoke to the devil and reminded him of the truth. We need to do the same. Our power and authority is in the name of Jesus.

The Holy Spirit will show you what's underneath your bad habits and will expose them for what they are. Once you receive the truth you can reject the lie and ask God to fill the voids deep within your soul. Bad habits take time to change so be patient and disciplined in the sanctification process. Keep submitting to God and he will enable you to develop strong, positive habits which lead to freedom in Christ.

God's Word...

When you repeat God's promises they will give you the power, strength and determination to break those bad habits. Joshua was told to meditate on God's word day and night so that he would obey Gods principles. By doing this God was telling him that he would be equipped, encouraged and empowered to do what He has called him to do (Joshua 1:5-9).

My point is, when we mediate on God's word it creates faith based self-talk based on God's truth. Self-talk is a lot like walking in faith, believing and hoping in what hasn't happened yet. When you do this you're acting in faith which allows you to become who you want to be. The idea is to create faith-based self-talk to help you break the bad habits that God is calling you to walk away from. Replace the bad habits with God's truth and watch your life change.

Take action…

1. Look up the following passages and paraphrase each one.
   - Rom. 12:1-2; James 4:7; 1 Peter 5:7; 1 Cor. 16:19; Psalm 34:10b
   - Matt. 12:41; Acts 2:38; Acts 3:19; Isaiah 55:7; Psalm 16:8
   - Gal. 5:22-23; Titus 2:12; Eph. 4:22-24; Col. 1:20; Deut. 33:27

Reflection

1. After reading today's devotion, I realize…
2. The key statements I need to remember and work on are…
3. The positive consequences of remembering and working on these statements will be…

DAY 49-50

TRANSFORMATION

The sacrifice you desire is a broken spirit. You will not reject a broken and repentant heart, O God. (Psalm 51:17)

Today I want to talk to you about **Transformation** and what it means.

Transforming means: to change the condition of something. When you reflect on this word I want you to associate it with redemption and painful feelings or regrets. Part of transformation is surrendering to God your pain and regret so it doesn't hold you back. God's forgiveness is redemption. When we receive this gift through Jesus we can find a way to turn our pain and regret around into forces that move us forward (Rom. 8:28).

Repression…

God can't change our lives, or heal our broken hearts, if we repress negative emotions or avoid feeling them. The problem with this is it only brings more pain and it prevents us from transforming our character and making the needed changes in our lives. God wants to take our despair and transform it into strength. When we experience a defeat the Holy Spirit will help us redirect its energy, or intent to destroy us, into a commitment to do better. The Holy Spirit shines light into the darkness and transforms it; this is redemption and sanctification.

As we learn from Paul's struggle with sin (Rom. 7:14-25) no matter how much we fight our pain, regrets or bad habits in our own strength, they don't go anywhere. But as soon as we ask Jesus for help He will shine his light and the darkness is no more. Jesus wants to transform our problems and painful situations so they can be used to advance God's kingdom. Transformation equals freedom.

12 Things you need to do to Transform your Life

Consider this…

1. So from this point forward I want to challenge you to feel your pain. What's the saying, "No Pain, No Gain."
2. You will experience God's healing power when you ask Him to help you feel any negative emotions that you might be repressing. Remember, your feelings are signals; they have a message for you. If you feel angry this could mean someone crossed your boundaries. If you're feeling guilty that means you might be violating a value or a belief that's important to you.
3. Don't rush your transformation. You're a work in progress and sanctification ends when you die.
4. Allow God to comfort you when you're hurting. Reach out to others.
5. Be open to the changes the Holy Spirit is guiding you to make.
6. Expect change. God will equip you during the sanctification.
7. Make sure you have realistic expectations of God, others and yourself.
8. Lean not on your own understanding. Seek and trust God.
9. Be willing to address your weaknesses
10. Be honest about you unmet needs
11. Be willing to be a victim so you can become a victor. Admit that you have been wronged or offended.
12. Be willing to break the chains of sin in your life. Get honest and be repentant about your habitual sin.

Keep in mind...

1. Pain can help you make the needed changes in your life... Psalm 51:17, Job 42:62.
2. This too shall pass
3. To Thine own self be true
4. Let go, let God
5. God will redeem you: Job 19:15, Psalm 78:35, Rev. 21:4-5, Psalm 5:3, Isaiah 54:5

Take Action...

1. Look up the following passages and paraphrase each one.
   □ 1Peter 2:21; John 13:15; Rom. 8:28-30; 1 Cor. 11:1; 2 Cor. 3:18; Gal. 3:27; 1 John 3:2-3; Matt 5:48; Eph. 5:1-2; Col. 1:21-22; Eph. 2:10; Col. 1:10; Col. 3:15-17; 2 Thess. 2:16-17; Heb. 10:24-25; James 2:14-26

Reflection

1. After reading today's devotion, I realize…
2. The key statements I need to remember and work on are…
3. The positive consequences of remembering and working on these statements are…

DAY 51-53

SALVATION IS GOD'S WAKE UP CALL

Do not conform to the pattern of this world, but be transformed by the renewing of your mind. Then you will be able to test and approve what God's will is—his good, pleasing and perfect will. (Romans 12:2)

I want to start this section out by reminding you about why God saved you, and what's involved in working out your salvation. For the next few days I want to share with you how salvation is God's way of waking you up, and what you need to consider as you work out your salvation.

1. *Choices...* Before Christ, you made some bad decisions and choices. God will help you to correct them by teaching you how to make right choices.

But first, He needs to show you the incorrect beliefs and values that you had that caused you to make those choices.

- •Looking back what lessons did you learn?

2. ***Looking back*** at your old life, what things do you never want to be part of your life again? What can you do to prevent history from repeating itself?

- •Salvation is the first step to improving your life. It's a fresh start.
- •God shows you what's working in your life and what isn't by transforming your mind.

3. ***Our Father...*** wants us to grow spiritually and heal emotionally. He wants to strengthen our character, refine our personality, meet our unmet needs, help us with our unfinished business of the past, and to heal the hurts that occurred before we received His Son so that we can become oaks of righteousness (Isaiah 61:1 -4).

- •As believers we need to realize that when we accepted Jesus into our life, our spirit became united with God, but our old nature (the soul: mind, will, emotions) remains. I've come to realize that this is where the pruning or healing process begins (Isaiah 64: 8, John 15:1-8).
- •God our Father will fill and heal any voids we experienced in our childhood, and with His love, grace, and truth, He will remove the need for any sin or idol we used to feel loved, needed, accepted, significant, secure and in control (Hebrews 10:14)
- •God gradually shows you a new way of looking at life, yourself, people and the world. Before you came to Christ you viewed yourself a certain way. When you're in Christ you view yourself a certain way.
- •Positive view of myself (New Man- in Christ):
- •Negative view of myself (Old Man-Before Christ):

Paradigms... When we turn our will over to God our whole paradigm changes

1. How you view people changes.
2. How you view the world changes.
3. Healthy view of new self (in Christ)...

- •Forgiven
- •Loved
- •Accepted
- •Significant
- •Having a purpose
- •Special
- •Strong
- •Courageous
- •Wise
- •Gentle

- Kind
- Loving
- Faithful
- Peaceful
- Giving
- Self-controlled
- Patient
- Joyful
- Accepting
- Secure
- Holy and blameless
- Adopted
- Confident in Christ
- Child of God
- Friend of God
- God as Daddy
- Friend of Christ
- Redeemed
- Restored
- Justified
- Protected
- Alive
- Part of a family
- Complete
- Changing and growing New creation
- Victorious
- (Feel free to add to the list)
-

4. How you treat yourself will change as you grow in Christ.
5. How you treat others will change as you grow in Christ.
6. How you conduct your relationships change as you grow in Christ.

Take action...

1. Look up the following passages and paraphrase each one.
   ☐ Isaiah 55:8-9; Prov. 14:12; Ezek. 36:26-27
   ☐ 1 Cor. 3:19-20; 1 John 2:15-17; Col. 1:10; 1 John 3:8
   ☐ Psalm 1:1; John 15:2-5; Eph. 4:22-24

DAY 54

DEFENSES WE USE AS ADULT CHILDREN

I appeal to you therefore, brothers, by the mercies of God, to present your bodies as a living sacrifice, holy and acceptable to God, which is your spiritual worship. Do not be conformed to this world, but be transformed by the renewal of your mind, that by testing you may discern what is the will of God, what is good and acceptable and perfect. (Rom. 12:1-2)

You said you never wanted to see me hurt. Did you close your eyes then when I cried? ~ Unknown

The sanctification process stops when we remain defensive and avoid how we truly feel. We use our defenses to cope with pain instead of relying on Jesus

Jesus wants you to trust Him and to put down your guard so He can heal the hurt you're hiding. Whatever defense(s) you use will prevent you from working out your salvation, which results in character defects and disobedience. Our defenses prevent us from seeing the truth or reality of our life and pain.

The Ways We Avoid Our Feelings

(This list was taken from **ACA Inner Peace group**)

Read through the list and check off what applies to you.

☐Agreeing	☐Justifying, Moralizing
☐Analyzing	☐Minimizing
☐Attacking, Aggression	☐Projecting
☐Being Smug, Superior or Arrogant	☐Questioning or Interrogating
☐Blaming, Accusing	☐Rationalizing
☐Complying	☐Sarcasm
☐Debating, Arguing	☐Shouting, Intimidating
☐Defiance	☐Silence
☐Denying	☐Sparring
☐Evading, Dodging	☐Staring
☐Explaining	☐Switching
☐Frowning	☐Theorizing
☐Glaring	☐Threatening
☐Intellectualizing	☐Verbalizing, Talking
☐Joking	☐Withdrawing

Self-Examination: How do I Cope with Negative Emotions?

Examine yourselves, to see whether you are in the faith. Test yourselves. Or do you not realize this about yourselves, that Jesus Christ is in you?—unless indeed you fail to meet the test! (2 Cor. 13:5)

Ask yourself:

1. Am I aware of my own feelings- such as sadness, anger, happiness, satisfaction, frustration – either as they occur or some time later?

2. Do I name these feelings for myself or express them to others?

3. When do I become aware of my feelings? Do they have to be strong and powerful to get my attention?

4. Do I believe I have a good relationship with myself? Explain.

5. How do I handle strong emotions?

6. Emotions I seem to struggle with are:

7. Is how I feel and think about myself constant (stable, regular, continuous)? Or does it change, depending on whom I'm with? Explain.

8. When do I experience feelings of shame or self-hatred? When? What triggers it? What do I do to keep it going?

9. What do I do to lessen those negative feelings?

10. I like the following things about myself:

Take action…

1. Look up the following passages and paraphrase each one.

   ☐Matt 5:3; Luke 6:20-21; Matt 5:6; Psalm 116:6; Psalm 51:17
   Isaiah 66:2; Psalm 34:18; Isaiah 57:15; Isaiah 61:1; Luke 1:53

Reflection

1. After reading today's devotion, I realize…
2. The key statements I need to remember and work on are…
3. The positive consequences of remembering and working on these statements will be…

DAY 55-57

LET GO OF SELF-DECEPTION

"You will know the truth and the truth will set you free." (John 8:32)

Self-Deception...

One of the worst things we can do is to deceive ourselves and cover up the truth about our struggles. When we pretend that everything is okay, or when we avoid our issues, we don't allow God in so He can help us grow spiritually and emotionally.

I realized that if I want to grow in Christ I need to make a commitment to fight the temptation to resurrect my old habits and to rely on my old coping methods.

Reality...

"Every time I close the door on reality it comes in through the windows." (Jennifer Yane) Accepting reality isn't always easy but it's a necessity if you want to grow into the person God wants you to be.

I'm curious, why is it hard for you to face the truth or accept certain realities? How many times has the Holy Spirit tried to show you the reality about something and you ignored it thinking it would just go away?

Listen, I know it's scary to think about what lies ahead or underneath the denial that you might have been in or under. Just remind yourself that **God is with you.** He already knows your fears and apprehensions. (Psalm 139) What's coming to your mind right now? Invite Jesus in so He can show you specifics.

You're a work in progress and God loves you deeply. (John 3:16) He wants to walk with you through your valleys and peaks. God's spirit will see you through as long as you stay surrendered, humble, and teachable to what God wants to do within your soul and life.

Keep in mind...

- It's not easy to accept our powerlessness. Jesus is there for you.
- The potter's wheel is where you get molded and re-shaped. When you're on the potter's wheel God will:

- Help you to come to terms with your addictions, obsessions, bad habits, hurts, and hang ups.
- Make you aware of, and feel the pain of, your obsessions and compulsions.
- Stop your racing thoughts and over-rehearsing of your regrets.
- Change your desires and help you to control your impulses.
- Help you to accept your weakness and brokenness without feeling guilt and shame about who you are as a person.
- In His loving grace and mercy, show you (without condemnation) how your addictions, sins, brokenness and immaturities have affected every area of your life.
- Encourage you to become more conscious and aware of your life.
- Deepen your hunger for Him.
- Teach you how to bond to others and deepen your relationships.
- Build and rebuild your character.
- Teach you how to make godly choices.
- Teach you how to take ownership and give you the courage you need to take responsibility for your life and calling.
- Address the character defects that have developed in you as a result of living independently from Him.
- Accept the bad parts and good parts of your personhood.
- God will help you to define your needs, wants, desires, values, limits, and decisions
- Show you your calling and purpose.
- Fill in your developmental voids so you can become and adult with childlike faith.

Defenses...

We learned in our formative years of life how to protect ourselves and how to live independently form God. Below is a list of defenses that I believe we inherited from our first parents Adam and Eve (Gen 3). Read through and check off the defense you use to cope, hide your hurt, sin and flaws, or to feel accepted, significant, loved, safe or secure.

God needs to work through the following defenses (I use these to cope) ...

☐**Denial** - a refusal to accept external reality because it is too threatening. There are examples of denial being adaptive (for example, it might be adaptive for a person who is dying to have some denial (1John 1:7-9)

☐**Distortion** - a gross reshaping of external reality to meet internal needs (2Cor. 4:4)

☐**Delusional Projection** - frank delusions about external reality, usually of a persecutory nature (John 8:12)

☐**Fantasy** - tendency to retreat into fantasy in order to resolve inner and outer conflicts (1Peter 1:13)

☐**Projection** - attributing one's own unacknowledged feelings to others; includes severe prejudice, severe jealousy, hyper-vigilance to external danger, and "injustice collecting". (Projection is a primitive form of paranoia, so it is common in today's world) Luke 10:38-42)

☐**Hypochondriasis** - the transformation of negative feelings towards others, into negative feelings toward self, pain, illness and anxiety

☐**Passive Aggressive Behavior** - aggression towards others expressed indirectly or passively (Rom. 12:10-11; Gal. 6:1)

☐**Acting Out Behavior** - direct expression of an unconscious wish or impulse to avoid being conscious of the emotion that accompanies it (Gal. 2:12)

The following Defenses have short-term advantages in coping, but they often cause long-term problems in relationships, work, and enjoyment of life for people who primarily use them as their *basic style of coping with the world.* Check off the defenses that you commonly use.

☐**Intellectualization** - separation of emotion from ideas; thinking about wishes in formal, affectively bland terms and not acting on them

☐**Repression** - seemingly inexplicable naivete, memory lapse, or lack of awareness of physical status; the emotion is conscious, but the idea behind it is absent (and, of course, Scarlet "I won't think about that today" O'Hara from Gone With The Wind) 1 John 3:16

☐**Reaction Formation** - behavior that is completely the opposite of what one really wants or feels (e.g, taking care of someone when what one really wants is to be taken care of; studying to be a pilot to cover-up being afraid to fly). Note - this can work in the short term as an effective strategy to cope, but will eventually break down. (Matt 7:1-5)

☐**Displacement** - separation of emotion from its real object and redirection of the intense emotion toward someone or something that is less offensive or threatening in order to avoid dealing directly with what is frightening or threatening (Heb. 5:11-6:1)

☐**Disassociation** - temporary and drastic modification of one's personal identity or character to avoid emotional distress (Prov. 6:16-18)

Ask yourself...

1. My favorite defense mechanism(s) are...because...
2. My defenses have helped me to...
3. My defenses have hurt me in the following ways...
4. For me to lower my defenses I need to...
5. _____defense affects my relationship with God in the following ways:
6. _____defenses have affected my relationships in the following ways:

Take action...

1. Look up the following passages and paraphrase each one.

   ☐Gen. 3:1-10; Num. 32:23; Josh. 7:21; 2 Kings 17:9; Job 24:13-17 Ezek. 8:12; Prov. 28:13; Isaiah 29:15; 2 Cor. 4:4; Psalm 82:5
   Isaiah 8:20; 2 Cor. 3:14-15; Eph. 4:18; Isaiah 9:2; Matt 4:16
   Psalm 107:13-14; Isaiah 29:18; Isaiah 49:8-9; Luke 1:78-79
   Acts 26:17-18; Col. 1:13; 1 Thess. 5:4-5; 1 Peter 2:9

2. My plans to work on my defenses are...
3. This week I will...

Reflection

1. After reading today's devotion, I realize...
2. The key statements I need to remember and work on are...
3. The positive consequences of remembering and working on these statements are...

Resource:

1. **Dr. Sanity http://drsanity.blogspot.com/2005/12/psychological-defense-mechanisms.html**

DAY 58-60

FACE REALITY

Be good to your servant, that I may live and obey your word.
Open my eyes to see the wonderful truths in your instructions. I am only a
foreigner in the land. Don't hide your commands from me!
I am always overwhelmed with a desire for your regulations.
(Psalm 119:17)

What is a face, really? Its own photo? Its make-up? Or is it a face as painted
by such or such painter? That which is in front? Inside? Behind? And the
rest? Doesn't everyone look at himself in his own particular way? Deformations
*simply do not exist. ~**Pablo Picasso***

Jesus speaking…

The truth will set you free (John 8:32) so you need to learn how to be open to the Spirit of Truth (John 14:16-17) and examine your soul. If you want to become more like Me [Jesus] abide in Me (John 15:1-8) and I will help you to define your purpose and become the person Our Father wants you to be.

Self-Awareness…

Self-awareness determines your tomorrows. Don't be afraid to look at your reality. You only have one chance at this life. You can make your life better; just take a look at it. Experience it. Be true to yourself. Self awareness and examination will help you release negative experiences that are stored in your mind and heart. Self awareness and examination increases your ability to take charge of your life. Remember, life is not a spectator sport.

Memories…

Your brain has stored memories and experiences that help can you or hurt you. Self-awareness and examination is a way to tap into your unconscious and subconscious mind. This is where your past is stored. If you don't take time to understand yourself, you could be living in the past and not even realize it.

You could be living off a set of beliefs and values that aren't your own. You could be living your life based on a lies and false perceptions. In order to experience healing, and joy in your soul and spirit, you need to look inside your hard drive (mind, brain) and allow God to erase the files and programs that aren't working for you, then re-write them – replace them with new files (beliefs and values). This is what I think Paul was saying in Romans 12:1-2:

"I APPEAL to you therefore, brethren, and beg of you in view of [all] the mercies of God, to make a decisive dedication of your bodies [presenting all your members and faculties] as a living sacrifice, holy (devoted, consecrated) and well pleasing to God, which is your reasonable (rational, intelligent) service and spiritual worship. Do not be conformed to this world (this age), [fashioned after and adapted to its external, superficial customs], but be transformed (changed) by the [entire] renewal of your mind [by its new ideals and its new attitude], so that you may prove [for yourselves] what is the good and acceptable and perfect will of God, even the thing which is good and acceptable and perfect [in His sight for you]."

Note: I want you to take the next few days, or however long it takes, to work on the questions. Take your time. Don't move on until you feel you have answered all the questions.

Consider This:

Daily practices that will help you to live consciously:

- ☑Take time each day to get in touch with your thoughts, feelings, needs and wants. I suggest you write them down. Writing them down is like putting your subconscious on paper.
- ☑Record your interactions with people. How did you do? How do you react? How do people treat you? Why do they treat you this way? What, if anything, needs to change?
- ☑Connect with others. Relationships show us a lot about ourselves.
   - o Who did I connect with today?
   - o Who did I avoid today? Why?
      - ▪ I felt…
      - ▪ I thought…
- ☑Start to define and live according to your beliefs and values. Think about all areas of your life (for instance: relationships – mother, father, friend coworker, husband, wife, sibling, boyfriend, girlfriend, citizen, etc…) spirituality, career, dreams, health, recreation, hobbies, character, personality, personal development, etc…
   - o My beliefs about _____ are:
   - o My values about _____ are:
- ☑Where do you see your life 5 years from now? 10 years from now?
- ☑See a life coach or counselor to teach you how to develop self-awareness.
- ☑Journal. "If your life is worth living, its worth recording." Anthony Robbins
   - o Journaling can help you to:
      - ▪ Put your thoughts into perspective

- ▪Express your pain and hurt
- ▪Brainstorm your dreams
- ▪Set goals
- ▪Get closer to God
- ▪See your negative habits
- ▪See your strengths
- ▪See what you want to change
- ▪Identify your accomplishments
- ▪Identify reasons why you're stuck
- ▪Understand yourself
- ▪Live out your beliefs and values
- ▪Become the person you want to be

☑Pray. Stay in touch with God. Apply your faith, live it out. "Keep the Faith." Read personal development books. I personally rely on the Bible.

- oB= Basic
- oI= Instructions
- oB= Before
- oL= Leaving
- oE= Earth

☑Meditation

☑ Be honest with yourself. Thomas Jefferson said it best, "Honesty is the first chapter in the book of wisdom."

- oMake list of things you don't like about yourself.
- oPay attention daily to how you lie to yourself and others.
- oConsequences I experienced because I lied are…
- oReason why I'm dishonest is…
- oWhen I'm dishonest I'm usually feeling…
- oIs there anything in my life that I'm feeling pressured to do? What comes to mind? Who comes to mind? How do I feel?
- o(My) Negative attitudes affecting me are…
- oBehaviors that are hurting me are…
- oThese negative attitudes and behaviors are linked to a memory (experience, event, and person). Try identifying the link. What can I do? What do I need to do?
- oWhat's preventing me from being the person I want to be and living the life I want to live? (Consider all areas: Health, career, relationships, finances, personal development, recreation, hobbies, spirituality, dreams, passions, and your bucket list).
  - ▪No goals
  - ▪Lack of risk taking

- ▪Lazy
- ▪Procrastination
- ▪Below average expectations
- ▪Boredom
- ▪No vision
- ▪Lack of resources
- ▪Fear
- ▪Lack of accountability
- ▪No support
  - oRelationships I'm not happy with are:
  - oRelationships I'm happy with are:
  - oI'm the happiest when I'm…
  - oI'm at my worst when…

☑Become aware of your physical condition.
  - oHow would you describe your physical condition?
  - oDo you have energy, enthusiasm, zeal when you wake up in the morning?
  - oDo you have longevity? Endurance?
  - oHow do you sleep?
  - oHow often do you exercise? Do you do cardio?
  - oDo you have regular bowel movements?
  - oHow often do you go to the doctor? What do they say about your physical health?
  - oAre you over weight? Underweight?
  - oHow's the blood pressure?
  - oHow's your cholesterol?
  - oWhat's your diet like?

☑Take a look at your mental and emotional health: Am I mentally healthy?
  - oAre you:
    - ☐Able to accept yourself unconditionally
    - ☐Able to separate your worth from your accomplishments
    - ☐Able to have fun and not always try to prove yourself
    - ☐Able to take healthy risks
    - ☐Curious and adventurous
    - ☐Able to face adversity and life's trials
    - ☐To accept that life can be unfair
    - ☐Able to work through your false sense of entitlement
    - ☐Able to tell what you can and cannot control
    - ☐Able to put your mistakes and failures in to perspective and learn from them

☐Able to accept responsibility instead of blaming

☐Able to take responsibility for your thoughts, actions and behaviors

☐Able to balance your self-interest with that of the interests of others

☐Able to see the importance of getting involved with your community to make it a better place

☐Able to take responsibility for your own life and purpose

☐Able to be inter-dependent

☐Able to lean on others for support when you need it

☐Able to tolerate other people's flaws, mistakes and failures

☐Able to work through life's uncertainties and unknowns

☐Involved with something outside of yourself

If you checked off all of the statements, you are considered to be mentally and emotionally healthy. The statements that you didn't check off require your attention and action.

Take action...

1. Look up the following passages and paraphrase each one.

   ☐2 Cor. 13:5; Haggai 1:5; Psalm 4:4; Psalm 19:12-14; Psalm 26:2; Psalm 139:23-24; Lam. 3:40-42; James 1:23-25; Rom. 2:1-4

Reflection

1. How would I describe my relationship with myself, people in my life and God?
2. What have I accomplished so far in my life? Am I where I want to be?
3. Do I have negative people in my life? If so, Who? How are they negative? What am I doing about it?
4. What kind of transitions am I making in my life (new beginnings)? How am I handling my new beginnings?
5. What bad habits do I need to work on?

REVIEW & REPAIR

Reshaping Your Soul

1. What did I learn this past month about myself, God and others?

2. What concepts or ideas stood out to me in the devotions? Why?

3. What adjustments do I need to make in my life?

4. What, if anything, needs to change about how I think, feel, and act?

5. What changes have I made so far? What actions have I taken?

6. How are people reacting to my changes?

7. Steps I will continue to take are…

8. I'm committed to…

9. My victories this week were…

10. God please help me with…

DAY 61

RECONCILE YOUR LIFE

For if their rejection [i.e., the Jew's rejection of Christ] be <u>the reconciliation of the world</u>, what will their acceptance be but life from the dead? Rom. 11:15

Jesus said, the truth will set us free (John 8:32) so does this mean all we need to do is to study God's word, memorize scripture, and all our emotional and spiritual problems will just go away?

Relationship with God…

God wants us to know the truth because freedom comes with it, but we can't have freedom if we're not in relationship with God. Just ask Paul (Romans 7: 24-25). There needs to be a connection, like the branch to the vine (John 15). The branch has a life because it's connected to the vine. **C.S Lewis said** "The Christian is in a different position from other people who are trying to be good.

The Christian thinks any good he does come from the Christ-life inside him. He does not think God will love us because we are good, but that God will make us good because He loves us..."

Reconciliation...

While you have your Bible out go to **2 Corinthians 5:18-19.** So what's this passage teaching you? What's one word that stands out to you? Yes, reconciliation. Like any other relationship we have, if we're not connecting, we really don't care about the truth or what the person has to say, even if they're right.

I think the Pharisees are a great example of what not to do. They knew the truth but they didn't have a relationship with God. They weren't reconciled with Him.

Your goal is to build or rebuild your relationship with God. Today I want you to spend time looking up the names of God. This will help you to get a healthy image of Him.

Take action...

1. Look up the following passages and paraphrase each one.

☐2 Cor. 5:18-21; Rom. 5:10; Col. 1:20; Heb. 9:14; 1 John 4:4

Reflection

1. After reading today's devotion, I realize...
2. The key statements I need to remember and work on are...
3. The positive consequences of remembering and working on these statements are...

SANCTIFICATION

&

YOUR CONCEPT OF GOD

And because you are sons, God has sent the Spirit of his Son into our hearts, crying, "Abba! Father!" (Galatians 4:6)

DAY 62-64

STOP HIDING AND TAKE A LOOK INSIDE

Have mercy on me, O God, because of your unfailing love.
Because of your great compassion, blot out the stain of my sins.
Wash me clean from my guilt. Purify me from my sin.
For I recognize my rebellion; it haunts me day and night. (Psalm 51:1-3)

Developing your faith…

Developing your faith means you need to open up your heart to God. I used to think that if I hide from God, my problems and sins would just go away. Now that I look back, I really couldn't function spiritually and emotionally when I was hiding in my sin and brokenness. I was isolating a part of me from God, and when I did that, a part of me started to die.

Casting your burdens…

I remember losing touch with what I thought and felt, and as far as my memories go I couldn't get the story straight anymore. I had to ask God to examine my soul so I could understand what I was feeling. God helped me to see my transgressions so I can start to heal spiritually and emotionally. It wasn't easy to admit my hurt and my sin to God, but I have to tell you, I felt so free afterwards! I truly felt blessed. I learned the importance of casting my burdens and sins onto God for His help and direction.

Releasing our burdens isn't always an easy thing to do and sometimes we just don't know where to start. So I made a checklist for you so you can evaluate your ability to cast your burdens on the Lord.

Release your burdens…

Instructions: Indicate the number that best describes your Thoughts, Attitudes, Feelings, Perceptions, Behaviors, Events

1. I never do
2. I occasionally do
3. I usually do
4. I always do

This assessment is based on:

☐Psalm 55:22 "Give your burdens to the LORD, and he will take care of you. He will not permit the godly to slip and fall."

----

1. I find myself becoming consumed with my problems, the problems of others, my obstacles or my broken dreams.

2. I realize that I can be happy even though my life isn't exactly the way I planned or want it to be.

3. I find myself frustrated a lot.

4. I can say, "God, I trust you."

5. I think about all the times God has been there for me.

6. I can say from my heart, "Father, I know You know what's best for me and it is well with my soul."

7. If things don't go the way I want them to I'm able to let go and get myself back to a place of peace and rest.

8. I'm content with where I am in my life.

9. I don't let others' discontentment affect my contentment.

10. I believe that, with God, all things are possible.

11. I cast my problems onto God and I begin to take responsibility for finding solutions.

12. I tell God exactly how I feel.

13. I focus on what I have instead of what I don't have.

14. I tell God what to do or how to do it.

15. I tell God that I won't be happy unless it turns out the way I want.

16. I can release the weight of my burdens.

17. I know when I haven't released the weight of my burdens.

18. I believe God is in control.

19. My fears cause me to lose faith.

20. I trust God wherever I am in my life.

21. I ask God for the strength to endure.

22. I don't mine leaning on my friends and/or family, or my church family.

23. God will take care of me in the most vicious storms of life.

Take action…

1. Look up the following passages and paraphrase each one.

☐Gal. 6:1-3; Gal. 2:1; Phil. 4:6; Matt. 11:28-29; John 14:6;
Isaiah 26:3; Matt 6:33; Psalm 55:22; Phil. 4:6-7; Psalm 94:18-19

Reflection

1. After reading today's devotion, I realize…
2. The key statements I need to remember and work on are…
3. The positive consequences of remembering and working on these statements will be…

DAY 65

EXPLORE HOW YOU VIEW GOD

Open your Bible to Luke 1:67-75. Take a few minutes to read.

How do you view God? How would you describe Him to a new believer? How would you describe Him to a nonbeliever? How would you describe Him to a child? What words would you use to describe what He did for you? Do you see Him as a father or do you see him as an unreachable God that is distant, punishing and critical, a taskmaster, moody, a killjoy, detached, etc.?

I want you to go online and look up positive and negative personality traits. Read through them and pick the ones that you would use to describe your heavenly father and write them in the space provided below. (If you're not sure where to start looking online for personality traits, I've given you some sites to try below)

PositiveNegative

Keep in mind:

1. How you view God is crucial because it determines how deep and connected you're going to be with Him. Also, it determines how submissive and obedient you're going to be, which determines the level of spiritual and emotional healing you're going to receive from Him.

Consider this…

1. Try these web sites:
   - www.gurusoftware.com/GuruNet/Personal/Factors.htm
   - http://cte.jhu.edu/techacademy/web/2000/kochan/charactertraits.html
   - http://www.thelists.org/list-of-personality-traits.html

Take action…

1. Look up the following passages and paraphrase each one.

   ☐Isaiah 6:1-4; Gen. 1:26-27; John 1:14,17; Col. 1:6

Reflection

1. After reading today's devotion, I realize…
2. The key statements I need to remember and work on are…
3. The positive consequences of remembering and working on these statements will be…

DAY 66-70

DEVELOP A HEALTHY, REALISTIC VIEW OF GOD

Our image of God is crucial for healing and character growth. Today I want you to read through the names of God so you can see how awesome your Father is.

Names of God…

Instructions: Read through the names of God and check off the names that you can personally relate to through your own experience. Journal your experience and share it.

☐Jehovah (Exodus 6:2,3) - The LORD	☐Jehovah Chereb (Deuteronomy 33:29)

☐Adonai Jehovah (Genesis 15:2)
- Lord GOD

☐Jehovah Adon Kol Ha-arets
(Joshua 3:11)
- The LORD, the Lord of
All the Earth

☐Jehovah Bore (Isaiah 40:28)
- The LORD Creator

☐Jehovah Maginnenu (Psalms 89:18)
- The LORD Our Defense

☐Jehovah Goelekh (Isaiah 49:26;
60:16)
- The LORD Thy Redeemer

☐Jehovah Hashopet (Judges 11:27)
- The LORD the Judge

☐Jehovah Hoshiah (Psalms 20:9)
- O LORD Save

☐Jehovah Shammah (Ezekiel 48:35)
The LORD Is There

☐Jehovah Tsidkenu (Jeremiah 23:6)
- The LORD Our Righteousness

☐Jehovah Tsuri (Psalms 19:14)
- O LORD My Strength

☐Jehovah Sali (Psalms 18:2)
- The LORD My Rock

☐Jehovah Shalom (Judges 6:24)
- The LORD (our) Peace

☐Jehovah Shammah (Ezekiel 48:35)
The LORD Is There

☐Jehovah Tsidkenu (Jeremiah 23:6)
- The LORD Our Righteousness

☐Jehovah Mephalti (Psalms 18:2)
- The LORD My Deliverer

☐Jehovah Mekaddishkem (Exodus
31:13)
- The LORD that Sanctifies You

☐Jehovah Metsudhathi (Psalms 18:2)
- The LORD My High Tower

- The LORD, the Sword

☐Jehovah Eli (Psalms 18:2)
- The LORD My GOD

☐Jehovah Elyon (Genesis 14:18-20)
- The LORD Most High

☐Jehovah Gibbor Milchamah (Psalms
24:8)
- The LORD Mighty In Battle

☐Jehovah Immeka (Judges 6:12)
- The LORD Is with You

☐Jehovah Izuz Wegibbor (Psalms
24:8)
- The LORD Strong and Mighty

☐Jehovah-jireth (Genesis 22:14)
- The LORD Shall Provide

☐Jehovah Kabodhi (Psalms 3:3)
- The LORD My GOD

☐Jehovah Kanna Shemo (Exodus
34:14)
- The LORD Whose Name Is
Jealous

☐Jehovah Keren-Yishi (Psalms 18:2)
- The LORD the Horn of My
Salvation

☐Jehovah Machsi (Psalms 91:9)
The LORD My Refuge

☐Jehovah Sabaoth (Tsebaoth) (I
Samuel 1:3)
- The LORD of Hosts

☐Jehovah Sali (Psalms 18:2)
- The LORD My Rock

☐Jehovah Shalom (Judges 6:24)
- The LORD (our) Peace

☐Jehovah Magen (Deuteronomy
33:29)
- The LORD the Shield

☐Jehovah Makkeh (Ezekiel 7:9)
- The LORD that Smiteth

☐Jehovah Mauzzam (Psalm 37:39)

☐Jehovah Moshiekh (Isaiah 49:26&60:16) - The LORD Your Savior	- The LORD their Strength
	☐Jehovah Mauzzi (Jeremiah 16:19) - The LORD my Fortress
☐Jehovah Nissi (Exodus 17:15) - The LORD My Banner	☐Ha-Melech Jehovah (Psalms 98:6) - The LORD the King
☐Jehovah Uzzi (Psalms 28:7) - The LORD My Strength	☐Jehovah Melech Olam (Psalms 10:16) - The LORD King Forever
☐Jehovah Roi (Psalms 23:1) - The LORD My Shepherd	☐Jehovah Ori (Psalms 27:1) - The LORD My Light

Keep in mind…

1. How you view God will influence how you work out your salvation, so it's extremely important to make sure your view or image of God is Biblically accurate.
2. As you develop a healthy view of God, you will notice your behaviors and attitudes change. How you feel about yourself will also change when your image of God is correct.
3. God loves you and He will act on your behalf. He will not leave you, nor will He forsake you. I know you might have felt like He did in some capacity, but He didn't. He was there through every experience.

Reflection

1. After reading today's devotion, I realize…
2. The key statements I need to remember and work on are…
3. The positive consequences of remembering and working on these statements will be…

LETTERS FROM GOD

Introduction

For the next several weeks you're going to read letters from God and Jesus that were written to help you understand and develop a healthy concept of God.

I believe God talks to me the same way I talk to my children, so I wrote these letters with that in mind (Matt. 7:9-11). In the same respect, the books in the

Bible are like letters for us to read so we can understand who our Heavenly Father is, and how to live our lives here on earth.

We are God's children and he is our Father. (Matt. 6:9). God wants to have a close, personal, intimate relationship with you. He wants you to see Him as "DAD." He wants us to attach and bond to Him like the branch attaches to the vine (John 15).

The letters address particular issues that can cause us to backslide and get stuck in the sanctification process. When we get stuck we separate and isolate from God's truth, love and grace.

My hope is that these letters will help you to heal those areas of your soul that's hurting and under developed, as well as help you to develop a Biblical concept of God. When we have the right perception of God, we no longer allow our fear of failure, guilt, shame, rejection, correction, discipline or rebuke affect us because we know that we are loved, accepted, approved of, secure and significant in Christ.

Before you start this section I want you to spend some time reading and paraphrasing the scriptures below. I believe that if we want to be healthy spiritually, mentally, emotionally and relationally, we need a healthy Biblical view of God.

Take Action…

1. Look up the following passages and paraphrase each one.

☐ 1Cor. 8:6; Matt. 5:48; Deut. 32:6,18; John 5:17-18; John 17:11
John 20:17; Rom. 15:6; Eph. 1:3;1 Peter 1:3; Psalm 103:13; Jer. 3:19
Psalm 68:5; Prov. 3:11-12; Heb. 12:5-6; 2 Cor. 6:18; Gal. 3:26
John 1:12-13; Rom. 8:17; Mark 14:36; Rom. 8:15; Gal. 4:6

DAY 71

A LETTER FROM GOD

You made all the delicate, inner parts of my body and knit me together in my mother's womb. Thank you for making me so wonderfully complex! Your workmanship is marvelous—how well I know it. You watched me as I was being formed in utter seclusion, as I was woven together in the dark of the womb. You saw me before I was born. Every day of my life was recorded in your book. (Psalm 139:13-16)

Our Father in heaven *let your name be kept holy. Let your kingdom come. Let your will be done on earth as it is done in heaven. Give us our daily bread today. Forgive us as we forgive others. Don't allow us to be tempted. Instead, rescue us from the evil one (Matt. 6:9-13)*

NEEDS AND WANTS

MY CHILD:

It's so important that you don't allow your heart to become bitter. Do you judge and condemn because you're hurt or broken? Are you angry? Talk to me! I'm here.

I noticed that you ignore your own needs and wants. Aren't your needs important too?

You seem to pay plenty of attention to other people's problems. I'm not always asking you to do this. I want you to love yourself too. Stop feeling guilty for paying attention to your own needs. Rebuke Satan when he tells you it's wrong to ask for help or support. You have needs too, and I want to take care of you. Stop taking care of yourself through helping others. Come to me.

You need help like everybody else. Yes, I tell you to deny yourself but that's between me and you. I will let you know when I want you to help others. Jesus came across a lot of people but he didn't help everybody directly. He was about my business and he did what I lead him to do.

Can you learn to trust more? I hear you think and say that other people want to harm you, or that it's not safe to trust others. This is what's making you bitter and depressed. Trust me.... You're right that some people can't be trusted, but if you give me your soul I will protect you. Find safety in me not in isolation or eating and drinking. Come to me.

Stay in an attitude of faith and victory. I want you to notice how your mistrust and martyrdom is affecting your life, your actions, and especially your thinking. Stop automatically assuming that others will be hurtful. Take your thoughts captive.

Love, Daddy

Take action…

1. Look up the following passages and paraphrase each one.

       ☐Matt. 6:33; Prov. 3:34; Gal. 6:5; Matt. 9:12-13; Eph.4:13
       2 Cor. 1:3-4; 1 John 4:16; Matt. 22:37-40; Matt. 5:3-5
       Matt.7:17-18

Reflection

1. After reading today's devotion, I realize…
2. The key statements I need to remember and work on are…
3. The positive consequences of remembering and working on these statements will be…

DAY 72

A LETTER FROM GOD

Let us hold tightly without wavering to the hope we affirm, for God can be trusted to keep his promise. (Hebrews 10:23)

TRUST ME

MY CHILD:

I know it's difficult sometimes to walk in love. I do understand your difficulties at times to do this. If you let me fill your heart with my love it will get easier to walk like my son, Jesus, did.

You are a leader in whatever you do. Whatever role I give you, I will give you power to influence others.

I like it when you practice generosity. Let others see my will through you and they will follow. Let this be your desire. Care more about others than yourself. I hear your heart and I will take care of you. You won't be depleted, it's just the opposite - you will be filled.

I'm loyal to you; be loyal to others through me, not yourself. When you're loyal through me you will have harmony, unity, peace and success.

I gave you free will so I expect you to do the same for others. If the people in your life are acting in ways that aren't pleasing to me or to you, pray for them. Release them to me. In some cases, you may need to confront them - but wait for my leading.

I understand that you're hurt and disappointed, but at some point you need to let it go. Rehearsing the situation over and over is making you more bitter and depressed. I've been trying to reach out to you but you're not hearing me because your mind is fixed on your pain and not on me. This is why you feel the way you do.

Everything will work out for the good if you keep your focus on my love and promises. I know you're frustrated but can you trust me? I know you think I could have prevented it... but I have a plan. Remember, my thoughts aren't like your thoughts and my ways aren't like your ways. My ways are higher and my words will not come back void.

People have choices and I've given everyone free will. I do protect you.... I pour grace and mercy into your life daily. I only allow what I think you can handle. I AM in control even though you might not think so.

Give me a chance to use this situation to your advantage. See it through my eyes.... release it to me, we can sort it out together. Don't forget that the adversary wants to keep you negative and powerless... but I want to set you free. Can you trust me?

Love, Daddy

Take action…

1. Look up the following passages and paraphrase each one.

   ☐Rom. 8:28; John 10:10; Matt. 6:33; Deut. 28:1-68

Reflection

1. After reading today's devotion, I realize…
2. The key statements I need to remember and work on are…
3. The positive consequences of remembering and working on these statements will be…

DAY 73

A LETTER FROM GOD

I am in them and you are in me. May they experience such perfect unity that the world will know that you sent me and that you love them as much as you love me. Father, I want these whom you have given me to be with me where I am. Then they can see all the glory you gave me because you loved me even before the world began! (John 17:23-24)

BY MY GRACE

MY CHILD:

Why are you struggling so much? Don't you think you're making life harder than it needs to be?

I've been watching you trying to live up to these standards that are impossible to meet without me. You've been idealistic lately. Every day doesn't have to be a struggle. I don't create them like that. Your day is what you make of it. I want you to rest assured that I'm in control. I want you to relax more and let your guard down. Hyper-vigilance is good but not all the time.

At one point you thought you could have worth by performing, or by martyrdom. Remember, this isn't your life any more. I love you without performing... I love you no matter what, and I love all my children equally.

Please stop burying or ignoring your own needs, desires and inclinations. Why are you giving in to others? Have you talked to me? Why are you preoccupied with rebelling against others? Are you hurt or angry about something? Did you ever stop and think that you might be resentful because you're doing something that I didn't want you to do in the first place? Talk to me!

You can have more peace if you stop reacting to others' needs, desires, and actions. Focus on your own. Focus on me. This is one reason why you lose sight of me.

Your struggles don't determine your worth, I do. If there isn't a struggle, don't create one. Let life happen. Enjoy the peaceful moments I give you. Enjoy people. Love them. Show them my love. Because you trust me, you can let life fall into place and just experience it. Doesn't it seem like when you try to control things you get off course?

We all need to be loved. Without it, nothing is right. I want you to know that you were created to be loved and adored. You have the right to be respected and cherished. I want you to know that getting close to other people is okay. Put your defenses down.

People need to love and accept you for who you are not what they want you to be. I love you as you are. My desire is that my children accept each other.

Be who you are. Don't pretend to be someone you're not, just to be loved. If you're not sure if others love you the way you want them to... take a look at my definition of Love.

Love is patient and kind. Love is not jealous or boastful or proud or rude. It does not demand its own way. It is not irritable, and it keeps no record of being wronged. It does not rejoice about injustice but rejoices whenever the truth wins out. Love never gives up, never loses faith, is always hopeful, and endures through every circumstance (1 Corinthians 13).

Love, Daddy

Take action…

    1. Look up the following passages and paraphrase each one.
          ☐Isaiah 55:6; Gal. 1:10,15-16; 1 Thess. 2:4; Rom. 7:14-25
                Acts 17:27; 1 Chron. 16:11; 1 Chron. 22:19; Psalm 14:2
                Acts 15:16-17; Amos 9:11-12; Heb. 11:6; Psalm 27:4-5
                Ezra 8:21-23; Rom. 15:7; Rom. 12:1; Eph. 5:8-10

Reflection

    1. After reading today's devotion, I realize…
    2. The key statements I need to remember and work on are…
    3. The positive consequences of remembering and working on these
       statements will be…

DAY 74

A LETTER FROM GOD

And we know that God causes everything to work together for the good of those who love God and are called according to his purpose for them.
(Romans 8:28)

EVERYTHING WORKS OUT IN THE END

MY CHILD:

If you want to heal you need to stop focusing on your hurts and disappointments. Focus your mind, will and emotions on me. Love me with all your heart.

I love you despite your mistakes. All I see is your potential. All I see is your heart and intentions. I see your pain. I know why you act the way you do. Others don't know your wounds like I do. Release them to me. Don't take it out on others. Don't punish yourself.

If you let me, I will turn it around, but you need to learn from the situation. I have a reason for everything I do. Your thoughts are not my thoughts.... your ways are not my ways..... I can see the BIG PICTURE.

Focus on what I can do. I can, and will, make your wrong right again. Trust me.

When you get hurt, repay evil with good. I will repay evildoers what they deserve. I spoke this to Paul when he was addressing Rome. I know it's difficult, but I want you to be at peace with your enemies. Through me you can do it. Always remember: you do this for ME.

I fill you with joy, and you can have it no matter the circumstance. You can have peace that surpasses all understanding.

Your past doesn't determine your future, I do. I have a plan for you, but it's hard for me to see it through if you're living in the past.

Love, Daddy

Take action…

1. Look up the following passages and paraphrase each one.
   ☐ John 14:16-17; Rom. 8:37; Rom. 16:20; 1Cor. 15:20, 25, 55-57
   1Thess. 4:16-17; Psalm 103:6; Psalm 119:50

Reflection

1. After reading today's devotion, I realize…
2. The key statements I need to remember and work on are…
3. The positive consequences of remembering and working on these statements will be…

DAY 75

A LETTER FROM GOD

Jesus gives <u>two</u> great commandments: (1) Love God with all your heart, soul, and mind; (2) Love your neighbor as yourself -- there is <u>no third command</u> to love yourself. Jesus is saying, "as you <u>already</u> love yourself" -- "as" is used in the same way in Eph 5:25,28,33, indicating a state of current existence, <u>not</u> a command. Jesus knows we already love ourselves and thereby commands us to love others with this same commitment. (Mt 22:36-40)

YOU'RE FEARFULLY AND WONDERFULLY MADE

MY CHILD:

Why don't you encourage yourself? Why don't you encourage others? I don't criticize you nor do I condemn you. So then why do you do this? Are you hurting? Are you mad at someone? Are you mad at me?

You've been acting out lately too. Why are you so negative? Talk to me, I can make your burden light. I accept you and I love you. I know you're not perfect; I created you from dirt and dust. I just want you to do the best you can each and every day. I see your potential and I know your future. For all of this to work out I need you to stop downing yourself. When you don't accept my design you don't accept me nor trust me.

I do want you to take your life seriously but I also don't want you to forget that you're just passing through. This isn't home.

Despite what anyone has told you, you are competent and you do have potential. I have a purpose for you but you have to let go of the past. I know growing up you didn't have much encouragement and I know you need to heal. I'm here now. Listen and believe my words when I say.... *YOU CAN DO ALL THINGS.*

Moses felt incompetent and he didn't accept himself. He expected failure, feared challenges, and in the beginning he shied away from my plans because he didn't accept himself. Any challenge I place before you is thought out. I just need you to see yourself through my eyes, not the eyes of man, or your past.

Love, Daddy

P.S. Never forget: I love you no matter what... You're my Child

Reshaping exercise...

The following sentence completions are designed to generate some thought and discussion on how you view yourself.

1. Loving myself means…
2. My greatest asset is…
3. I need to improve…
4. I regret…
5. My best accomplishment is…
6. Compared to others, I think I am…
7. I am…
8. It's easy to love myself because…
9. It's hard to love myself because…

Take action…

1. Look up the following passages and paraphrase each one.
   ☐ 2 Cor. 12:9-10; Eph. 1:4; Rom. 8:13-17; Col. 2:9-10
      Mark 10:27; Matt. 19:26; 2 Cor. 5:17-21; Rom. 5:17; Phil. 4:13
      1 Sam. 2:10; Dan. 2:27-28; 2 Cor. 13:3-4; Phil 4:13; 2 Tim. 1:7
      1 Peter 4:11; 2 Thess. 1:11

Reflection

1. After reading today's devotion, I realize…
2. The key statements I need to remember and work on are…
3. The positive consequences of remembering and working on these statements are…

DAY 76

A LETTER FROM GOD

Take delight in the LORD,
and he will give you your heart's desires. (Psalm 37:4)

GOOD ENOUGH

MY CHILD:

Life is mundane. As you know it's repetitive. You get up, go to work, go to school, come home, eat, and go to bed. Life can get monotonous. I designed it that way. Life on earth isn't meant to last forever. If you if you think you can find your peace in this world, in pleasure or in relationships, you're going to be sadly disappointed. I like how you take care of yourself but that too, in time, will decline. Your peace can't be in the external things. Your focus needs to be balanced. Your soul needs to be your focus. Your focus needs to be on me and my promises. My love is unconditional.

Don't let your desires get the best of you, even the ones I place in your heart. I have a perfect time for them to come to pass. My time is what matters, not yours. Live by this truth and you receive the peace that surpasses all understanding. I created the systems of life. You need to live by them just like everybody else. Why are you so upset and frustrated? You sit there disappointed about your life. Why? Don't you see how much I've given you? Isn't my son enough for you? Isn't eternity enough? What more do you want? Want me as much as you want your desires and pleasures.

Do you know why you lack time for me? You want too many things. You lose sight of me, the creator. You focus too much on the creation. You can't have both my child. I have what you need. I will bless your heart, but this life isn't about you. It's about my kingdom. It's about eternal life. I need you to follow through with your assignment.

Discontentment floods you because you fix your soul, your identity, on the very thing you don't have, or that you've lost. Letting your heart be filled with what was or what might me be, will lead to frustration and pain. Lean on my love, lean on my promises. Is my love good enough for you? I have what you need because I made you. I am the great I AM. I'm your maker and your creator.

Love, Daddy

Take action…

1. Look up the following passages and paraphrase each one.

   ☐ Ecc. 1:2; Ecc. 3:19; Ecc. 12:8; Jer. 29:11; Psalm 127:1-2; Ecc. 2:17
   Ecc. 6:7; 1 Peter 1:18; Psalm 81:10; John 1:16; John 10:10; Eph. 4:13
   Col. 2:10; John 6:35; Job 20:5; 1 Peter 2:2; John 7:37; Rev. 22:17

Reflection

1. After reading today's devotion, I realize…
2. The key statements I need to remember and work on are…

3. The positive consequences of remembering and working on these statements will be…

DAY 77

A LETTER FROM GOD

Never pay back evil with more evil. Do things in such a way that everyone can see you are honorable. Do all that you can to live in peace with everyone (Rom. 12:17-18)

REPAY EVIL WITH GOOD

MY CHILD:

I know you're upset but you have to let me in. If you take this on yourself you're going to end up making the wrong choice. I hear your thoughts. Repaying her isn't the answer. I know she hurt you but stop and think about it. What will you gain if you repay her with evil?

I understand that you're hurt and disappointed but at some point you need to let it go. Rehearsing the situation over and over is making you more bitter and depressed. I've been trying to reach out to you but you're not hearing me because your mind is fixed on your pain and not on me. This is why you feel the way you do.

Everything will work out for the good if you keep your focus on my love and promises. I know you're frustrated but can you trust me? I know you think I could have prevented it but I have a plan. Remember, my thoughts aren't like your thoughts and my ways aren't like your ways. My ways are higher and my words will not come back void.

People have choices and I've given everyone free will. I do protect you. I pour grace and mercy into your life daily. I only allow what I think you can handle. I AM in control you even though you might not think so.

Give me a chance to use this situation to your advantage. See it through my eyes.... release it to me, we can sort it out together. Don't forget that the adversary wants to keep you negative and powerless, but I want to set you free. Can you trust me?

For starters, this isn't the way I do things. In fact it's just the opposite. I want you to release the offense to me. Give them to me and repay them with your honesty and unconditional love. Set your boundaries and tell them what needs to change. Just don't repay them with vengeance. This will not work. Vengeance is mine and it always will be. I know what's going on within her soul. Pray for her and I will give you wisdom and insight. I will guide in the way that you should go.

If you let me pay back what others deserve you're taking the high road. Let me have control. My conviction is much better than your condemnation.

I said it in Isaiah.... I will repay you for unfair treatment. I will handle any injustices. I will restore your life, just give it time and let go of control. Don't let the thought of vengeance blind you. Keep your eyes fixed on me and follow my ways.

Love, Daddy

Take action...

1. Look up the following passages and paraphrase each one.
    ☐Matt. 5:38-45; Luke 18:7-8; Deut. 32:43; 1 Sam. 24:12; 2 Kings 9:7 Psalm
        18:47; Rev. 6:10; Rev. 19:2; Isaiah 54:17

Reflection

1. After reading today's devotion, I realize...
2. The key statements I need to remember and work on are...
3. The positive consequences of remembering and working on these
   statements will be...

DAY 78

A LETTER FROM GOD

The LORD says, "I will guide you along the best pathway for your life.
I will advise you and watch over you.
⁹ Do not be like a senseless horse or mule
that needs a bit and bridle to keep it under control."(Psalm 32:9-10)

RECEIVE MY PEACE

MY CHILD:

For you to heal and transform from the inside out you need to be honest and face the truth about whatever's going on in your life.

Dishonesty prevents inner healing. The only way to receive my peace that surpasses all understanding is to stop protecting yourself. The Holy Spirit wants to shine light in your darkness so you can heal and transform.

I want you to drop your defensive attitude because it doesn't bring peace.... only chaos. I know you might be afraid to let your guard down, but you need to learn how to trust me. David didn't want to face the truth. He might have thought that his situation would take care of itself. He couldn't deny that he had a problem because I wouldn't let him, and I made sure that it was always at the fore front of his mind so he could heal and change.

Don't lose your peace over making a mistake because all I ask is that you learn from your mistakes. If you're not happy, talk to me, tell me about it. Blaming others will only frustrate you more; accept responsibility and own your part. You don't have to be dishonest anymore; there's a better way of obtaining peace of mind.

*Love, **Daddy***

Take action…

1. Look up the following passages and paraphrase each one
   ☐Rom. 5:1; Rom. 8:1,31-39; 1 Cor. 1:2-3; 1 John 4:7-8; 1 Thess. 3:12   2
   Tim. 1:7; 1 John 4:16,19; Gal. 3:21-25; Rom. 6:1-14; Rom. 7:1-6
   Gal. 3:13; Gal. 4:5,21-31

Reflection

1. After reading today's devotion, I realize…
2. The key statements I need to remember and work on are…
3. The positive consequences of remembering and working on these
   statements will be…

DAY 79

A LETTER FROM GOD

*Others were given in exchange for you. I traded their lives for yours
because you are precious to me. You are honored, and I love you.*
(Isaiah 43:4)

LOVE THROUGH ME

MY CHILD:

When you're in me, you're full of love. Love was intended to be free. When
you separate from me, notice how you put conditions on the love you give.
When you allow me to fill you with my loving kindness it flows out to others.
Loving others through me purifies your motives. Remember, I want them to see
me, not you.

If others hurt you, you're not as devastated by it because you loved them through
me. My love guards your heart. Do your best not to put expectations on others
when you show them love and mercy. Remember, you do this for me, through
me. Some people don't know how to receive love and compassion. Some will
take advantage. When this happens draw a line in the sand. I don't want you to
be taken advantage of. If you feel others are taking advantage of you, tell them
exactly how. Speak the truth in love.

As I said, you love each other[1] because I loved you first. Trying to love others
without me, often leads to feeling hurt and bitter. Love will overflow when you
connect to my spirit. Attach yourself to the vine. Let me flow through you like a
stream.

You are precious to me. You are honored, and I love you. I will protect you and
help you through your afflictions. I promise you strength, hope, mercy and

favor. You will experience valleys because they're part of life, my child. Take heart and follow Jesus. My son modeled for you how to go through trials and hard times. Line your heart up to his. Live out his words, for this shows him how you love him. This can be done when you put me first. Love me with your heart, soul, mind and strength.

Love, Daddy

Take ction…

1. Look up the following passages and paraphrase each one.
   ☐Deut. 7:7-8; Ezek. 16:1-14; Rom. 5:8; Eph. 2:4-5; Rom. 8:38-39
      2 Cor. 13:14; 2 John 3; Matt. 5:44-45; Hosea 3:1; 1 John 2:15;
      1 John 4:7-8,11-12

Reflection

1. After reading today's devotion, I realize…
2. The key statements I need to remember and work on are…
3. The positive consequences of remembering and working on these statements will be…

DAY 80

A LETTER FROM GOD

He humbled himself in obedience to God
and died a criminal's death on a cross. (Philippians 2:8)

YOU GAIN MORE THROUGH ME

MY CHILD:

You don't lose when you love, you gain. If you're losing your peace loving others, check your motivation. Do you love in order to get something? Are you seeking acceptance? Loving others is supposed to leave you feeling free and empowered.

If you need to feel loved come to me. I will fill your cup; I will take away your thirst and hunger. The world cannot give you what your soul is looking for. Your soul was designed to want ME, the great I Am.

Life is empty without me so I sent Jesus, my only begotten son, to empty himself so I could redeem humanity. Many of my children seek relief through wine, drugs and food, only to feel emptier than before. Earthly things will not satisfy you. I alone, can fill that void. If only they would practice patience and tolerance.

My children want to escape their feelings. They only want to feel pleasure. Pain is where we meet. When will they get it? I'm the joy they want. I'm everlasting. I'm forever. Drinking from my well is free. I provide everything you need. I am JEHOVAH-ROHI, your shepherd.

My son gave up his divine privileges to take the humble position of a servant, and was born as a human being. When he appeared in human form he humbled himself in obedience to me. Jesus died a criminal's death on a cross so that you can be filled with my love and grace.

Love, Daddy

Take action…

1. Look up the following passages and paraphrase each one.
   ☐Micah 6:8; James 4:10; 1 Peter 3:8; Lev. 26:41; Deut. 8:2,16
   1 Kings 11:39; 2 Chron. 28:19; Prov. 8:13; Psalm 101:5; Psalm 131:1
   Rom. 12:3; 1 Cor. 13:4; Gal. 6:14

Reflection

1. After reading today's devotion, I realize…
2. The key statements I need to remember and work on are…
3. The positive consequences of remembering and working on these statements will be…

DAY 81

A LETTER FROM GOD

Therefore, since we are surrounded by such a huge crowd of witnesses to the life of faith, let us strip off every weight that slows us down, especially the sin that so easily trips us up. And let us run with endurance the race God has set before us. We do this by keeping our eyes on Jesus, the champion who initiates and perfects our faith. Because of the joy awaiting him, he endured the cross, disregarding its shame. Now he is seated in the place of honor beside God's throne. (Hebrews 12:1-2)

YOU HAVE A REBELLIOUS SPIRIT

MY CHILD:

For a long time you lived with blinders. You didn't want to acknowledge how you were living the life I gave you. You have so much potential but because of your disobedience I've been unable to bless you. I want you to think about the time you wasted in your life. What interferes with our relationship? What do you value more than my love? Now that I have your attention, I want you to take ownership of the choices and decisions you have made.

I did give you free will because I love you and I want you to make your own choice when it comes to loving me. I will not force you to love me or to serve me. This is your choice and each choice has its consequences.

Child, strip off every weight that slows you down, especially the sin that so easily trips you up. I know life can be hard but I will give you the strength and endurance to run and finish the race I set before you. Look at your life – what choices have you made that you regret? What disturbs you the most?

If you have a tendency to blame others for your behaviors, stop. You're my child and you're not a victim. Take ownership for how you've been living. You know right from wrong. Let go of your way of gaining and receiving approval, acceptance, control and security. It only separates you from me.

Love, Daddy

Take action...

1. Look up the following passages and paraphrase each one.
   Jer. 33:8; Dan. 9:5-9; 1 Sam. 15:23; Prov. 21:4; James 4:16
   Mark 7:22-23; Rom. 1:29-30; 2 Cor. 12:20; 2 Tim. 3:1-2; 1 John 2:16
   Neh. 9:16-17,29; Job 36:8-9; Psalm 5:5; Psalm 119:85; Hos. 5:4-5
   Hos. 7:10; Zeph. 3:1-4

Reflection

1. After reading today's devotion, I realize…
2. The key statements I need to remember and work on are…
3. The positive consequences of remembering and working on these statements will be…

DAY 82

A LETTER FROM GOD

Pride leads to conflict;
those who take advice are wise. (Proverbs 13:10)

QUIET YOUR EGO

MY CHILD:

Your life is so unmanageable because you edge me out. Learn to be still. You're so afraid. Listen to my voice. Remove the distraction so you can hear me. Spend more time in the Word. You can't hear me because you're not listening with your heart. Get out of your head. I have an answer but you're too busy to hear it. In fact, do you already have the answer? Do you want me to conform to you?

Have the courage to listen to me. Sometimes the truth hurts, but I promise you it will set you free. Are you running from what you know is right? Where does avoidance get you? What do you gain from it? Seek me first. Put your hope in me. I will purify your heart and make you like my son. My hope will bring you peace and contentment, as well as restoration.

Remember, it's not a battle of flesh and blood. Satan loves to play on your pride. You need my help to fight against the evil forces and principalities that exist in the spiritual realm. You're not just dealing with your addictive behaviors. Don't be fooled. You need me because I created you and know what you need. You will find wisdom in my advice.

Love, Daddy

Take action…

1. Look up the following passages and paraphrase each one.
   ☐1 Sam. 12:14-15; Num. 14:9; Num. 17:10; Psalm 2:10-12; Ezek. 2:8   1
       Sam. 15:10-11; 1 Thess. 4:8; 1 Sam. 15:23,26; Psalm 50:17
       Prov. 1:24-25; Prov. 5:12; Psalm 81:11-13; Isaiah 8:6; Isaiah 30:1-2
       Luke 7:30; Heb. 7:25; John 6:40; Rom. 8:2-3; 1 Cor. 15:22
       Heb. 7:26-28; 1 Peter 3:18

Reflection

1. After reading today's devotion, I realize…
2. The key statements I need to remember and work on are…
3. The positive consequences of remembering and working on these statements will be…

DAY 83

A LETTER FROM GOD

And have you forgotten the encouraging words God spoke to you as his children? He said, "My child, don't make light of the LORD's discipline, and don't give up when he corrects you. For the LORD disciplines those he loves, and he punishes each one he accepts as his child. (Hebrews 12:5-12)

BE TEACHABLE

MY CHILD:

I want you to know that I'm loving and caring. I want you to trust me. I can give you the wisdom and insight you need to heal. You didn't have the best role models growing up. Yes, they did the best they could with what they had, but they didn't seek me. I'm your true Father. You might be upset with me because your life isn't working right now, but I needed to stop you. You were killing yourself. You're my child and I want you back. I correct you and discipline you because I love you… you're my child and I correct those I love. I know my discipline is painful but, in time, you will reap a harvest. Let me train you. I will use my servants as an extension of my love. Let me be the power greater than yourself. Let me restore your sanity.

Open your mind to me. Remain teachable. Consider my way of living. If you're mad at me, tell me. I know you're going through a lot right now. You want to change your life and it's scary. You've been living by your rules and now you're realizing they need to change.

You're my child... You might blame me for your addiction, hurt, loss and life. You might say, "I wouldn't have this problem if certain things didn't happen." If your parent's only, if he/she didn't die, or if you didn't lose your job you wouldn't have turned to your addictive behavior(s). I understand you needed to find a way to cope with your losses or pain. You wanted instant relief and gratification. Just realize that this isn't working anymore and that I have a better way. If you want to heal and grow, remain teachable and humble.

Love, Daddy

Take action...

1. Look up the following passages and paraphrase each one.

   Exod. 15:26; Deut. 5:27; Acts 8:30-31; Mark 4:10; Mark 9:11,28
   John 5:30; John 8:26-28

Reflection

1. After reading today's devotion, I realize...
2. The key statements I need to remember and work on are...
3. The positive consequences of remembering and working on these statements will be...

DAY 84

A LETTER FROM GOD

Confess your sins to each other and pray for each other so that you may be healed. The earnest prayer of a righteous person has great power and produces wonderful results. (James 5:16)

FEEL YOUR FEELINGS

MY CHILD:

You don't have to act like everything is alright. Feel what you feel. I gave my children emotions so I can show them what I want or need them to do. If someone asks you how you are or how you feel, tell them the truth. Don't lie. If you're sad, happy, mad, hurt or joyful, say so. The more you deny how you feel the more inadequate and inferior you're going to feel. It's hard to love yourself when you deny your emotions. Emotions make you feel alive.

I want you to feel and experience your emotions because they show you what you're thinking. Stop feeling shame or guilt when you feel negative emotions. My child, feel them. Talk to me about what's going on. I want to hear from you.

I gave you the ability to feel so you can be aware of what is right or wrong in your life. Your feelings can motivate you to change and seek healing. The worst thing you can do is deny them, avoid them, or escape them. Feelings can inspire you to live a different life.

Some of my children are misled by what they feel because they live by them (their feelings) instead of living by my word (truth) and promises. The more you understand your emotions the less likely it is that you'll be deceived by them. If you line up what you feel with my truth and respect how you feel, I can guide you and direct you. With my help, you can face and admit your feelings. Confession is good for your soul.

Love, Daddy

Take action...

1. Look up the following passages and paraphrase each one.

   ☐Prov. 25:28; Eph. 4:26; Eph. 5:18; Col. 3:8; 1 Tim. 2:8; James 1:19-20
   Psalm 73:16-17; Psalm 119:78; Rom. 8:28; Josh. 7:20-21

Reflection

   1. After reading today's devotion, I realize...
   2. The key statements I need to remember and work on are...
   3. The positive consequences of remembering and working on these statements will be...

DAY 85

A LETTER FROM GOD

For everyone has sinned; we all fall short of God's glorious standard.
(Rom. 3:23)

ADMIT YOU'RE WRONG

MY CHILD:

Have you ever felt left out because you made a mistake or failed at something? Have you ever felt like everyone else is "in" and you're left out?

My children have a tendency to isolate from people when they make a mistake instead of admitting their wrongs and saying "I'm sorry, I was wrong," or "I made a mistake." For some, those words are very hard to say.

I want to encourage you not to separate yourself from me when you make a mistake. I don't stop loving you, in fact, I embrace you. I won't leave you discouraged. If everyone in your life turns against you, I won't. My love is unfailing and never ending. Hang on to me and we'll get through the storm.

Love, Daddy

Consider this…

If you sin or make a mistake, all you need to do is admit it. Be sure to settle your accounts so this way you don't feel left out. Hugh White said, "When you make a mistake, don't look back at it long. Take the reason of the thing into your mind and then look forward. Mistakes are lessons of wisdom. The past cannot be changed. The future is yet in your power."

Take action…

1. Look up the following passages and paraphrase each one.

☐Prov. 28:13; 1 John 1:9; Lev. 16:20-22; Lev. 26:40-42; 2 Sam. 12:13 Psalm 32:3-5; Luke 19:8; John 8:11; Jer. 4:3-4; Luke 19:1-10; John 5:14 Rom. 6:11-14; 1 Peter 2:11; Acts 3:19; 2 Chron. 6:36-39; Isaiah 55:7

Reflection

1. After reading today's devotion, I realize…
2. The key statements I need to remember and work on are…
3. The positive consequences of remembering and working on these statements will be…

DAY 86

A LETTER FROM GOD

Trust in the LORD with all your heart; do not depend on your own understanding. Seek his will in all you do, and he will show you which path to take. Don't be impressed with your own wisdom. Instead, fear the LORD and turn away from evil. Then you will have healing for your body and strength for your bones. (Proverbs 3:5-8)

SLOW DOWN

MY CHILD:

Your mind would be clear if you learn to be still and focus on my small still voice. Slow down and let me minister to you. I know your life was surrounded by chaos. Abide in me and I will give you peace. Talk to me about your choices and decisions. Life gets confusing without my guidance.

Your thinking is complicated. Let me help you. You don't have to rush your decisions. Let's figure out what you will reap when you sow that choice. If you don't slow down you're going to overwhelm yourself. Make sure you align your choices to my words. Live out your values not your emotions. Be quick to listen and slow to speak.

If you let me, I will help you by guiding you and directing your steps. I will give you wisdom, just ask. I will not rebuke you for asking. But when you ask me, put your faith in me alone. Be loyal to me and don't doubt me. Take my promises to heart.

Love, Daddy

Take action...

1. Look up the following passages and paraphrase each one.

   □Psalm 23:1-3; Psalm 25:4-5,8-9,12; Prov. 9:10; 2 Tim. 3:16-17
   Acts 16:3; Acts 20:3,16; 1 Cor. 16:8-9; James 1:5-6

Reflection

1. After reading today's devotion, I realize...
2. The key statements I need to remember and work on are...
3. The positive consequences of remembering and working on these statements will be...

DAY 87

A LETTER FROM GOD

"So don't worry about tomorrow, for tomorrow will bring its own worries. Today's trouble is enough for today. (Matt. 6:34)

KEEP IT SIMPLE

MY CHILD:

You're making your storm bigger than it needs to be. Try to relax. I can quiet your storm but you need to surrender. I reach out to you and you ignore me. Why? I keep reminding you that worry will do nothing for you. Turn your worry into faith and trust in me. I was there for you before, and I will be there for you this time. Quiet your mind.

Fix your mind on me, and you will have perfect peace. I've put people in your life… reach out to them. I will work through them. I see the big picture. I have a plan and purpose for you. Trust me. The grace I give you is for today, not tomorrow. Your restoration will come when you have faith in me and my love.

Love, Daddy

Take action…

1. Look up the following passages and paraphrase each one.

  ☐Psalm 23:2-3; Prov. 17:1; Ecc. 4:6; Matt. 11:28-30; Deut. 1:21
    Psalm 23:4; Prov. 3:25-26; Matt. 10:29-31; Rom. 8:1,31-39
    1 Cor. 1:2-3; Psalm 94:18-19; Psalm 139:23; 1 Peter 5:7

Reflection

  1. After reading today's devotion, I realize…
  2. The key statements I need to remember and work on are…
  3. The positive consequences of remembering and working on these
    statements will be…

DAY 88

A LETTER FROM GOD

That's why I take pleasure in my weaknesses and in the insults, hardships, persecutions, and troubles that I suffer for Christ. For when I am weak, then I am strong. (2 Corinthians 12:10)

I WILL TRANSFORM YOUR LIFE

MY CHILD:

I know you want to grow into the person I made you to be. To be this person you need learn how to love truth. I want to help you to be open to what I'm going to show you. I need to do this so you can understand why you do what you do. I want you to take the time to understand why you do what you do. We need to do this together. Naturally, you don't want to do this because it's not in your nature. Some truth will be hard to face and admit. Lean on me and I will see you through your darkness.

Stay in today and look forward to what lies ahead. Try to accept where you are at this moment no matter how afraid you might be. You're going to respond in your old way as I show you the truth about your life and the choices you've made. Don't let this upset you. It's good pain and doesn't last as long. When you don't accept the truth I show you, this only prolongs and lengthens your pain. When you're weak, I am strong. In your willingness to be transformed, I will give you strength and courage to face your hurts and pain. You don't have to act like you know the truth about everything, because you don't. Be willing to let your resentment and fears go so my truth makes sense to you.

I will deliver you from the sin that invades your life by filling your void with my love. Let me purify you and renew your heart and mind. I know you want a new life and purpose. When you mourn I will comfort you. When you walk through the fire I will strength you. When you walk through the valley I will be by your side.

Love, Daddy

Take action...

1. Look up the following passages and paraphrase each one.

    ☐Eph. 3:16,20; 2 Thess. 2:16-17; 1 Tim. 1:12; 2 Tim. 1:7; Gal. 6:14
       Heb. 13:6; Rom. 8:3-4; 2 Cor. 5:17; Gal. 5:16

Reflection

    1. After reading today's devotion, I realize...
    2. The key statements I need to remember and work on are...
    3. The positive consequences of remembering and working on these
       statements will be...

DAY 89

A LETTER FROM GOD

Help me understand the meaning of your commandments,
and I will meditate on your wonderful deeds. (Psalm 119:27)

CHANGE HOW YOU THINK

MY CHILD:

If you want to heal and change you need to stop being so negative. You need to stop giving yourself negative messages about others and yourself. Let me help you renew your mind. I need you to stop confirming to the message you've received throughout the years. The problem is that your mind conflicts with mine. We need to work through the beliefs you hold that don't line up with mine. The beliefs you have about yourself make you feel shameful, inferior, hopeless, helpless, inadequate and bitter. Because of your hurt and pain, you created a set of beliefs and values just so you can survive and get through each day.

I can help you see when you're being rebellious. When I do, you'll feel a sense of conviction, not condemnation. Your beliefs mislead you and, as a result, you become a slave to many lusts and pleasures. Your beliefs can fill you with evil and envy, and hatred for yourself and others. This is why I want you to stop copying the behaviors and customs of this world, and let me transform you into a new person by changing the way you think. Then you will learn to know my will for you, which is good, and pleasing, and perfect.

Take your thoughts captive. Line them up with my words. Pay attention to what you're thinking about. Record them and compare them to how I talk to you. My people perish for lack of knowledge. Your inner life is very important. I want to help you understand the meaning of my design and my commandments, and I need you to meditate on them so I can wash your heart and mind clean. When you think about my words you will see my wonderful deeds and come to realize how much I love you.

Love, Daddy

Take action...

1. Look up the following passages and paraphrase each one.

    ☐Matt. 5:48; Heb. 6:1; Deut. 6:6-7; Deut. 11:18; Josh. 1:8
       Psalm 119:15,23,78,97; Rom. 1:21; Eph. 4:17-19; Matt. 6:31-34
       Phil. 2:4; 2 Cor. 10:12; 1 Peter 1:13-14

Reflection

    1. After reading today's devotion, I realize…
    2. The key statements I need to remember and work on are…
    3. The positive consequences of remembering and working on these statements will be…

DAY 90

A LETTER FROM GOD

A person standing alone can be attacked and defeated, but two can stand back-to-back and conquer. Three are even better, for a triple-braided cord is not easily broken. (Ecc. 4:12)

LET ME HELP YOU

MY CHILD:

How do you expect to change if you see yourself in a negative way, or if your opinion of yourself is not based on how I view you? I believe in you and I think you're precious. You are my child and I formed you in my hands. I will put people in your life to believe in you and to be your fan. It's me working through them. Listen to them and trust them. Be open to suggestions. Lean on this person. As you know, my son received help carrying His cross! What makes you different? Look around, who's been reaching out to you? Think about the people in your life, who can you lean on? Who sees the good in you? Who sees you potential? Who encourages you?

I know it's not easy to ask for help or admit that you have a need, especially when you're used to living independently. Many people have a hard time admitting that they need help, love, validation or guidance, for one reason or another. Some of my children believe that they have to figure things out on their own because asking for help suggests weakness, or lack of control. I'm in those people, child. Don't fear rejection. I don't want you to stay stuck because you're afraid to face reality and take responsibility.

I didn't design you, or life for that matter, to be lived alone. Sometimes you might reach out to others and they're busy. In these times I want you to only want me. I want to spend time with you. Don't think you're being rejected or abandoned - that's not the case. I will not leave you, nor will I abandon you. You're special to me.

Love, Daddy

Take action...

1. Look up the following passages and paraphrase each one.

   ☐Rev. 21:3; Psalm 127:4; Prov. 17:6,17; Prov. 18:24; Prov. 27:10; Ecc. 4:9-12

Reflection

1. After reading today's devotion, I realize...
2. The key statements I need to remember and work on are...
3. The positive consequences of remembering and working on these statements will be...

REVIEW & REPAIR

Reshaping Your Soul

1. What did I learn this past month about myself, God and others?

2. What concepts or ideas stood out to me in the devotions? Why?

3. What adjustments do I need to make in my life?

4. What, if anything, needs to change about how I think, feel, and act?

5. What changes have I made so far? What actions have I taken?

6. How are people reacting to my changes?

7. Steps I will continue to take are…

8. I'm committed to…

9. My victories this week were…

10. God please help me with…

DAY 91

A LETTER FROM GOD

Paul tells us: "God is faithful, and he will not let you be tested beyond your strength but with your testing he will also provide the way out so that you may be able to endure it." (1 Corinthians 10:13)

FEEL YOUR HURT

MY CHILD…

I created hurt so you can only go so far in ruining your life. Hurt puts limits on the extent of pain you can cause yourself, and what others can cause you. When my children finally accept and experience the hurt or pain, they change. They start to listen to me or cry out to me.

I created hurt so you can avoid dangerous things and dangerous people. Hurt tells you that you're broken and wounded. It tells you that you're not whole. It tells you that you're not in my will, or you're being disobedient.

Through pain and hurt I teach you lessons and, most importantly, I get your attention. Hurt encourages you to grow and change. When you allow yourself to feel hurt and deal with the issues, you will become more like my son... Jesus.

When you're hurt I want you to express it. I want you to tell me all about. Some of the hurt you feel might be brought on by your own choices. Other times the hurt you feel might be ME trying to get your attention because I need you to do something for me, or to prevent you from further danger.

Satan wants you to deny your hurt and pain because he doesn't want you to grow. He wants you to destroy your life. He knows pain creates limits. He wants you to go beyond your limits so you separate from me. Many of my children stop talking to me because they're hurt, and Satan lies to them by getting them to think it's my fault entirely.

Hurt tells you when someone is untrustworthy or harmful. Hurt will tell you what's important to you. It tells you what you like, don't like, need, want, desire, etc. When you don't follow my way you feel hurt, pain, and a loss of peace.

See hurt as signal or a private message from me to you. Don't ignore it. Work through it, and talk to me and others about it.

Love, Daddy

Take action…

1. Look up the following passages and paraphrase each one.

    ☐Deut. 32:6,18; Isaiah 64:8; Acts 17:24-28; Psalm 103:13; Jer. 3:19;   2
    Cor. 1:3

Reflection

    1. After reading today's devotion, I realize…
    2. The key statements I need to remember and work on are…
    3. The positive consequences of remembering and working on these statements will be…

DAY 92

A LETTER FROM GOD

So there is a special rest still waiting for the people of God. [10] For all who have entered into God's rest have rested from their labors, just as God did after creating the world. So let us do our best to enter that rest. But if we disobey God, as the people of Israel did, we will fall. (Hebrews 4:9-11)

SPEND MORE TIME WITH ME

MY CHILD:

I love it when you spend time with me and you allow yourself to be quiet and silent. I want you to think more about where you want to go in life. Before me, you just did what you thought was right. I will speak words of hope and courage to you. Meditate on my words. Let them sink deep within your heart.

I know you're thankful, so tell me. When you have gratitude your spirit is up, and you become full of joy. Think about what you have, not what you don't have. Want what I have given you. Be content. When you walk away from quite time with me, you will feel focused, loved and challenged. I want you to live a quiet life marked by godliness and dignity.

Give thanks for my mercy and love. I provide for you a way out of your hurt, pain, brokenness and sin. Praise me in your quite time. I will give you rest while you wait for your miracle, or for your prayer to be answered. I love how you believe in me and place all your hope in my love. I know some things might be hard for you to accept, but I need you to be reconciled to it. I know at times it might be hard for you to walk that narrow road with me, but keep in mind it will work out for your good, and for my glory. Like King David, I need you to trust me and wait patiently. When you're quiet I can give you peace, but I need you to be open and submissive. I will never give you what you can't bear or handle.

Love, Daddy

Take action…

1. Look up the following passages and paraphrase each one.

   ☐2 Cor. 8:7,22; Titus 3:1,8,14; 1 Peter 3:13; Psalm 73:25;
   Psalm 119:81,131; John 7:37; Rev. 21:6; Rev. 22:17

Reflection

   1. After reading today's devotion, I realize…
   2. The key statements I need to remember and work on are…

3. The positive consequences of remembering and working on these statements will be…

DAY 93

A LETTER FROM GOD

And we know that God causes everything to work together for the good of those who love God and are called according to his purpose for them. (Romans 8:28)

DISCOURAGEMENT IS A CHOICE

MY CHILD:

I can see that you're discouraged. Your life is changing and you feel like you don't have control, but you do. In me you have what you need to make it through your loss. I will give you the inner strength and understanding to make it through. It's normal to feel despair when you are disappointed. Come to me and I will give you peace to calm your troubled heart.

Sometimes I will bring you to situations where all you can do is place your hope in me. Sometimes the only solution is to fall on your knees and pray. Don't lose heart, I am with you. Don't leave my side. Remind me of my promises. Remember what I have done for you in the past. Remember our past victories.

When you receive bad news you might feel a flood of emotions like grief, pain, fear, anger, betrayal, hate, guilt, helplessness, bitterness, sadness, anxiety or regret. This is part of being human. You have to hear them, feel them and express them, so that in time you can hear my promises. Talk to me and don't run from me. I will help you; I will give your soul what it needs to make it through the storm. Stand on the Rock. I am the firm foundation, and always remember that I will make sure everything works together for your good because you love me. I've called you to fulfill a purpose for me so I will give you what you need. All my children go through some form of suffering from time to time. My very own son has suffered beyond measure. He understands how it feels to grieve. He understands what it's like to be rejected, abandoned, despised and persecuted.

When hard times come, I don't abandon you, I'm right by your side. I'm your shadow. Be determined and confess my goodness and love for you. I will give you peace and grace to always make it through the storms.

It's okay to feel upset when an expectation hasn't been met, but allowing your soul to become discouraged is wrong. Staying discouraged is a choice just like happiness or depression. Surrender you soul to me before you fall into self-pity. I will help you work through your pain and sense of powerlessness. I have what you need for I am the LORD, and there is none else, the way, the truth, and the life.

Love, Daddy

Take action...

1. Look up the following passages and paraphrase each one.

   ☐Rom. 8:28; Gen. 27:41; Gen. 37:34; Gen. 50:3-4; Deut. 34:8; Jer. 4:28; Luke 8:13; 1 Peter 1:6-7; Rev. 2:10; Isaiah 49:13; 2 Cor. 1:3-4

Reflection

1. After reading today's devotion, I realize…
2. The key statements I need to remember and work on are…
3. The positive consequences of remembering and working on these statements will be

DAY 94

A LETTER FROM JESUS

Therefore if any person is [ingrafted] in Christ (the Messiah) he is a new creation (a new creature altogether); the old [previous moral and spiritual condition] has passed away. Behold, the fresh and new has come! (2 Corinthians 5:17)

YOU'RE NOT THE SAME ANYMORE

Today you're going to read a letter addressing the importance of seeing yourself through God's eyes. *Note: This letter is written from my interpretation of scripture.*

You are a different person now and the more you connect to me the more you're going to realize it. When you spend time with me your memories will heal and your opinion about yourself will change. You don't have to be unsure of yourself anymore. I want you to see yourself as a person who is worthwhile and capable of achieving their goals. I want you to have an abundant life. I saved you for a purpose. I died for a purpose, and that purpose is to set you free from all the lies you believe about yourself. I need you to work hard at this each and every day. Think about the Israelites: many of them didn't make it because they viewed my Father in the wrong way. They had a bad attitude which caused them to be disobedient and go in the wrong direction. The way that seemed right to them lead to death and they never got a chance to experience what God had for them and their family for future generations.

I want you to start seeing yourself as God's child… loved and special. You have been made for good works. Take on this attitude and, I guarantee, you will be successful. You now have the ability to be like me. I tell you this because you will stop the sanctification process if you don't change how you view yourself. If you don't see yourself as I see you, your personality will not change. My Father created it so that your self-image is connected to your behaviors, personality, and what you can achieve in life. You can only go as far as your self-image can take you. As a man thinks, so he is.

Love, Jesus

Take action…

1. Look up the following passages and paraphrase each one.

   ☐Matt. 10:40 See also Matt. 18:5; Matt. 25:40; Eph. 1:1; Phil. 1:1; Rom. 8:10; 2 Cor. 5:17; Rom. 4:23-25

Reflection

1. After reading today's devotion, I realize…
2. The key statements I need to remember and work on are…
3. The positive consequences of remembering and working on these statements will be…

DAY 95

A LETTER FROM JESUS

...So is my word that goes out from my mouth: It will not return to me empty, but will accomplish what I desire and achieve the purpose for which I sent it.
(Isaiah 55:11)

BE CONFIDENT BECAUSE OF WHOSE YOU ARE

Today you're going to read a letter teaching you how to build godly confidence. *Note: This letter is written from my interpretation of scripture.*

The way to build confidence is to take action. What good is it, dear brothers and sisters, if you say you have faith but don't show it by your actions? Can that kind of faith save anyone? Face your fears. I'm not saying that you need to perform to be loved and accepted. I'm reminding you of what I said before, those who love me obey my commands.

The longer you don't take action, the stronger your self-doubt becomes, which in turn causes you to feel lowly and insecure. If you use your fears to take action you will understand your identity and who you are in ME. I felt fear on my way to the cross while in the garden of Gethsemane.

On a daily basis, fill your mind with God's promises. Take your thoughts captive and walk out the truth. Eliminate the negative thoughts. Satan will do what he can to deter your efforts. Satan attacks your mind, so protect it with the helmet of salvation. Fight off the thoughts and voices that say "you can't," "why bother," or, "it's impossible." Store up promises in your memory bank so the Holy Spirit can remind you of them, and encourage you to move forward.

~ Jesus

Take action...

    1. Look up the following passages and paraphrase each one.

           Phil. 4:13; Heb. 13:6; Prov. 3:6; Phil. 1:6

Reflection

> 1. After reading today's devotion, I realize…
> 2. The key statements I need to remember and work on are…
> 3. The positive consequences of remembering and working on these statements will be…

DAY 96

A LETTER FROM JESUS

I can do all things through him who strengthens me. (Phil. 4:13)

JESUS WILL GIVE YOU CONFIDENCE

Today you're going to read a letter sharing with you how God empowers you to do the impossible. *Note: This letter is written from my interpretation of scripture.*

I have placed in your soul and spirit all the confidence and strength you need to do the impossible. Our father's power can give you the ability to conquer anything that he has called you to do.

I want you to take the narrow road, which means I want you to take healthy risks when my spirit leads you to. Remove the "I can't" attitude or the "fear of looking stupid attitude" and get out of the boat. I'm going to give you the opportunity to build your confidence and courage. I'm going to nudge you to do things you never thought you can do. Failure is a part of life so don't fear it. Look at Thomas Edison: our Father called him to create the first light bulb. It took him 2000 tries. If you fail, it has nothing to do with who you are as a person, it's separate.

My goal is to help you to feel positive about yourself. I will send you the reassurances you need to build your "can-do" attitude. I will equip you, encourage, and empower you, to do the tasks God has given you.

Love, Jesus

Ask yourself:

1. Do I lack confidence?
2. Do I have a "can-do" attitude?
3. Do I give up too easily?

Keep in mind:

1. Avoid negative self-talk
2. Keep your mind positive
3. You don't have to fear change
4. Avoid pessimism
5. Because of Jesus:

    ☐You can believe in yourself

    ☐You have a purpose

    ☐You're no longer rejected

    ☐You can accept that you have weaknesses, without condemnation

    ☐You have strengths and skills

    ☐You can take risks without fearing failure... Just pray, and do your best

    ☐If you lose you still win

    ☐Don't compare yourself to any one... you're unique

    ☐Let go of the past

Take action...

1. Look up the following passages and paraphrase each one.

    ☐Heb. 4:16; Josh. 1:9; Rom. 12:3; Acts 1:8; Deut. 31:6;   2 Cor. 12:9

Reflection

1. After reading today's devotion, I realize...
2. The key statements I need to remember and work on are...
3. The positive consequences of remembering and working on these statements will be...

DAY 97

A LETTER FROM JESUS

But if we walk in the light, as he is in the light, we have fellowship with one another, and the blood of Jesus his Son cleanses us from all sin. (1 John 1:7)

MY BLOOD SHOWS YOU HOW MUCH YOU'RE WORTH. -JESUS

Today you're going to read a letter addressing how much you're worth. *Note: This letter is written from my interpretation of scripture.*

I want you to remind yourself of why I died for you. I believe in you and I have a purpose for you here on earth. I'm the answer to your question, "Why am I here?"

Don't ever think of yourself as a failure. Your past mistakes don't define you. The reason you have a problem with failure is because you weren't designed to fail. You were designed for success, peace and joy. Because of sin you know failure, loss and pain; but your failure doesn't define your worth, I do. I will not condemn you.

I want you to see your failures and mistakes as an opportunity to get it right the next time. Focus on your blessings. Recall all the times you were victorious. When you fail you're going to feel bad, but this doesn't mean you **are** bad. Allow your emotions to surface. Try to fix the problem, and seek and pray for solutions.

Love, Jesus

Ask yourself:

1. Do I define myself based on my accomplishments?
2. Do I think of myself as a failure in certain areas of my life?
3. Do I celebrate my victories?
4. What can I do to turn my failures into successes?
5. Do I ask the Holy Spirit to help me work through my emotions when I fall short?

Take action…

1. Look up the following passages and paraphrase each one.

☐1 John 1:9; Phil. 4:13; 2 Cor. 5:17; Rom. 8:1; Rom. 5:8; Matt. 3:8; Gen
6:8

Reflection

1. After reading today's devotion, I realize…
2. The key statements I need to remember and work on are…
3. The positive consequences of remembering and working on these
   statements will be…

DAY 98

A LETTER FROM JESUS

*Be strong and courageous. Do not fear or be in dread of them, for it is
the LORD your God who goes with you. He will not leave you or forsake you."*
(Deut. 31:6)

DON'T DREAD

Today you're going to read a letter addressing how much Jesus loves you and
how he empowers you to do God's will. *Note: This letter is written from my
interpretation of scripture.*

I will never leave you. I will never neglect you. I have always paid attention to
you, even when you were growing up. I know you've felt neglected at times but
I was right there with you. I don't want you to neglect yourself. I want you to
love yourself and know that you are dear to my heart. You were not an accident.
I made you for my purpose.

I want things to matter to you. You matter. You have an influence on people
around you. Stop thinking that life is short. I want you to make the most out of
it now. Today I want you to stop taking the path of least resistance. Have
expectations. Ask and you shall receive.

You are not invisible. I see you and so do others. If you have to confront others don't fear being abandoned, I will be with you. I know you want to be settled and avoid conflict, but you can't. You live in a fallen world and things are going to upset you. So don't numb your feelings, wants and needs from me or others.

Love, Jesus

Ask yourself:

1. Do I feel threatened by significant changes in my life?
2. Have I been going along with others to keep the peace?
3. Have I been procrastinating lately? If so, with what?
4. Am I setting goals and following through step by step?
5. What areas of my life do I need to set goals in?

Practice Healthy Self-Talk

1. *Because of Jesus:*
   o I am confident that I will be able to let others see and hear me.

   o I will be able to do what it takes to become visible.

   o I will be able to take the necessary risks to stop hiding from others and myself.

   o I know I can do it.

Take action…

1. Look up the following passages and paraphrase each one.
   ☐ 1 Chron. 29:12; Psalm 89:20-21; Isaiah 41:10; Isaiah 49:13; Jer. 29:11; Zech. 1:17; Acts 20:32; 1 Peter 5:10; 1 Sam. 17:34-50; Prov. 28:1; 2 Cor. 3:12

Reflection

1. After reading today's devotion, I realize…
2. The key statements I need to remember and work on are…
3. The positive consequences of remembering and working on these statements will be…

DAY 99

A LETTER FROM JESUS

And we know that for those who love God all things work together for good, for those who are called according to his purpose (Romans 8:28)

TRUST GOD DESPITE YOUR CIRCUMSTANCES

Today you're going to read a letter encouraging you to trust God. *Note: This letter is written from my interpretation of scripture.*

OUR FATHER wants you to enjoy life every day but some don't know how to do that for one reason or another. Some of my children don't know how to let go of disappointments because they choose to hang onto them. They don't trust our Father to see them through hard times and adversity because they run the other way.

Our Father wants you to run to Him and jump onto his lap. When God called you to be his child, His goal as your Father is to teach you the right way to process and handle tough times that you have experienced in the past, as well as tough times that are right around the corner. He wants to teach you how to enjoy life no matter what (James 1:2-4). This means you need to put aside what you think you know about life and include our Father in the situation, circumstance or problem (Romans 12:1-3).

Love, Jesus

Enjoying Life...

Believe it or not, we have the ability to enjoy life no matter what season we're in (Ecclesiastes 3). Our Father will teach us, we just need to go to Him with childlike faith. We need to be open to learning new ways of dealing with life. God saved us to teach us His way. He wants to re-parent you in the areas you need it. He will teach you how to enjoy life regardless of what you're going through (sickness, financial issues, job loss, relationship loss, or other troubles, etc.).

Regardless of where we're at today we can function even if life isn't going our way. Happiness isn't a prerequisite to serving our Father (Acts 20:19). Paul relied on his Father in heaven to get him through, so can you. We can follow the "Cloud of Witnesses" (Hebrews 12:1-3) by doing what they did. Let's follow in the footsteps of Christ today.

Take action...

1. Look up the following passages and paraphrase each one.
   ☐1 Peter 1:6-7; 1 Cor. 10:9; Heb. 3:7-11; Psalm 95:7-11; Gal. 6:4;   1 Peter 1:6; 1 Peter 4:12-16; 2 Peter 2:4-9; Rev. 3:10

Ask yourself:

1. Am I enjoying life no matter what?
2. Am I able to enjoy my life regardless of what's going on around me?
3. What did my parents teach me about disappointments? How was I taught to handle them?
4. Does my life seem to stop when I experience a setback?

Reflection

1. After reading today's devotion, I realize...
2. The key statements I need to remember and work on are...
3. The positive consequences of remembering and working on these statements will be...

DAY 100

A LETTER FROM JESUS

Do not fear, for I am with you; Do not anxiously look about you, for I am your God. I will strengthen you, surely I will help you, Surely I will uphold you with My righteous right hand. (Isaiah 41:10)

JESUS WILL GIVE YOU THE COURAGE YOU NEED

Today you're going to read a letter reminding you that through him you can have the courage to do what God has called you to do. *Note: This letter is written from my interpretation of scripture.*

I don't want you to fear the future any more. Some of my children dread the future because they don't realize that I'm watching over them. Yes, I ask you to do things through faith because I want to see if you trust me. If you keep your eyes on me and my Father's promises, the Holy Spirit will guide you and strengthen you.

My Father had to remind me when I was in the Garden of Gethsemane not to fear or be anxious. Once I made a decision to trust him and rely on his strength I was empowered by the Holy Spirit. I felt courageous when I surrendered my fears, and my confidence grew.

Love, Jesus

Keep in mind...

- o Wait and hope for and expect the Lord; be brave and of good courage and let your heart be stout and enduring. Yes, wait for and hope for and expect the Lord. **Psalm 27:14**
- o Say to those who are of a fearful and hasty heart, Be strong, fear not! Behold, your God will come with vengeance; with the recompense of God He will come and save you. **Isaiah 35:4**
- o For I the Lord your God hold your right hand; I am the Lord, Who says to you, Fear not; I will help you! **Isaiah 41:13**
- o So we take comfort and are encouraged and confidently and boldly say, The Lord is my Helper; I will not be seized with alarm [I will not fear or dread or be terrified]. What can man do to me? **Hebrews 13:6**

Reflection

1. After reading today's devotion, I realize...
2. The key statements I need to remember and work on are...
3. The positive consequences of remembering and working on these statements will be...

DAY 101

A LETTER FROM JESUS

Am I now trying to win the approval of men, or of God? Or am I trying to please men? If I were still trying to please men, I would not be a servant of Christ (Gal 1:10)

YOU NO LONGER NEED THE APPROVAL OF OTHERS

Today you're going to read a letter encouraging you not seek man's approval. *Note: This letter is written from my interpretation of scripture.*

I paid the price for your need to be approved and valued. I know you have a tendency to want the approval of others but you don't need it. The only approval you need is mine. Satan will try to distract you by performing for others or people pleasing. That's the world's way.

I know you want to be loved, liked, needed and appreciated, but not at the expense of our relationship. It's okay to want to receive praise but remember, it doesn't give you any more worth than the next person. The praise and reassurance comes from me. If you want to know how special you are, read your Bible.

You no longer need to search for the approval of man, not even your parents, spouse, boss, pastor, or anyone with authority. You're equal. If you start to hide your real self you're going down the wrong path. You don't need people to tell you you're great, OK, or special. You just are. I made you that way. I love you and died for you. You're in me now.

Because I love you and approve of you… you no longer have to:

1. Criticize yourself for imperfections
2. Please others just to feel loved. Connect to me
3. Fear rejection. When you're connected to me you won't want the approval of others

I want you to start relating to yourself with the conviction that you have value, worth, and significance. Love yourself through me. It might feel awkward at first. Don't wait until you feel it, just do it because it's a fact. It's the truth. You no longer need to feel defeated. You're approved of and loved by God.

Love, Jesus

Take action…

    1. Look up the following passages and paraphrase each one.
        □2 Cor. 5:9; Gal. 6:8; Col. 1:10; Col. 3:20; 1 Thess. 4:1; 1 Tim. 2:1-3; 1
           Tim. 5:4; Gal. 1:10,15-16; 1 Thess. 2:4; Psalm 37:23

Reflection

      1. After reading today's devotion, I realize…
      2. The key statements I need to remember and work on are…
      3. The positive consequences of remembering and working on these
         statements will be…

DAY 102-103

A LETTER FROM JESUS

Accept one another, then, just as Christ accepted you, in order to bring praise to God. (Rom. 15:7)

JESUS ACCEPTS YOU NO MATTER WHAT

Today you're going to read a letter reminding you of the importance of accepting yourself. *Note: This letter is written from my interpretation of scripture.*

The reason I want you to accept yourself is because, when you do, you will find yourself encouraged and empowered. Take time to encourage yourself today and don't reject or criticize yourself. Learn to accept the fact that you might fall short and not please everyone. I don't condemn you so don't condemn yourself. I don't expect you to be perfect. What I expect is that you come to me for help, and to admit your faults and failures.

Satan will use the spirit of criticism to get you to feel discouraged. He wants you to focus on your shortcomings and the shortcomings of others. Don't fall for it. Make it a point to accept yourself and others today (Rom. 15:7).

Do your best today, that's it. God isn't keeping score. I'm not keeping score. I already know what you're going to do before you do it (past, present and future). I want you to be happy. Live by grace and truth, not just grace, or not just truth. I'm both of them.

Love, Jesus

Ask yourself:

1. When I fail what do I say to myself about myself?
2. Do I often feel guilty about who I am?
3. What don't I accept about myself?
4. Am I compassionate with myself?
5. Do I set my standards too high? Do I set myself up to fail?

Keep in mind:

1. Jesus wants you to obey His word because He loves you. His commands have your best interest in mind. Through Him and His spirit you can obey him!
2. God delivered you from legalism, idealism and perfectionism… you're in His grace now.

Take action…

1. Look up the following scriptures and paraphrase each one.
   ☐John 14:15; Luke 11:28; Matt. 7:13-14; Rom. 8:1

Reflection

1. After reading today's devotion, I realize…
2. The key statements I need to remember and work on are…
3. The positive consequences of remembering and working on these statements will be…

DAY 104-105

A LETTER FROM JESUS

"For I know the plans I have for you," declares the LORD, "plans to prosper you and not to harm you, plans to give you hope and a future" (Jeremiah 29:11)

YOU HAVE A GREAT FUTURE THAT AWAITS YOU

Today you're going to read a letter reminding you of the awesome plan God has for your life. Jesus wants you to stay on God's potter's wheel so he can continue to mold you into the vessel He created you to be. *Note: This letter is written from my interpretation of scripture.*

I want you to start seeing yourself in a different way. I want you to see yourself as the person I designed you to be: a winner, a champion and an achiever. See yourself accomplishing your goals. Love how you look because I made you and formed you. I gave you your life and I designed a plan specifically for you. Embrace your life because I died for it. I have given you the responsibility to create your self-image based on what my Father thinks of you. If you see yourself as loved, worthwhile, intelligent, valued and needed, you will become that person. You don't have to feel unsure of yourself anymore. You have place in life now. I want you to get rid of all the negative labels that you have for yourself. Stop making comparisons because I made you uniquely, no two people are the same. Don't envy others and don't be jealous, because I have given you gifts, talents and abilities that will take you to the Promised Land my father has prepared for you.

Take time and visualize the life you want. Pray and seek my face because I am listening. You must believe this. I know you have a lot of plans in your mind, but it's my purpose for you that will stand (Proverbs 19:21). If you do it your way your life will be mediocre.

I want you to take on my attitude. I have come down from heaven not to do my own will and purpose, but to do the will and purpose of Him Who sent me (John 6:38). It's going to take you time, and a lot of hard work, to change how you view yourself. Be patient. Make sure that you make the time to mediate on God's word and claim the Father's promises. The more you line up your image with what the Father says about you, the closer you are to achieving your goals, dreams and purpose. Nothing will get in your way.

Love, Jesus

Take action...

    1. Look up the following passages and paraphrase each one.
        ☐Jer. 29:11; Psalm 138:8; Col.1:16; Prov. 21:5; James 4:13-15

Reflection

1. After reading today's devotion, I realize…
2. The key statements I need to remember and work on are…
3. The positive consequences of remembering and working on these statements will be…

DAY 106-108

LETTERS FROM GOD & JESUS

THE CONCLUSION

For the last several weeks we've been exploring how much God loves you and the importance of seeing yourself as a new person. To wrap up this section, I put together a checklist that will help you to see if you're finding your worth, significance, acceptance, security and identity through Jesus. Review it and check off what currently applies to you. The statements you don't check off might be the ones you need to work on. Take your time with this. You might want to take a day or two to go through it. Enjoy!

KNOWING WHO YOU ARE IN CHRIST

"I have been crucified with Christ; it is no longer I who live, but Christ lives in me; and the life which I now live in the flesh I live by faith in the Son of God, who loved me and gave Himself for me." (Galatians 2:20)

In Christ we have a love that can never be fathomed, a life that can never die, a peace that can never be understood, a rest that can never be disturbed, a joy that can never be diminished, a hope that can never be disappointed, a glory that can never be clouded, a light that can never be darkened, and a spiritual resource that can never be exhausted. (Anonymous)

Knowing your identity in Christ is essential if you want to become the person God created you to be.

Instructions: Check off the statements that you can truly agree with. Complete the reflection questions after each section.

Because I know who I am in Christ:

☐I don't have to blame other people for my mistakes and failures.

☐I don't fear that God will punish me for my mistakes and sin. I know I'm covered by the blood of Christ.

☐I worry less and have more peace of mind

☐Things don't have to be perfect

☐I'm less depressed and more hopeful

☐I'm less self-critical and condemning

☐My accomplishments don't define me. I'm successful as I am. My success doesn't make me better than others

☐I don't fear looking incompetent

☐I'm okay with losing because I know you have to lose to win

☐I don't fear what God will do to me

☐I don't judge because I know I have my own issues

☐I know God is loving and kind

☐I know God loves me no matter what

☐I don't live in the past; I'm learning how to let it go

☐I believe God will restore my life

☐I don't feel inadequate anymore

☐I have less shame because Jesus has forgiven me for all of my bad choices

☐My past doesn't determine my future

☐I walk in my inheritance and forgiveness. I believe that I'm pleasing to God

☐I don't fear punishment from others

☐Shame and guilt are a thing of the past

☐It's acceptable to make a mistake

☐I don't have to have high standards. I know I can't reach the ideal without God's grace.

☐I'm not a loser if I have a bad day or don't do everything perfectly

☐I no longer believe that the ideal is what's real

☐I don't have "all or nothing" thinking anymore

☐I accept that I'm human

☐I no longer believe that I'm not good enough

☐I set realistic goals

☐I'm more flexible

☐I accept that we all fall short of God's glory. Imperfections are acceptable

☐I can go slow and easy, one day at a time

☐I have realistic expectations of God, others, and myself

☐I enjoy my accomplishments because I know I don't have to perform in order to be loved by God

☐I can be adaptable

☐I don't have to be controlling

☐I accept what I can't change

☐I no longer withdraw from God when I sin or fail

☐I no longer isolate from the body of Christ when I fall into sin. I can confess my sin and not fear their judgment because I know God forgives me for my past, present and future sins

☐I'm no longer hopeless or helpless

☐I can accept feedback and criticism

☐I know I have a purpose and plan

☐I'm accepted, loved, significant and secure

☐I know that God will bind my broken heart

☐I want to do what's right, now

☐I care about what God thinks and feels

☐I see God as my Father

☐I can be open and vulnerable

☐I trust others more

☐I want to please God

☐I know I'm His child

☐I'm more merciful, compassionate and kind

☐I have more confidence knowing that I can do all things through Jesus

☐I don't seek approval or security from people

☐I can be assertive

☐I can say no

☐I no longer feel inferior to others

☐I feel deserving from God

☐I like how I look physically

☐I no longer feel bad if I can't make someone happy, especially when I try

☐I no longer have a compulsion to please others

☐I no longer fear letting my loved ones down

☐I'm comfortable with my gifts, talents and abilities

☐I don't avoid conflict

☐I face my problems instead of denying them

☐I make my own choices and decisions

☐I can handle pressure, adversity, trials and hardships, because I'm standing on the rock

☐My worth is no longer defined by the people in my life

☐I can handle other people being mad at me or disappointed in me

☐I can accept that not everybody is going to like me

☐I give and receive in balance

☐I don't have to work harder to make things better for people. All I have to do is share the burden

Keep in mind… What the Bible says about your identity in Christ

☐Psalm 1:3: He shall be like a tree planted by rivers of water, that brings forth its fruit in its season, whose leaf also shall not wither; and whatever he does shall prosper.

☐Romans 8:14-16: For as many as are led by the Spirit of God, these are sons of God.
>For you did not receive the spirit of bondage again to fear but you received the Spirit of <u>adoption</u> by whom we cry out "Abba Father." The Spirit Himself bears witness with our spirit that we are children of God.

☐2 Corinthians 5:17: Therefore, if anyone is in Christ, he is a new creation; old things have passed away; behold, all things have become new.

☐2 Corinthians 5:21 : For He made Him who knew no sin to be sin for us that we might become the righteousness of God in Him.

☐Galatians 2:20: "I have been crucified with Christ; it is no longer I who live, but Christ lives in me; and the life which I now live in the flesh I live by faith in the Son of God, who loved me and gave Himself for me."

☐Ephesians 2:6: ...and raised us up together and made us sit together in the heavenly places in Christ Jesus

☐1 Peter 2:9: But you are a chosen generation, a royal priesthood, a holy nation, and His own special people, that you may proclaim the praises of Him who called you out of darkness into His marvelous light.

☐Romans 8:31-39 I am free from any condemnation brought against me and I cannot be separated from the love of God. *What, then, shall we say in response to this? If God is for us, who can be against us? He who did not spare his own Son, but gave him up for us all how will he not also, along with him, graciously give us all things? Who will bring any charge against those whom God has chosen? It is God who justifies. Who is he that condemns? Christ Jesus, who died more than that, who was raised to life is at the right hand of God and is also interceding for us. Who shall separate us from the love of Christ? Shall trouble or hardship or persecution or famine or nakedness or danger or sword? As it is written: "For your sake we face death all day long; we are considered as sheep to be slaughter." No, in all these things we are more than conquerors through him who loved us. For I am convinced that neither death nor life, neither angels nor demons, neither the present nor the future, nor any powers, neither height nor depth, nor anything else in all creation, will be able to separate us from the love of God that is in Christ Jesus our Lord.*

☐Philippians 3:20 I am a citizen of heaven.
>*But our citizenship is in heaven. And we eagerly await a Saviour from there, the Lord Jesus Christ,*

☐2 Timothy 1:7 I have not been given a spirit of fear but of power, love and a sound mind.
>*For God did not give us a spirit of timidity, but a spirit of power, of love and of self-discipline.*

☐1 John 5:18 I am born of God and the evil one cannot touch me.
>*We know that anyone born of God does not continue to sin; the one who was born of God keeps him safe, and the evil one cannot harm him.*

☐Ephesians 2:10 I am God's workmanship.
For we are God's workmanship, created in Christ Jesus to do good works, which God prepared in advance for us to do.
☐Ephesians 3:12 I may approach God with freedom and confidence.
In him and through faith in him we may approach God with freedom and confidence.
☐Philippians 4:13 I can do all things through Christ, who strengthens me.
I can do everything through him who gives me strength.

Reflection

    1. After reading today's checklist I realize…

    2. The key statements I need to remember and work on are…

    3. What can I do to change the areas I need to work on?

    4. What kind of support and accountability do I need?

    5. The positive consequences of remembering and working on these statements are…

SANCTIFICATION

&

FAITH

And this is the way to have eternal life—to know you, the only true God, and Jesus Christ, the one you sent to earth. (John 17:3)

We are made right with God by placing our faith in Jesus Christ. And this is true for everyone who believes, no matter who we are (Ro 3:22)

DAY 109-112

WHAT IS FAITH?

Now faith is the substance of things hoped for, the evidence of things not seen
(Heb. 11:1)

Today I want you to think about think about the amount of confidence you have in God, as well as your commitment to God.

Faith is defined as:

1. Confidence or trust in a person or thing.
2. Belief that is not based on proof.
3. Belief and full confidence in God's promises and word

Ask yourself:

1. How has my faith grown in the last 6 months? In the last year?
2. In what areas of my life do I need stronger faith? (Career, finances, relationships, etc.)
3. What prevents my faith from growing?
4. Do I love God unconditionally? Do I trust him?
5. Do I walk away from God because things don't go my way?
6. Do I need to strengthen my commitment to God?

Take action...

1. Look up the following passages and paraphrase each one.
   ☐John 14:1; Heb. 11:6; Psalm 40:4; James 2:14-26; Jer. 17:7-8; John 5:24; John 6:28-29; Rom. 1:5; Heb. 4:2; Luke 8:15

Keep in mind:

1. True faith is seen in obedient action, love, and continuing good works.
2. A deeper faith in God will help eliminate our anxiety, depression and anger.
3. Anxiety, worry, depression and anger come from a lack of faith and confidence in God, self and others.
4. Faith is: *F*= Full - *A*= Assurance - *I*= In - *T*= The - *H*= Heart

Reflection

1. After reading today's devotion, I realize…
2. The key statements I need to remember and work on are…
3. The positive consequences of remembering and working on these statements will be…

DAY 113-114

FAITH RELEASES GOD'S POWER

"You don't have enough faith," Jesus told them. "I tell you the truth, if you had faith even as small as a mustard seed, you could say to this mountain, 'Move from here to there,' and it would move. Nothing would be impossible.
(Matthew 17:20)

"What do you mean, 'If I can'?" Jesus asked. "Anything is possible if a person believes."

So, in other words, God's power is released through faith.

Doubt…

Jesus wants you to stop doubting and believe. When He was in the garden He experienced doubt for a minute and He expressed that doubt to his father. He prayed and released His will, or choice. Why? Because He had 100% faith in His Father. Jesus is telling us that He can help. We all have a mission, plan, adversities and hardships to go through in life and Jesus wants you and I to reach out to Him, not turn from Him. Life is full of challenges and tests, and without belief and trust in God, life becomes impossible to bear.

Risk Taking…

How do you and I receive God's blessing? By placing our confidence in Him and trusting Him. Think about Peter for a minute… when he got out of the boat he had a deep faith and confidence in Jesus, but what did he do? He took his eyes and mind off of Him and he sank. We have to keep our eyes and mind on God's words and believe them and apply them despite of how we feel.

We need to celebrate that God will not abandon us (Psalm 27). We no longer have to feel like God, or others won't help us, or that God is going to leave us. He won't ... it's a promise. God tells us that He will never leave us nor forsake us... regardless of what you or I do. God will be there when you and I need Him the most. He is dependable.

Don't avoid a close relationship with God because you fear He might leave or abandon you. Maybe you experienced this on earth by a parent or someone you love.... but this doesn't happen in heaven. Cling to God not man. God is available, dependable, reliable and willing to help you. You and I just need to be patient as He works behind the scenes.

Ask yourself:

1. How do I know when I'm losing faith? How does my personality change?
2. How do I do with unanswered prayer? Or when God answers in a way that opposes what I think I need? How do I act? Are my actions helpful or harmful? What, if anything, do I need to change?
3. Do I fear abandonment? Was I abandoned by someone and does it affect my relationship with God?
4. Do I feel at a gut level that important people in my life, such as significant others, are going to leave, drop me for someone better, or die, or that others in my life aren't dependable and won't be there when I need them the most?

To Do:

1. Look up 3 scriptures that confirm that God needs your faith in him to do the impossible.
2. Confirm in God's Word that He will never leave you.
3. Explore the possibility that you might have abandonment issues.

Take action...

1. Look up the following passages and paraphrase each one.
   Acts 16:5; 2 Cor. 10:15; Rev. 2:19; Luke 17:5; Psalm 131:2;   1
      Peter 1:14; Psalm 18:2-3; Psalm 9:9-10; Psalm 115:9-11; Psalm
      144:1-2; Psalm 13:5

Reflection

1. After reading today's devotion, I realize…
2. The key statements I need to remember and work on are…
3. The positive consequences of remembering and working on these statements will be…

DAY 115-117

RELY ON GOD'S GRACE NOT JUST HIS COMMANDS

So the trouble is not with the law, for it is spiritual and good. The trouble is with me, for I am all too human, a slave to sin. (Rom. 7:14)

Today I want you to think about the importance of relying on God's grace to help you live out His principles. Many people get stuck in the sanctification process because they think they have to follow God's commands perfectly. I think this is a big problem among Christians. God doesn't make us perform in order to be loved and accepted. He wants us to surrender to Him so He can give us the desire and power to please Him.

Peter's Story

Peter was struggling to understand his sin nature. He really wanted to change but he couldn't. His struggle was much like the Apostle Paul's as recorded in Romans 7:15-17. Peter came in for a session and said, "I don't understand Mike, I want to change, I want to do what is right but I don't do it. I take three steps forward and then ten backwards."

Peter's struggle is not unique. He was relying on his own willpower and strength. He was applying God's principles but he wasn't relying on God's grace and mercy to help him make changes from the inside out.

Ask yourself:

1. Have I been making poor choices lately? If so, describe them. What are the causes? Share your insights with your support network.

2. Am I admitting my weaknesses? Am I giving into my weaknesses? If so which ones? What are you hoping to gain by giving in to them?

3. O, what a wretched, miserable person I am…" In what areas of my life do I feel this way? Explain.

4. Am I hiding? Do I wear masks? If so, why? What makes me want to hide or pretend?

5. Am I trying to control others? If so, what's causing this? What can I do to let go?

6. Am I trying to hide my problems?

7. Am I hurt or sad about anything?

8. Am I escaping my hurt and pain by minimizing or avoiding it?

9. Am I dealing with the people, places and things that frustrate me? If so how?

10. Am I applying God's principles to my relationships and struggles?

11. Do I need to strengthen my commitment to God?

Take action…

1. Look up the following passages and paraphrase each one.
   2 Cor. 12:8-9; 1 Peter 5:10; Matt. 15:19; Mark 7:21-22; Rom. 7:14-15; 1 Cor. 1:8; Eph. 4:24; Col. 3:10; Phil. 1:6; 1 John 3:2; Rom. 8:29; 2 Cor. 3:18

Reflection

1. After reading today's devotion, I realize…
2. The key statements I need to remember and work on are…
3. The positive consequences of remembering and working on these statements will be…

DAY 118-120

ACCEPT YOUR NEED FOR GOD

Let us then with confidence draw near to the throne of grace, that we may receive mercy and find grace to help in time of need. (Heb. 4:16)

God's in Charge...

I don't think it became apparent to the prodigal son that he needed his father until he lost everything. When he came to his senses, he realized what he did.

Isn't that the case for most of us?

Today I would like you to open your Bible to Luke 15:18 and think about what this verse means in the context of "Oh no, I made a mistake; my father was right."

Have you ever had an experience like the lost son? Discovering that God is the one in charge? He realized that his ways were wrong and that God's ways were right. He finally realized that God was in charge. The lost son had to admit that he was powerless in order to return to his father.

As you can see in the story, it took pain for him to come to his senses and to return home. I must admit, the lost son put up a fight trying to avoid and escape the reality of his situation. I think Jesus was teaching him Matt 5:3. What about you?

Consider this...

Complete the following sentences

1. I'm rebellious in the following areas of my life...

2. I'm struggling to give up the following behaviors...

3. It's hard for me to ask God to....

4. When I let go and let God, He always....

5. I've been making the following bad choices lately_____ and here's the reason why...

6. I need to stop controlling the following issues in my life...

7. I'm going to let go of the following things and ask for help from God and others:

I created journal entries that I think the prodigal son would have written as he was in the process of coming to his senses.

Read through the Prodigal Son's journal and think about what might be true for you.

The Prodigal Son's Journal

In order to change my life I needed to...

1. Face the truth about myself, my life and my choices
2. Accept that our father has designed life to be lived a certain way and that I need to follow his ways not my own. God's ways guarantee success, peace, joy, and happiness
3. Be poor in spirit in order to change and grow. I had to let down my pride and personal independence.
4. Mourn my loss and accept responsibility for my behaviors.
5. Face the reality that I blew everything that my father gave me and now I have to start over.
6. Be humble before my father and resist Satan's lies for me to fight temptation and to return home. I couldn't do it on my own (James 4:7)
7. Admit to myself that I needed to depend on my father, and when I did he lifted me up
8. Realize that the truth does equal freedom and going through pain is worth it in the long run. Being separated from my father hurt me more than it did to return home because at home is where I receive love, grace, support, truth and direction. Why did I ever doubt that?

9. Look at the wrong things I have done, not just from my mind but from my heart. I needed to experience sorrow and deep grief for my behaviors, attitudes and choices (James 4:7-10) in order for them to change.

10. Grieve the following issues:

   a. The fact that I spent the inheritance my father worked so hard to give me.
   b. My self-image
   c. Starting over
   d. What I could have had if I had just stayed home
   e. My old ways of coping
   f. The strain and barriers between my brother and I

Take action...

1. Look up the following passages and paraphrase each one.

☐2 Cor. 6:1; 1 Cor. 2:1-5; 2 Cor. 9:8; Heb. 2:14; Heb. 4:15; Heb. 5:2; James 4:6; 2 Peter 3:17-18; 1 Peter 4:10; Phil. 2:13; 2 Peter 1:3

Reflection

1. After reading today's devotion, I realize…
2. The key statements I need to remember and work on are…
3. The positive consequences of remembering and working on these statements will be…

REVIEW & REPAIR

Reshaping Your Soul

1. What did I learn this past month about myself, God and others?

2. What concepts or ideas stood out to me in the devotions? Why?

3. What adjustments do I need to make in my life?

4. What, if anything, needs to change about how I think, feel and act?

5. What changes have I made so far? What actions have I taken?

6. How are people reacting to my changes?

7. Steps I will continue to take are…

8. I'm committed to…

9. My victories this week were…

10. God please help me with…

DAY 121-122

REMOVE ANY BARRIERS

Not many days later, the younger son gathered all he had and took a journey into a far country, and there he squandered his property in reckless living.[14] And when he had spent everything, a severe famine arose in that country, and he began to be in need. (Luke 15:13-14)

A moment with the Prodigal

I had to admit that I was broken and poor in spirit. The only way I was going to heal was if I confessed to God that I had sinned. I had to come to the end of myself so I could ask for help. I had to stop deceiving myself.

I realized that letting go of my lifestyle would bring me new life and new beginnings. I had to stop clinging to my failures and sin. I think my regrets prevented me from returning home and restoring my relationship with my father. When I was clinging to my mistakes and regrets I was breaking union with God which, in turn, affected how I though felt and behaved. I felt so powerless and hopeless. *(Luke 15:17-19)*

Charles H. Brent said, "Peace comes when there is no cloud between us and God. Peace is the consequence of forgiveness, God's removal of that which obscures His face and so breaks union with Him."

Today I want you to ask yourself the following questions:

1. If I'm struggling, what prevents me from going to God and others?

2. Do I have a cloud between myself and God? If so, what am I doing to bring sunshine? Am I claiming God's promises? If not, why not?

3. What do I need to confess today?

Take action…

1. Look up the following passages and paraphrase each one.
   Rom. 6:19; 2 Cor. 7:1; Gal. 5:16,25; Eph. 5:15-16; Col. 3:5; James 1:17; James 4:6; Jude 24

Reflection

1. After reading today's devotion, I realize…
2. The key statements I need to remember and work on are…
3. The positive consequences of remembering and working on these
   statements will be

DAY 123-124

LET GO OF YOUR NEGATIVE IMAGE

*Trust in the LORD with all your heart,
and do not lean on your own understanding. (Proverbs 3:5)*

Let Go and Let God…

You need to see yourself through our Father's eyes. I can tell you this, your life will not change if you continue to shame and antagonize yourself with your regrets and mistakes.

Your past doesn't have to define who you are as a person. It's your story and testimony. Take responsibility and ownership for the one life you have and stop hiding behind your past, character defects and disease. I love the story about the man by the pool in John 5:1-13. This man was a paraplegic for 38 years and Jesus told him to get up and stop making excuses has to why he couldn't. He was weighed down by his shame and guilt. He felt like a victim so he acted like one and Jesus said, "Do you want to get well? Pick up your mat and carry it." In other words, take responsibility - I have a new life for you.

Refocus…

Let go of all your excuses and the reasons why you can't change. Stop looking at what you did and start to look at who you are and what God has done for you. Look at what it says in Col. 3:3-5 "**For you died to this life, and your real life is hidden with Christ in God. And when Christ, who is your life, is revealed to the whole world, you will share in all his glory. So put to death the sinful, earthly things lurking within you.**" This includes your negative self-image. Let go of the dead dog image. In recovery, you have a new life and a new self.

I know it took years for you to develop this image to keep your addictions alive. You had to establish a set of values and beliefs systems to pull off your old lifestyle. Well, those days are over. You turned your will over to God, so let go and do what you need to do to heal and get well. Pick up you mat and get stepping.

Take action…

> 1. Look up the following passages and paraphrase each one.
>   - Deut. 4:30-31; Luke 1:16-17
>   - Deut. 30:2-3,10; Luke 22:32; James 5:19-20; Hosea 12:6; Matt. 18:3-4
>   - Gal. 5:22-24; Eph. 4:1; Eph. 5:8-11; 1 Peter 2:11-12; Luke 7:11-15; John 11:1-44

Reflection

> 1. After reading today's devotion, I realize…
> 2. The key statements I need to remember and work on are…
> 3. The positive consequences of remembering and working on these statements will be…

DAY 125-126

LEARN TO ASK FOR HELP

My help comes from the Lord, who made heaven and earth (Psalm 121:2)

Asking for help does not mean we are weak or incompetent. It usually indicates an advanced level of honesty and intelligence. ~ Anne Wilson Schaef

Feeling Vulnerable…

I must admit, it's not easy asking for help or admitting that you have a need, especially when you're used to living independently. Many people have a hard time admitting that they need help, love, validation or guidance for one reason or another. Some people believe that they have to figure things out on their own because asking for help suggests weakness, or a lack of control. Some people fear rejection. Believe it or not, some people just want to stay stuck because they're afraid to face reality and take responsibility.

Today I want you to think about how hard, or how easy it is for you to ask for help or admit that you have a need.

Open your Bible to Luke 15 and read the story of the Lost Son. Focus on verses 14-19. As you read the story I want you to think about his struggle to ask for help, and how it was hard for him to admit that he was in serious trouble. What emotions do you think were preventing him from returning home? What was he thinking? Remember, your feelings are a mirror to your thoughts, and as a man thinks so he is (Prov. 23:7).

Consider this…

Complete the following sentences:

1. The following thoughts keep me from relying on God…

2. The following behaviors keep me independent from God…

3. When I feel _____ I run from God instead to God

4. When I'm afraid to admit I need help from God I will…

5. I can go to the following people to ask for help (1 Peter 4:10)…

6. I will talk to the following people about this devotion…

Take action…

1. Look up the following passages and paraphrase each one.
   □ Heb. 4:16; Exod. 14:31; Deut. 8:3; Psalm 4:5; Gal. 6:2; Ecc. 4:9-12; Psalm 55:14; Acts 4:24; Acts 12:12; James 5:16; Heb. 10:24-25; Job 29:12-17; Job 30:25; Prov. 14:31

Reflection

1. After reading today's devotion, I realize…
2. The key statements I need to remember and work on are…

3. The positive consequences of remembering and working on these
   statements will be…

DAY 127-128

GOD IS WORKING IN YOU

*For God is working in you, giving you the desire and the power to do what
pleases him. (Phil. 2:13)*

Work in Progress…

How does it make you feel knowing that your Father in heaven is working in
you, giving you the desire to obey Him and the power to do what pleases Him?
This truth about our Abba Father takes away all the excuses we might have about
not being able to change a particular habit, immaturity, or overcome our
brokenness, hurt, loss or childhood wounds.

Our Father provides different ways for us to grow spiritually. Everyone has a
different sanctification process. His divine power will give you everything you
need for living a godly life (2 Peter 1:3).

Power to Change…

Do you believe that you have the power to change and that Jesus has promises
for you to cling to that will give you hope and inspiration? For example, when I
have problems with my thinking and it becomes negative and pessimistic, I
practice and apply Philippians 4:8 with the help of the Holy Spirit. When I'm
facing temptation I rely on the Holy Spirit to help me apply 1 Corinthians 10:13
to my situation. All we need is the desire (which God gives us) and love for our
Father, not allegiance to the law (Matt 22:37-40). Our obedience needs to come
out of our respect and love for our Father. It needs to be stronger than our love
for particular sins and habits.

Paul's Memoir
c.61 A.D.
Phil 2:13

I wanted to remind my brothers and sisters that we need to imitate and follow the pattern of Jesus. I want them to stay humble and united as one body. But as we know, pride gets in the way. Euodia and Syntyche weren't getting along. I was trying to tell them that to make any relationship work we need to be united in spirit and purpose. The tests and trials are God's way of making us stronger in character. As we live day to day God is sanctifying us and it's our responsibility to work out our salvation. We don't have to rely on our own strength to do the things we can't do ourselves, as God's children we rely on His power, might and spirit (Zech. 4:6).

The best way that I could explain this was to use Jesus as the role model so they could understand how to be humble; and to remind them that all they do is for Jesus and not to try to please men. Instead of fighting I wanted them to see that they need to put off the old man and to put on the new man, and that our Father will help them through His grace and mercy.

In my ministry I came across a lot of Christians who love the principles of Christianity but when it comes down to changing internally, they rebel. They didn't understand that God made the rules and He's the one in charge. Also we were designed for dependency. I've learned (Rom. 7, 2 Cor. 12) that I need to give God my will. I don't have control over my habits, my emotions, or my urges and desires. Once I realized that I couldn't follow the law and keep my promise to God, I needed to surrender my will and choices to Him. In other words I asked Jesus to take my life (Rom. 7:25).

Consider this...

Today think about one behavior or attitude that you want to change and search the Scriptures to find the promises God has for you pertaining to the thing you want to change. Remember God is for you, and not against you, and make sure that you apply the benefits of those promises to your life every day (2 Peter 1:5).

Take action...

1. Look up the following passages and paraphrase each one.
        □Col. 2:19; Eph. 4:13-15 See also 1 Cor. 3:1-2; 1 Cor. 13:11;   1
        Cor. 14:20; Heb. 5:12-14; 1 Peter 2:2; 1 Peter 2:1

Reflection

1. After reading today's devotion, I realize…
2. The key statements I need to remember and work on are…
3. The positive consequences of remembering and working on these statements will be…

DAY 129-131

ATTITUDES THAT PREVENT GOD'S PRESENCE IN YOUR LIFE

For just as by one man's disobedience (failing to hear, heedlessness, and carelessness) the many were constituted sinners, so by one Man's obedience the many will be constituted righteous (made acceptable to God, brought into right standing with Him) (Rom. 5:19)

Today I want to discuss with you some possible reasons why you might get stuck in the sanctification process. Read through the following attitudes and see what might apply to you.

The following attitudes can prevent God's presence in your life:

1. You fail to live out God's principles.
2. You are unwilling to explore your inner emotional world.
3. You don't allow yourself to accept loneliness, hurt, and other painful feelings.
4. You over-play the "Martyr" role to the point of depression.
5. You envy others and become self-absorbed.
6. You target others for blame and criticism.
7. You mistrust people's motives and become calloused.
8. You think of yourself as independent.
9. You feel too ashamed to ask for help so your pride gets the best of you. (James 4:6-10)

The Sovereign LORD will wipe away the tears from all faces. (Isaiah 25:8)

Reshaping Exercise…

I was thinking about reasons why I lack peace of mind; here's what I came up with. See if you can add to the list. Circle what applies to you and find ways to improve. Perhaps do the opposite!

51 Reasons why some people <u>get stuck in the sanctification process</u> and lose the <u>joy of their salvation</u>:

1. I argue instead of talk
2. I don't say what I really feel
3. I don't ask for what I want or need
4. I ignore my soul
5. I stop praying
6. I disconnect from God
7. I ignore my values and beliefs
8. I compare myself to others
9. I fight
10. I become defensive
11. I'd rather be right then happy
12. I play the expert role
13. I think I know it all
14. I teach others, not myself
15. I lack gratitude
16. I'm always competing
17. I ignore what others have to say
18. I don't take advice
19. I think I need to be perfect
20. I don't repent when I say I'm sorry
21. I lie
22. I deceive myself
23. I pretend
24. I isolate and withdraw
25. I numb out
26. I lose faith and hope
27. I hide from love and grace
28. I rescue
29. I fix
30. I worry about stupid stuff
31. I'm always striving for something
32. I'm not in the present
33. I live in the future
34. I don't trust
35. I feel shame and guilt
36. I feel insecure
37. I don't ask for forgiveness
38. I don't receive forgiveness from God
39. I fix my mind on what is wrong

40. I don't follow my gut
41. I pressure myself
42. I live off deadlines
43. I don't rest or have fun
44. I seek approval...NOTICE ME.... LOOK AT ME AREN'T I SPECIAL
45. I don't focus on the positive enough
46. I think others are out to get me
47. I see the worst in others
48. I have unrelenting standards
49. I don't like to fail
50. I don't risk
51. Grandiosity and entitlement take over my soul

Take action...

1. Look up the following passages and paraphrase each one.
   ☐Deut. 26:16; Deut. 32:46; Rom. 6:16-18; 1 Peter 1:14-16; Matt. 7:24-27; James 1:22; Josh 24:24; Rom. 6:17

Ask yourself:

Why do I lose my peace of mind?

Reflection

1. After reading today's devotion, I realize…
2. The key statements I need to remember and work on are…
3. The positive consequences of remembering and working on these statements are…

DAY 132-134

LIVE BY GODLY PRINCIPLES

And he declared to you his covenant, which he commanded you to perform, that is, the Ten Commandments,[a] and he wrote them on two tablets of stone. (Deut. 4:13)

All scripture is given by inspiration of God, and is profitable for doctrine, for reproof, for correction, for instruction in righteousness. (2 Tim. 3:16)

So he was there with the LORD forty days and forty nights. He neither ate bread nor drank water. And he wrote on the tablets the words of the covenant, the Ten Commandments. (Exod. 34:28)

Today we are going to take a look at what it means to live by God's principles, and what you believe about reading God's Word. I'm going to start off with examples of some principles God wants us to follow. After you read through the list I want you to answer the questions below.

Godly Principles...

1. God created principles to organize the human world
2. God created principles for the physical world.
3. God created principles for the spiritual world.
4. Living a life based on God's principles will bring blessings here on earth and/or in heaven.
5. God's principles (ethics, ideologies or philosophies):
    - Honesty
    - Love
    - Integrity
    - Peace
    - Forgiveness
    - Service
    - Commitment: Keep your promises to God, self and others
    - Humility
    - Persistence
    - Courage
    - Faith
    - Hope
    - Endurance
    - Trust
    - Responsibility
    - Thankfulness

- •Gratitude
- •Support and encouragement
- •Family

Ask yourself:

1. Based on the list above, what principles are you currently living out consistently? Make a list.
2. Based on the list above, what principles do you struggle to live by? What are the reasons? What can you do about it?

Take action...

1. Look up the following passages and paraphrase each one.
   □2 Tim. 3:14-15; Psalm 19:7-11; John 20:30-31; Rom. 10:8; Rom. 15:4; 1 John 5:13; Psalm 1:1-3; Matt. 4:4; John 15:5-8; 2 Cor. 1:19-22

READING THE BIBLE

Cause me to understand the way of your precepts that I may meditate on your wonderful deeds. (Psalm 119:27)

Instructions: Check off the statements that are true for you. Complete the reflection questions after each section.

I believe the Bible:

□Teaches me the truth about God, others and myself

□Shows me what values I need to live by

□Teaches me how to live my life

□Is used for my correction and discipline so I can grow and change

□Is my compass to live a life pleasing to God

□Teaches me how to be upright and righteous

□Helps me to resist temptation and turn from evil

☐Helps me break the cycle of my sin, bad habits and hang ups

☐Helps me resist the devil. Scriptures are the sword of truth. I need the Bible for spiritual warfare

☐Helps me to grow because it allows me to see how other followers of God lived their life and how they dealt with different circumstances and situations (Heb. 11).

☐Brings comfort, strength and hope

☐Offers encouragement

☐Shows me why, what, how I go wrong (rebel, sin, get off course)

☐Provides me with a standard to live by

☐Is meant to be read with the Holy Spirit

☐Needs to be read daily. Memorizing scriptures, setting up quiet times, doing word studies and topical studies on areas where I need to grow are major factors to help me grow, change and heal.

Reflection

1. After reading today's checklist I realize…
2. The key statements I need to remember and work on are…
3. What can I do to change the areas I need to work on?
4. What kind of support and accountability do I need?
5. The positive consequences of remembering and working on these statements are…

DAY 135-136

STAY CONNECTED TO GOD

"Teacher, this woman has been caught in the act of adultery (John 8:4)

He stood up and said to them, "Let him who is without sin among you be the first to throw a stone at her." And once more he bent down and wrote on the ground. But when they heard it, they went away one by one, beginning with the

older ones, and Jesus was left alone with the woman standing before him.
(John 8:7-9)

The story about the adulteress has so many messages for us to apply to our lives. One message in particular is God's unconditional love and His desire to be in relationship with us. Jesus wasn't only trying to reconnect to the adulteress He was trying to get the crowd and the Pharisees to reconnect to God too. They apparently had a distorted image of Him. We need to work through any distorted images of God we have so that we don't get stuck in the sanctification process.

Today let's use our imaginations and think about what the adulteress might have thought and felt when God was calling her back home. Here's what I think she might have said if I asked her, "What was your life like before God? What prevented you from connecting to God?"

A Moment with the Adulteress

(John 7:53-8:11)

I knew I wasn't in relationship with God. I was disconnected and alone. My life wasn't where God and I knew it could be. I must say, when I was held accountable before God for adultery, my life started to turn around. This was a turning point in my life. I believe that it was the best, yet scariest, day of my life.

I understand now that God wanted me to return to relationship with Him. He saw my pain and the emptiness I carried inside, and because He loves me, He wanted to save me.

For a long time I was trying to provide for myself. I would always try to fill my emptiness on my own. But now I don't have to. God's unconditional love fills my soul and spirit.

When Jesus said, *"Where are your accusers? Didn't even one of them condemn you?"* I felt my heart melt and I heard chains break off my soul and spirit. I was so ashamed up until Jesus said that to me. Jesus knew I wanted to change but I was too ashamed to do anything about it. Jesus took the initiative to reconnect to me so He could save my soul and spirit.

Today I want you to ask yourself the following questions:

1. Is God trying to reconnect to me in some way?

2. Am I experiencing shame in any area of my life? If so, what area? If you're hiding it, don't. Share it with a trusted friend, pastor, and mentor.

3. What does unconditional love mean to me?

Take action...

1. Look up the following passages and paraphrase each one.
   Exod. 19:5; Deut. 5:32-33; Deut. 10:12-13; Deut. 29:9; Isaiah 1:26; Rom. 6:16-18; 1 Peter 1:14-16; 1 John 1:9; Psalm 32:1-5; Heb. 9:14; Heb. 10:22; Hab. 1:13; John 9:31

Reflection

1. After reading today's devotion, I realize...
2. The key statements I need to remember and work on are...
3. The positive consequences of remembering and working on these statements will be...

DAY 137-138

MAKE SURE YOU'RE CONNECTED TO GOD

Go to a quiet place & still your thoughts & emotions. ("Be still & know that I am God." Psalm 46:10)

Often times we think we are walking in our faith but then God shows us that we're not. Today I want you to make sure that you're as connected to God as you think you are.

Scott's story

Scott thought he was connected to God but, as he discovered, he was shutting God's grace out. He was doing spiritual things but he wasn't happy, nor was he experiencing joy. He was depressed at the end of each day. He was exhausted and stressed. He was allowing himself to become frustrated over little things.

His temptations were starting to grow. He stopped reaching out for help. In fact, he felt like he had to keep his struggles a secret. His pride was leading to self-deception. He was becoming more and more closed down but wasn't admitting it. Scott's heart was divided and he became double minded.

Ask yourself:

1. How can I relate to Scott's story?

2. How often do I pray? Is it enough? What have I been praying for? Am I asking God to help me with certain struggles?

3. How often do I read and meditate on God's word? Is it enough?

4. Am I going to church regularly? If so, is it enough?

5. Am I connecting to others (the body of Christ, a mentor, small groups)? If so, is enough?

6. Am I distracted? Am I putting other things before time with God?

7. Am I shutting out the Holy Spirit? Is He speaking to me about making changes in my attitudes or behaviors? Am I ignoring Him? If so, why? What can I do to start listening?

8. Am I asking God to help me with my temptations, feelings, bad habits, hurts? If not, why not?

Take action...

1. Look up the following passages and paraphrase each one.
   ☐Psalm 37:7; Isaiah 30:15; Exod. 14:14; Matt. 6:6; Psalm 1:1-3; Psalm 119:15-16; James 3:13; Psalm 119:11; Gal. 6:7-9 See also Rom. 6:11-14; John 15:4-5

Reflection

1. After reading today's devotion, I realize...
2. The key statements I need to remember and work on are...
3. The positive consequences of remembering and working on these statements will be...

DAY 139-141

LIVING OUT YOUR FAITH

Faith without works is dead. (James 2:17)

Taking our Spiritual Pulse

Lisa's Story

Lisa was going to church faithfully. Every Sunday she would sit in the front row right next to the pastor and his wife. She was involved in two different ministries. She attended small groups faithfully; in fact, she led one for several months. Despite her activities she wasn't connected to God. She wasn't living out her faith from Monday to Saturday. Lisa had a hard time admitting that she had needs and struggles. She started to feel more and more anxious and resentful. Lisa was drifting away from God and didn't even realize it.

Ask yourself:

     1. In what ways can I relate to Lisa's story?

     2. Am I drifting away? If so, in what area(s) of my life?

     3. How do I know I'm drifting away? What are the signs?

     4. What can I do to reconnect?

Instructions: Read through the list and check off what you think you need to work on.

In order to stay connected to God we need to:

     ☐Surrender every area of our lives to God (emotions, mind, relationships, finances, health, career, etc.).

     ☐Pray and ask God for help

     ☐Ask others for help

     ☐Stay connected to the flock; the body of Christ

☐Be submissive to God

☐See God as the Boss

☐Resolve conflicts

☐Depend and trust

☐Release control to God

☐Face adversity, trials, hardships

☐Let go of our illusion of control

☐Stop judging

Take action…

1. Look up the following passages and paraphrase each one
   ☐Prov. 3:5-6; James 4:8 See also Psalm 145:18; Jer. 3:22; Jer. 30:21-22; Zech. 1:3; Mal. 3:7; Heb. 7:19; Psalm 119:17,65; Psalm 125:1-4; Jer. 32:41; Micah 2:7; Zech. 8:14-15; Acts 10:37-38; Psalm 34:14

Reflection

1. After reading today's devotion, I realize…
2. The key statements I need to remember and work on are…
3. The positive consequences of remembering and working on these statements will be…

DAY 142-143

FIGHT THE GOOD FIGHT

Fight the good fight for the true faith. Hold tightly to the eternal life to which God has called you, which you have confessed so well before many witnesses.
(1 Tim. 6:12)

I think many Christians are overboard on belief but bankrupt on obedience. A big part of developing our faith is following God's Word not only in good times but also in bad times. It seems that we have a tendency to look at our problems and take our eyes off Jesus. When we do this we sink. We can't do much apart from Jesus. We need to live out our values and beliefs unconditionally. The fact of the matter is, living by our feelings will prove to be futile in the long run.

Ask yourself:

1. Am I fighting the good fight?
2. What areas of my life do I need to be more obedient in?
3. Does my faith match my actions?
4. Bad habits I need to let go of are...
5. Problems and losses that I can't seem to let go of are...

Keep in mind:

1. If you are willing and obedient, you shall eat the good of the land. (Isaiah 1:19)
2. It was character that got us out of bed, commitment that moved us into action and discipline that enabled us to follow through. (Zig Ziglar)

Take action...

1. Look up the following passages and paraphrase each one.
   ☐John 15:4; Eph. 4:15; John 13:15; Rom. 12:1-2; Rom. 13:14; Col. 2:6-7; Col. 1:10-12; 1 Cor. 15:58; Phil. 1:27; Gal. 5:1; Phil. 4:1; 2 Thess. 2:15; 2 Tim. 3:14; 2 Tim. 4:5

Reflection

1. After reading today's devotion, I realize...
2. The key statements I need to remember and work on are...
3. The positive consequences of remembering and working on these statements will be...

DAY 144

REJOICE IN THE LORD

Come and see what our God has done, what awesome miracles he performs for people! He made a dry path through the Red Sea, and his people went across on foot. There we rejoiced in him. (Psalm 66:5-6)

A way to deepen your faith is to rejoice in the Lord. Rejoice means a feeling of great happiness and the utterance of sounds expressing great joy.

Express Your Love

As God's child I'm called to express my love and gratitude to my Father regardless of my situation. Paul tells us to be full of joy in the Lord. I say it again—rejoice! Let everyone see that you are considerate in all you do. Remember, the Lord is coming soon. (Phil. 4:4-5)

Rejoicing in the Lord is a Sign of Faith

When I sing to my Father and celebrate His goodness and love for me, I'm not to worry about the situation I'm in. I trust Him. Rejoicing takes my mind off myself and my circumstances and puts my attention back on the Lord where it should be.

Paul reminds us not to worry about anything; instead, pray about everything. Tell God what you need, and thank him for all he has done. ***Then you will experience God's peace***, which exceeds anything we can understand. His peace ***will guard your hearts and minds*** as you live in Christ Jesus.

Confess Your Needs

When I release my needs to God I love the peace I feel. For me, it's not a one step deal. Some days I'm able to let go, and other days I release my cares and concerns and within matter of minutes they come back to me. When this happens I just keep releasing and rejoicing.

It amazes me that when Paul wrote Philippians 4 he was in prison. Like Paul I'm trying to live my life inside out instead of outside in. It's easy to get discouraged because of our circumstances. If we keep the right attitude and perspective we can keep our faith in any situation.

Take action…

1. Look up the following passages and paraphrase each one.
   ☐Phil. 4:6; Psalm 66:1; Psalm 68:4; Psalm 95:1-2; Psalm 105:1-3; Psalm 35:9-10; Psalm 103:1-5; Isaiah 40:28-31; Matt. 11:28-30; 2 Cor. 4:16-18; Phil. 4:12-13; Psalm 34:18; Psalm 42:5; Lam. 3:20-23; Rom. 8:28-39

Reflection

1. After reading today's devotion, I realize…
2. The key statements I need to remember and work on are…
3. The positive consequences of remembering and working on these statements will be…

SANCTIFICATION

&

TRUTH

He is the Holy Spirit, who leads into all truth. The world cannot receive him, because it isn't looking for him and doesn't recognize him. But you know him, because he lives with you now and later will be in you. (John 14:17)

And you will know the truth, and the truth will set you free." (John 8:32)

DAY 145-146

TRUTH WILL SET YOU FREE

When he finally came to his senses, he said to himself, 'At home even the hired servants have food enough to spare, and here I am dying of hunger! [18] *I will go home to my father and say, "Father, I have sinned against both heaven and you,* [19] *and I am no longer worthy of being called your son. Please take me on as a hired servant." '(Luke 15:17-19)*

Telling the truth is the best thing you can do. We need to learn not to look the other way. Reality just doesn't disappear no matter how hard you try to ignore it. Your issues, losses, sins and bad habits don't get better on their own. Jesus said that apart from Him we can do nothing. (John 15:5) We need Him to help us to be strong enough to face our struggles.

When you deny the truth about how you feel you will gradually separate yourself from God. You will become lonely and distant. With a distorted view of reality, you're not going to see the problems or circumstances through God's eyes.

The prodigal son was experiencing this very thing. His mind was clouded, confused and irrational. (Luke 15:15-17) He lost touch with truth and started to doubt himself. The more he denied the truth the more impulsive he became. The lost son hid his emotions for so long that he started to question his goodness. Because he ran from the truth his procrastination and silence increased his suffering.

FACING THE TRUTH

Then you will know the truth, and the truth will set you free." (John 8:32)

Instructions: Check off the statements that are true for you. Complete the reflection questions after each section.

- ☐ I realize that truth and honesty are essential for my healing, change and growth
- ☐ I work hard on not ignoring my character defects
- ☐ Surrender is key to my healing and change
- ☐ I'm not scared of the truth because I know I'm loved by God and others
- ☐ Truth will set me free.
- ☐ Truth isn't meant to hurt me, it's purpose is to help me become more like Christ

☐Truth is my compass. It shows me which path to take in life and relationships

☐I believe Truth is everywhere: People, places and things (circumstances, loss, the Bible and the Holy Spirit)

☐Speaking the truth is essential to my growth, healing and refining my character

☐It doesn't make sense to lie to myself

☐I admit to failures and grow from them

☐Blaming gets me no where

☐I seek God's wisdom and insight

☐I know my weakness and immaturities that prevent me from being like Christ

☐Facing my past doesn't scare me

☐I know I need God's help if I want to grow and develop my character

☐God wants me to see the truth so I can be more like Christ

☐I see truth, and accountability to it, as a form of comfort because I have people in my life that allow me to be brutally honest about my struggles without condemning me

☐Truth gives me guidance and helps me to see what I need to own and take responsibility for. Truth allows me to see the part I played in a problem.

☐I want truth in my life because it helps me to reach my full potential in Christ

☐Truth is a bitter sweet, but I want it and need it

☐I need to know that others love me in order for me to receive the truth from them

☐Truth brings me out of darkness so I can heal and grow

Take Action…

1. Look up the following passages and paraphrase each one.

   ☐Eph. 4:25; John 3:33; John 4:37; Heb. 9:24; John 1:9; John 4:23; Psalm 51:4; Rom. 3:7; Rom. 15:8; 1 John 5:20; Psalm 15:1-2; 2 Cor. 4:2; Prov. 17:26; Prov. 29:10,27

Reflection

1. After reading today's checklist I realize…
2. The key statements I need to remember and work on are…
3. What can I do to change the areas I need to work on?
4. What kind of support and accountability do I need?
5. The positive consequences of remembering and working on these statements are…

DAY 147-148

ADMIT THE TRUTH

Man is least himself when he talks in his own person. Give him a mask, and he will tell you the truth. ~Oscar Wilde

"Cling to your faith in Christ, and keep your conscience clear. For some people have deliberately violated their consciences; as a result, their faith has been shipwrecked." (1 Timothy 1:19)

JIM'S STORY

Don't Stay Stuck...

At first it was hard for Jim to admit the truth. He wasn't happy for a long time. He had lost his purpose. He stopped dreaming. He couldn't figure out where he went wrong in his life. You could say he was stuck.

Some people stay stuck in relationships that are broken or jobs that make them miserable. Day in and day out they slowly lose their identity. They put on a smile, but inside they're dying.

We need to admit to ourselves that we're not happy. We gain nothing when we push the truth, and our feelings, down deep within our souls. Jim developed a life style around his self-deception. He became so emotionally dishonest with himself that he didn't even know what his real feelings were anymore.

Honesty...

Jim's first step toward a new life was getting honest with himself. He needed to let go of the guilt he was feeling over all the mistakes and bad choices he had made throughout his life. In order to heal from emotional wounds we need to be honest with ourselves.

Jim would have to stop blaming others and take a good look inside himself in order to begin to experience healing and change.

Jim's life will change when he looks at his life as it is and gets honest about the part he played in it. The key is not to drown our feelings in food, drugs, alcohol, sex and unhealthy relationships. Working out our salvation means we take responsibility for our habits, hurts and hang-ups, and feel them, grieve them and ask Jesus to give us the strength and courage to let them go.

Take Responsibility...

If you feel stuck, take some time to determine when it all started. Did anything trigger it? Are you avoiding responsibility for something? Have you experienced any changes recently? Make sure that you're honest with your emotions and that you're facing your fears. Keep close to honest people, people who are willing to face reality and find a solution to their problems.

Like Jim, we can make our problems worse because we avoid our issues and before you know it, our relationships, dreams and careers fall apart. When we avoid our problems we end up feeling miserable and irritated which, in turn, creates a whole new set of problems.

Michelangelo once said, "There is an angel in the stone, and I am trying to let him out." Open up so you can learn how to love, and deal with, the thorn in your side.

Take Action...

1. Look up the following passages and paraphrase each one.

□Eph. 1:17-19; Matt. 5:3; Phil. 2:3-5; Psalm 139:23-24; Prov. 18:15; Isaiah 50:4-5 Acts 8:30-31; Psalm 15:1-2; 2 Cor. 4:2; John 8:32; Isaiah 48:1; Jer. 5:3; Jer. 7:28; Jer. 9:3

Reflection

1. After reading today's devotion, I realize...
2. The key statements I need to remember and work on are...
3. The positive consequences of remembering and working on these statements will be...

Day 149-150

BE WILLING TO FACE THE TRUTH

"The plans of the righteous are just, but the advice of the wicked is deceitful."
(Proverbs 12:5)

Dishonesty prevents you from being transformed...

For you to heal and transform from the inside out you need to be honest and face the truth about whatever's going on in your life.

Dishonesty prevents inner healing. The only way to receive the peace that surpasses all understanding is to stop protecting yourself. The Holy Spirit wants to shine light in your darkness so you can heal and transform.

Jesus wants us to drop our defensive attitude because it doesn't bring peace, it only brings chaos. I know you might be afraid to let your guard down but you need to learn how to trust God.

And you will know the truth, and the truth will set you free... Jesus

Honesty will transform your life…

5 Benefits of Honesty

1. In order to transform and change your life you need to come out of denial and face the truth and the reality of the situation. I can understand the benefit of denial but it does have a shelf life. We can't stay in it forever.
2. There's peace on the other side of the pain.
3. When you face the truth, the powerlessness and helplessness goes away. Truth empowers you.... dishonesty weakens you.
4. There's hope and strength in seeking the truth.
5. David didn't want to face the truth. He might have thought that his situation would take care of itself. He couldn't deny that he had a problem because.... a) God wouldn't let him, and B) it was always at the forefront of his mind (Psalm 32).

Ask yourself:

1. Do I accept responsibility for my actions?
2. Can I handle constrictive criticism?
3. Am I teachable?
4. Do I make excuses for my actions?
5. Do I secretly fear any confrontation that may prove I'm bad?
6. Do I need to be right most of the time?

Let go of:

1. Your fear to admit failure and mistakes
2. Pretending to be happy… if you don't, how can God heal and transform you?
3. Don't pretend you planned your sin, failure or mistake

4. The need to hide the truth, because you're only telling others that you're too weak to take care of yourself

5. Blaming others for your mistakes. Blamers fear imperfections

6. Bragging, it only shows that you're insecure

7. Dishonesty… Jesus came to set you free… Jesus Christ has come to open the eyes of the blind, free the captives from prison and release those who sit in dark dungeons.

Take Action…

1. Look up the following passages and paraphrase each one.

 ☐ 1 Cor. 3:18-20; Heb. 12:5-12; Prov. 12:22; Exod. 20:16; Deut. 5:20; Exod. 23:1,7; Prov. 12:19; Prov. 13:5; Prov. 14:25; Prov. 19:5,9; Eph. 4:25; Rev. 22:14-15

Reflection

1. After reading today's devotion, I realize…
2. The key statements I need to remember and work on are…
3. The positive consequences of remembering and working on these statements will be…

REVIEW & REPAIR

Reshaping Your Soul

1. What did I learn this past month about myself, God and others?

2. What concepts or ideas stood out to me in the devotions? Why?

3. What adjustments do I need to make in my life?

4. What, if anything, needs to change about how I think, feel, and act?

5. What changes have I made so far? What actions have I taken?

6. How are people reacting to my changes?

7. Steps I will continue to take are…

8. I'm committed to…

9. My victories this week were…

10. God please help me with…

DAY 151-152

DON'T DENY YOUR PAIN

Examine yourselves, to see whether you are in the faith. Test yourselves. Or do you not realize this about yourselves, that Jesus Christ is in you?—unless indeed you fail to meet the test! (2 Cor. 13:5)

Denial…

At first the Lost Son denied his hurt and pain. He wasn't willing to admit he made a bad choice until he came to his senses. He finally took an honest look at his life and the situation he had gotten himself into.

A closer look…

Self-examination is essential if you want to heal and become whole. Through self-examination the Holy Spirit will show you what you need to change or deal with. Taking responsibility for your hurt and pain will lead to internal changes, character growth and needed personality changes. For instance, I think the Lost Son was all about the moment and wanted to ignore the realities and pains of life. The Lost Son saw life as one big party and he didn't care who he had to hurt to make it a reality. When he came to his senses you can see how his personality started to shift. He started to address his pain and choices which, in turn, caused him to repent and eventually become more responsible.

Ask yourself:

1. Am I avoiding taking responsibility for my hurt and pain?
2. Do I need to work on hurt caused by someone else?

> 3. Do I self-examine enough? Am I in tune with my feelings, thoughts and actions?
> 4. Has someone hurt me and I'm too scared to admit it, or even talk about it?

Keep in mind:

1. Come and listen, all you who fear God, and I will tell you what He did for me (Psalm 66:16)

   a.God will restore you and heal your soul

   b.God will redeem all the areas that are broken

   c.God will renew your life

   d.God will redeem you when you take responsibility for your pain, loss and sin

Take Action

1. Take time to pray and ask the Holy Spirit to show you repressed pain, hurt or sin that might exist.
2. Keep a journal and write out what the Spirit shows you.
3. Journal daily
4. When you're hurt don't deny it. Go to the person after you prayed and talk about it.
5. Look up the following passages and paraphrase each one.

   ☐Psalm 44:20-21; Psalm 90:8; Psalm 101:5; Psalm 139:1-15; Psalm 51:17; Psalm 147:3; Heb. 12:2; Deut. 21:23; Matt. 27:39-44; Heb. 6:6

Reflection

1. After reading today's devotion, I realize…
2. The key statements I need to remember and work on are…
3. The positive consequences of remembering and working on these statements will be…

DAY 153-154

TAKE EMOTIONAL RISKS

So stop telling lies. Let us tell our neighbors the truth. (Eph. 4:25-26)

Speak the truth...

The last thing you want to do is to hold back what you feel, intellectualize, or deny what you feel. When you do this you will automatically become defensive and lose sight of yourself, what you value and believe. In other words you lose faith, hope and love.

We Sink...

When Peter got out of the boat he took his eyes off of Jesus and focused on the waves (circumstances, feelings, and/or problems). When he did this what happened? He started to sink. What did Jesus say to him? Where's your faith?

I believe Jesus wanted to show Peter that he didn't have as much faith in his heart as he did in his mind. The truth is, you don't know how much faith you have in God until the waves start to crash down on you.

Emotions...

God gave you your emotions so learn how to express them. Speak the truth in love. If you hold your emotions in and don't communicate what you truly feel, you might end up in situations you don't want to be in, or worse, pursuing the wrong goal. Don't make choices out of anger, guilt, shame, fear or pain.

Learn to manage your hurt, fear, and anger, then depression and guilt will no longer be a problem.

Ask yourself:

1. How do I feel today?
2. What's making me feel this way?
3. What need is this feeling pointing to?
4. When I feel this way how do I act?
5. Feelings are a reflection of what I'm thinking, so what am I thinking to make me feel this way?
6. Have I talked to God about how I feel?
7. Has someone offended me or hurt me? Do I need to tell them how the offense made me feel?
8. Do I believe I have a right to share how I feel?

Take Action...

1. Look up the following passages and paraphrase each one.

☐Prov. 25:28; Eph. 4:26; Eph. 5:18; Col. 3:8; 1 Tim. 2:8; James 1:19-20; Psalm 15:1-2; 2 Cor. 4:2

Reflection

1. After reading today's devotion, I realize...
2. The key statements I need to remember and work on are...
3. The positive consequences of remembering and working on these statements will be...

DAY 155-156

ADMIT YOUR FEAR

When I am afraid, I put my trust in you. In God, whose word I praise, in God I trust; I shall not be afraid. What can flesh do to me? (Psalm 5:3-4)

Jesus admitted His fear...

Jesus taught us how to deal with fear when He was in the garden trying to work out His purpose with God. He knew He was about to experience loss and injury. This wasn't an imagined fear, it was real. Like Jesus, we have the ability to imagine what might happen as well as feel it. I think in this case Jesus saw in His mind what the walk to Calvary was going to be like physically, emotionally and mentally.

Jesus didn't pretend that He wasn't afraid, worried or anxious, and nor should you. He didn't cover his fear. He wasn't afraid to admit His anxiety and concerns, either to His Father or to His good friends that fell asleep. This shows us that it's not weak, unmanly, or out of control to admit our fear and anxieties. In fact it's just the opposite. It's a sign of strength to admit and accept your humanness, potential loss or injury.

Face your fears...

Like Jesus, you need to face your fears head on regardless of how weak you feel. Just put yourself in Jesus' sandals.... carrying that 300lb cross and being whipped and abused up a hill to be nailed to a cross. Wow, that's facing fear head on. Fight the temptation to cover your fears and face what you need to face head on. God provided the strength for Jesus and He will do the same for you. But first, you need to accept and admit your fear, worry, stress and anxiety to God and one other person.

I know for some people it feels like a trip to Calvary when they have to tell someone how they feel, or what they need and want. Again, the key is to face your fears.

Ask yourself:

      1. Are my fears real or imagined?

      2. Can I name my fear?

      3. Am I imagining the worst?

      4. Do I believe that real strength is the absence of fear?

      5. Do I act fearless? If so why?

      6. Fears I need to face are...

      7. Solutions to my fears are...

Take Action...

   1. Look up the following passages and paraphrase each one.

      □Psalm 50:15; Lam. 3:55; Matt. 26:39; Psalm 143:1; Heb. 4:16; John 12:27; John 13:21; Heb. 5:7; 1 Peter 5:6; Psalm 94:19; Matt. 11:28; 1 Peter 5:7

Reflection

   1. After reading today's devotion, I realize...

   2. The key statements I need to remember and work on are...

   3. The positive consequences of remembering and working on these statements will be...

DAY 157-158

STOP DENYING YOUR BROKENNESS

A Psalm of David, when Nathan the prophet went to him, after he had gone in to Bathsheba. Have mercy on me, O God, according to your steadfast love; according to your abundant mercy blot out my transgressions. Wash me thoroughly from my iniquity, and cleanse me from my sin! For I know my transgressions, and my sin is ever before me. Against you, you only, have I sinned and done what is evil in your sight, so that you may be justified in your words and blameless in your judgment. Behold, I was brought forth in iniquity, and in sin did my mother conceive me. ... (Psalm 51)

Rebellion...

At first, David didn't want to take responsibility for his hurt and brokenness. He didn't want to admit his role and disappointment. He might have had a hard time believing that he could be hurt by his own sin. I think he had a hard time accepting that he was vulnerable and powerless. It wasn't until he recognized his rebellion and admitted that his pain and sin was haunting him day and night; he stopped denying his brokenness (Psalm 51).

Withholding hurt...

When you withhold your hurt you gradually lose your joy and peace. Admitting your hurt is the beginning of your healing. Repressing your hurt will prevent you from becoming the person God wants you to be.

Ask yourself:

1. Do I see that my hurt can't protect me from further hurt?
2. When have I become reckless because I avoided my hurt and brokenness?
3. Do I pretend that I'm not hurt?
4. Is it hard for me to express my hurt to God and others?
5. God help me with...

Keep in mind

1. Jesus wants you to mourn
2. Satan knows...
    a. that a broken heart can and will hold you back from taking part in building real, vulnerable and loving relationships
    b. If you don't surrender your hurt to Christ, your sense of self-worth will be affected, which can stop you from believing in yourself and who God created you to be.

    c.If your spirit is broken, peace, joy and love appear unreal and unreachable.

3. Surrender your hurt and will to God and watch your brokenness heal.
4. Paul would tell you that God will use your brokenness and hurt to expose your need for Him.
5. God's final goal is your spiritual success and victory.

Reflection

1. After reading today's devotion, I realize…
2. The key statements I need to remember and work on are…
3. The positive consequences of remembering and working on these statements will be…

DAY 159-160

LET GO OF YOUR SECRETS

Tell your sins to each other. And pray for each other so you may be healed. The prayer from the heart of a man right with God has much power.
(James 5:16)

James tells us to confess our faults and sins to one another because if we hold in our pain and shortcomings we disconnect from God and others. When a person represses or suppresses their pain and hurt they run the risk of becoming emotionally and mentally unstable.

God didn't design us to hold in our hurt and sin. We weren't designed to handle the bad that we experience in life. There's no internal mechanism within us to absorb pain and sin. This is why we need a Savior, and why we need to practice the spiritual discipline of confession.

Consider this…

When we practice confession the following things happen…

- We have a clean slate. We're made new. It's hard to go through life carrying our baggage around with us.
- We prosper and find mercy from God and others.
- We develop character and confidence.
- We become real people instead of ideal people. Ideal comes when you're in heaven.
- Our attachment to God and others becomes deeper and more intimate.
- We don't have to live in guilt and shame.
- We get to tear down the rear view mirror and look forward to what lies ahead instead of living in the past.
- It helps with the grieving and mourning process. It un-complicates grief.
- Confession prevents us from living in condemnation.
- We stop the "CON."
- It puts the healing process in motion.
- Our self-worth develops and we start to respect others and ourselves.
- Ends the blame game so we can take responsibility for our part in our issues.
- Frees us from isolation.
- Allows us to experience forgiveness from God and others.
- Confession helps us to forgive ourselves, meaning we receive and accept God's forgiveness.
- We become restored, redeemed and reconciled to God, others and ourselves.

Confession is a win/win. Do it today and don't delay. Get whatever it is off your chest and cleanse your soul.

Sick as your secrets...

You know the slogan ... you're as sick as your secrets. James tells us to confess our sin, hurts and bad habits to our mentors and sponsors. You need to do this so you can stop carrying those heavy burdens. God wants to know your worries and the concerns you have. You might be thinking, "He already knows how I feel". This is true but, the thing is, He wants you to ask for help. He wants you to rely on Him because He is a power greater than you.

Hiding...

You need to take the power away from the secret. That's what David did in Psalm 51 and Psalm 32. Secrets weigh you down with guilt, pain, shame, bitterness, and fear. How can you grow when you keep secrets?

Finally, I confessed all my sins to you and stopped trying to hide my guilt.
I said to myself, "I will confess my rebellion to the LORD." And you forgave me!
All my guilt is gone. (Psalm 32:5)

Just for today...

    1. I will tell on myself to my pastor, friend, spouse, mentor or sponsor.
    2. I will make a list of secrets and share them with God and one other person
    3. I will let go of the old self

Take Action...

    1. Look up the following passages and paraphrase each one: Ecc. 12:14; 1 John 1:8-9; Psa. 32:5-6; Eph. 5:11-12; Prov. 11:13; Luke 19:8; Acts 19:18-19

Reflection

    1. After reading today's devotion, I realize...
    2. The key statements I need to remember and work on are...
    3. The positive consequences of remembering and working on these
       statements will be...

SACTIFICATION

&

RELATIONSHIPS

Two people are better off than one, for they can help each other succeed. If one person falls, the other can reach out and help. But someone who falls alone is in real trouble. (Ecclesiastes 4:9-10)

Now these are the gifts Christ gave to the church: the apostles, the prophets, the evangelists, and the pastors and teachers. Their responsibility is to equip God's people to do his work and build up the church, the body of Christ. This will continue until we all come to such unity in our faith and knowledge of God's Son that we will be mature in the Lord, measuring up to the full and complete standard of Christ. (Ephesians 4:11-13)

DAY 161-162

GOD DESIGNED US TO NEED RELATIONSHIPS

Today I want you to acknowledge your need for relationship. God designed you to need Him and other people. Take some time to read the following scriptures:

1. 1 Corinthians 12:12-27
2. Ecclesiastes 4:9-12
3. Matthew 22:37-39
4. Romans 12:5,15
5. Romans 15:14
6. 1 Corinthians 12:25
7. 1 Thessalonians 5:11
8. Ephesians 4:2
9. James 5:16
10. Galatians 6:2
11. 1 Peter 4:10

Reflection:

1, After reading today's scriptures on relationships, I realize…

2. The key passages I need to remember and work on are…

3. The positive consequences of remembering and working on these truths will be…

DAY 163

OPENING UP TO OTHERS

Be kind to one another, tenderhearted, forgiving one another, as God in Christ forgave you. (Eph. 4:32)

The Present…

I want you to take some time today to think about your past. If you're struggling to open up your heart to others in the present, there's a good chance that you might have to work through some hurt and anger to learn how to trust people again.

God will use the people in your life today to help you heal from the hurt caused by people in your past. People will help you work through the sanctification process – this is why it's essential that you work through whatever is shutting you down.

Ask yourself:

1. Do I have a difficult time trusting others? If yes, describe why?
2. I don't like people who....
3. My relationship with _____ really affected my ability to _____.
4. I feel _____ about myself because of my relationship with_____.
5. I still need to forgive_____.
6. Who do I want to get even with?
7. Do my past relationships affect my ability to connect with God?
8. I stopped becoming vulnerable, trusting, open, honest about my feelings and needs because of_____ (or when_____).

Take Action...

1. Look up the following passages and paraphrase each one
   ☐John 13:34-35; Col. 3:13-14; 1 Peter 1:22; Gal. 6:2; Luke 6:37; Matt. 5:38-48; Luke 6:27-36

Reflection:

1. After reading today's devotion, I realize…
2. The key statements I need to remember and work on are…
3. The positive consequences of remembering and working on these statements will be…

DAY 164

BEAUTIFUL PEARL

Therefore strengthen the hands which hang down, and the feeble knees, [13] *and make straight paths for your feet, so that what is lame may not be dislocated, but rather be healed. Pursue peace with all people, and holiness, without which no one will see the Lord: looking carefully lest anyone fall short of the grace of God; lest any root of bitterness springing up cause trouble, and by this many become defiled. (Hebrews 12:12-15)*

I like long walks, especially when they are taken by people that annoy me.
- Fred Allen

Lessons from an Oyster

There once was an oyster whose story I tell...
Who found that some sand... Had got into his shell...
It was only a grain, but it gave him great pain.
For oysters have feelings...Although they're so plain.
Now, did he berate the harsh workings of fate...?
That had brought him to such a deplorable state?
Did he curse at the government, Cry for election...?
And claim that the sea should... Have given him protection?
'No,' he said to himself as he lay on a shell,
since I cannot remove it, I shall try to improve it.
Now the years have rolled 'round, as the years always do...
And he came to his ultimate Destiny stew.
And the small grain of sand that had bothered him so,
was a beautiful pearl all richly aglow.
Now the tale has a moral, for isn't it grand...
What an oyster can do with a morsel of sand?
What couldn't we do ...If we'd only begin,
with some of the things that get under our skin?
(Author Unknown)

Today think about the things you're struggling with. What are you frustrated about, angry about, or annoyed about? It's so important that you deal with this because if you don't, you will get stuck in the sanctification/pruning process.

We all have areas of our lives that cause use stress or aggravation. We all have people we have to deal with every day that annoy us. The key thing is to keep your peace (Romans 12). You can only control yourself. God gives us peace like no one else can. We need to work on the things that cause our hearts to be troubled. We need to learn how to deal with that piece of sand that enters into our shell. It's there for a reason.

What can you learn from this oyster?

Take Action...

    1. Look up the following passages and paraphrase each one.

        ☐   Matt. 5:9; Prov. 12:20; Rom. 14:19; Ecc. 10:4; Rom. 12:18; Titus 1:6; Heb. 12:14; James 3:17

Reflection

    1. After reading today's devotion, I realize...

    2. The key statements I need to remember and work on are...

    3. The positive consequences of remembering and working on these statements will be...

DAY 165

BUILD UP YOUR SUPPORT NETWORK

Two are better than one, because they have a good [more satisfying] reward for their labor; [10]For if they fall, the one will lift up his fellow. But woe to him who is alone when he falls and has not another to lift him up! [11]Again, if two lie down together, then they have warmth; but how can one be warm alone? [12]And though a man might prevail against him who is alone, two will withstand him. A threefold cord is not quickly broken. (Ecc. 4:9-12)

Today we're going to discuss the importance of building a support network that will hold you accountable and be there when your cross gets heavy.

Stephanie's Story

Accepting my limitations has always been hard for me. If you told me I couldn't do it I would try to find a way to prove you wrong. I'm learning that there's one thing I can't prove people wrong in and that's trying to stay clean and sober alone. As hard as it is to say this in writing, it's the truth that saved my life.

Self-will leads to self-indulgence. Because of my addictive behaviors I was foolish and disobedient. I was misled and became a slave to many lusts and pleasures. My life was full of evil and envy, and I started to hate myself and others. You could say I was a fool and rebelled against God.

Ask for help…

A healthier way of thinking and acting is to allow yourself to receive the help and love you need. You weren't designed to live alone. You have limitations on your strength and abilities. Self-will takes you only so far. God uses people to help His children and the sooner you accept it the better off you will be. Stop copying the behavior and customs of this world, but let God transform you into a new person by changing the way you think. Then you will learn to know God's will for you which is good and pleasing and perfect (Rom. 12:1-2).

We all need a power greater than ourselves. If you have reservations talk with someone about them. Clarify your image of God. Do your best to be open-minded. Take a chance and trust God because when you do you will find new strength. You will soar high on wings like eagles. You will run and not grow weary. You will walk and not faint (Isaiah 40:30-31).

Connect with those you trust. Take more time feeling your feelings and sharing them. Stop intellectualizing them and trying to figure them out in your head. When you do this you forget about what you're feeling then in a day or two you will find yourself getting angry or resentful over the very thing you thought you figured out. Part of working out your salvation and growing up is sharing and connecting to people and emotions.

Practice

　　1. Keep a feelings journal so you can inventory what you feel daily.
　　2. Take time to listen to the message behind the emotion(s)

Take Action…

　　1. Look up the following passages and paraphrase each one.
　　　　☐Heb. 10:32-34 See also 2 Cor. 1:7; Phil. 1:27-30; Phil. 4:14; Heb. 11:25; Phil. 4:14-16

Reflection

　　1. After reading today's devotion, I realize…

2. The key statements I need to remember and work on are…

3. The positive consequences of remembering and working on these statements will be…

DAY 165

CONNECT TO THE BODY OF CHRIST

From whom the whole body, joined and held together by every joint with which it is equipped, when each part is working properly, makes the body grow so that it builds itself up in love. (Eph. 4:16)

It's hard for anybody to live this life alone. The fact of the matter is, you weren't designed to. You were designed to connect to the body of Christ. There are no lone rangers in the kingdom of God. When you try to accomplish your goals and purpose alone you're only going to frustrate yourself. God has placed certain people in the body of Christ to help you accomplish your purpose. God will also use people outside the church to help you accomplish your purpose and dreams.

Solomon said it best, two are better than one (Ecc. 4:9-12). The body of Christ can help you develop self-discipline and self-control, especially in those areas that you may struggle with the most. The body can provide love, feedback, accountability, stress relief, resources, or any help that you might need at a particular time or season in your life.

It's important that you recognize when you need help and aren't afraid to ask for it. Remember, you have not because you ask not. You're designed to share your purpose and dreams with others. In fact, you were designed to bring honor and glory to God with your gifts, talents and abilities.

Take Action…

1. Look up the following passages and paraphrase each one.
   ☐Gen. 2:18 See also Psalm 127:4; Prov. 17:6,17; Prov. 18:24; Prov. 27:10; Ecc. 4:9-12; Gal. 3:28; Eph. 2:14-16,19; Job 2:11-13; Prov. 17:17

Keep in mind:

1. As a believer, when you connect to the body of Christ you will receive spiritual life, love and care that you need, along with access to a variety of resources.
    o Remember the words of Paul - we go astray when we disconnect from Christ who is the body, we are joined together in His body by His strong sinews, and we grow only as we get our nourishment and strength from God (Col. 2: 19). God's primary way of revealing Himself and helping you is through people.

Reflection

1. After reading today's devotion, I realize…
2. The key statements I need to remember and work on are…
3. The positive consequences of remembering and working on these statements will be…

DAY 166

WE NEED EACH OTHER

So that there should be no division in the body, but that its parts should have equal concern for each other. (1 Cor. 12:25)

The fact of the matter is, you and I need relationships. We need to have more than our hobbies, interests and passions, we need connection. So many of us fill our lives with things, accomplishments and ambitions, but end up feeling empty and lonely at the end of the day.

We all get hurt and disappointed by life and the people we love, but we need to push through and deal with our anger and hurt. If we don't, we start to isolate from God and others. We try to sustain without connecting to others but we eventually crash because we were not designed to go it alone.

This is when depression and despair set into our souls and we start to lose our faith and hope. This is a scary place to be because if you and I stay here long enough, we forget about what we need and want from God and others.

God has given us needs and wants and if we think, even for a minute, that we can stay detached from people and get these needs met we are sadly mistaken. We forget that God's primary way of revealing Himself to us is through people (relationships).

Ask Yourself:

1. Am I isolating or detached from others because I'm hurt or think I can live my life without relationships?
2. Am I depressed? If so, why?
3. When was the last time I told someone what I needed?
4. I want....
5. I need....
6. God help me to.....
7. Do I think my past determines my future when it comes to connecting with people and developing relationships?
8. Am I satisfied with my connections and relationships?

Take Action...

1. Look up the following passages and paraphrase each one.

  ☐   1 Cor. 12:25-26; Eph. 3:17-21; Col. 2:19
  ☐   See also 1 Cor. 10:16-17; Eph. 4:15-16

Reflection

1. After reading today's devotion, I realize...
2. The key statements I need to remember and work on are...
3. The positive consequences of remembering and working on these statements will be...

I created a checklist to help you to see the reasons why you need to connect to the body of Christ, and so you can see where you might be falling short in this area. Remember, we all need help carrying our cross - two are better than one. God's primary way of revealing Himself to you is through people.

CONNECTING TO THE BODY OF CHRIST

But God has put the body together, giving greater honor to the parts that lacked it so that there should be no division in the body, but that its parts should have equal concern for each other. If one part suffers, every part suffers with it; if one part is honored, every part rejoices with it. Now you are the body of Christ, and each one of you is a part of it. (1 Cor. 12:24-27)

Instructions: Check off the statements that are true for you. Complete the reflection questions after each section.

☐ I have a support team

☐ I'm connected (open, honest, vulnerable, trusting, sharing my secrets) to people in the body of believers

☐ I have accountability

☐ I have people in my life who inspire me

☐ I have people in my life who show me grace, mercy and compassion

☐ I have people in my life who aren't afraid to tell me the truth

☐ I have people in my life who give me courage and hope when I'm down

☐ I have people in my life that will not co-sign my sin, hang ups, bad habits and pity parties

☐ I have people in my life that I allow to discipline me and hold me accountable

☐ I disclose my sin and practice confession with my support team

☐ I have people that pray for me specifically

☐ I attend prayer groups and Bible studies

☐ I attend meetings (AA, NA)

☐ I have people in my life that hold me accountable to my values

☐ I let people into my world. I share the secrets of my soul with trusted friends

☐ I desire and welcome feedback from the people in my life

☐ I have people in the body of Christ that I admire and model my life after

Reflection

1. After reading today's checklist I realize…
2. The key statements I need to remember and work on are…
3. What can I do to change the areas I need to work on?
4. What kind of support and accountability do I need?
5. The positive consequences of remembering and working on these statements are…

SANCTIFICATION

&

HEALTHY SELF-IMAGE

God said, "Now we will make humans, and they will be like us. We will let them rule the fish, the birds, and all other living creatures." (Gen. 1:26)

Thank you for making me so wonderfully complex! Your workmanship is marvelous—how well I know it. (Psalm 139:14)

DAY 167

ALLOW GOD TO RESHAPE YOUR SELF-IMAGE

For you formed my inward parts; you knitted me together in my mother's womb. I praise you, for I am fearfully and wonderfully made. Wonderful are your works; my soul knows it very well. (Psalm 139:13-14)

Self –Image…

God wants to reshape your self-image. He wants you to have a new paradigm of yourself. This is part of the sanctification process. Before you received Christ as your Savior you had an existing view of yourself. This view was developed from how your parents or caretakers treated you, what they said to you, how they reacted when you made a mistake or failed, and beliefs and values they taught you growing up.

Your self-image was developed by how people treated you as a child. As a child, you accepted this as truth because you didn't know any better.

We don't usually question our beliefs until we become teenagers or adults. Many of us come to the Lord wounded from our past. Why? Because we grew up with imperfect parents and imperfect families.

Part of the sanctification process is God helping you change your self-image. He wants to teach you the truth about yourself. He wants to heal any aspect of your self-image that doesn't line up with His word and His truth. Remember, you were created in His image.

Take Action…

1. Look up the following passages and paraphrase each one.

  ☐ Jer. 1:5; Gal. 1:15; Isaiah 43:1; John 10:3; 1 Cor. 8:3; 1 Cor. 12:21; Gal. 4:9; 2 Tim. 2:19

Keep in mind…

1. You are loveable
2. God will show you just how lovable you are
3. Your needs are important to God

4. God sees you as unique and special despite what others may have said

5. God will heal the void inside you, and will give you confidence

Reflection

1. After reading today's devotion, I realize…
2. The key statements I need to remember and work on are…
3. The positive consequences of remembering and working on these statements will be…

DAY 168

PLACE YOUR HOPE IN CHRIST

May the God of hope fill you with all joy and peace in believing, so that by the power of the Holy Spirit you may abound in hope. (Rom. 15:13)

Be Optimistic…

Optimism and a positive attitude are key components to your personal growth and working out your salvation. You can do all things through Jesus. God has designed you to face your past, present and future with confidence. The more knowledge you have of God the more hopeful you will be.

David is a prime example of having an optimistic attitude. Why? Because he placed his confidence in God. He confessed, "I am like an olive tree, thriving in the house of God. I trust in God's unfailing love forever and ever." (Psalm 52:8) Pay attention to the self-talk confirming his beliefs and values.

Peter said, "In his kindness God called you to eternal glory by means of Jesus Christ. After you have suffered a little while, He will restore, support, and strengthen you, and He will place you on a firm foundation. All power is forever and ever. Amen." (1 Peter 5:10-11) Peter is reminding you that life isn't always going to be easy.

You're going to have good days and bad days and how you react to them is crucial. For every action you take, there'll be a reaction. Peter is telling you that your life and your successes will mirror how you think, how you use your skills and talents.

Accept responsibility…

Regardless of what's going on, God wants you to accept responsibility for all your choices and to exercise self-control. In order to do this you need to take a good look at your attitudes.   Are they positive most the time or negative most the time? Remember, your attitude will determine your altitude. Again it comes down to a matter of choice and attitude.

You need to have confidence in what God can do. (Psalm 27:1-3) God designed you with the ability to have a positive and optimistic attitude in any situation. Place your soul in His hands and see what happens.

Your attitude will determine your personality and the growth of your character. I want to leave you with this thought: your attitude determines your success, and your past does not determine your future. Place your hope and confidence in Christ and watch Him change your life; watch Him turn you into the person you were designed to be.

Take Action…

    1. Look up the following passages and paraphrase each one.

        ☐ Psalm 131:3; 1 Tim. 6:17 See also Psalm 31:24; Psalm 130:7; Rom. 12:12; Heb. 10:23

Reflection

    1. After reading today's devotion, I realize…
    2. The key statements I need to remember and work on are…
    3. The positive consequences of remembering and working on these statements will be…

DAY 169

REASSURE YOURSELF IN CHRIST

"Do one thing every day that scares you."
~ Eleanor Roosevelt

Love others as you love yourself. (Mark 12:30-31)

Sometimes we grow up with low self-esteem because we didn't take enough risks. Growing up we needed to feel a sense of accomplishment. This is why some people develop the "I can't" attitude or "I'm terrible at that" attitude.

Because of Jesus we can start to do things that we're not used to doing. Through the Holy Spirit we can get out of our comfort zone.

Encourage yourself. Face your fears. Remind yourself that failure is part of risking and becoming successful at whatever you want to accomplish in life.

It's important to learn how to reassure yourself. We need to be our own cheerleader at times. If you have friends that take interest in your life, share with them your accomplishments, dreams and goals. We all have that little boy or girl inside us that cries out "Hey look at me, look at what I did." Ask them to encourage you as you take risks and get out of your comfort zone. This is so important, especially if you didn't grow up with encouraging parents.

Consider this…

1. Encourage yourself as you take a risk
2. Share with a friend your dreams, goals, aspirations, and accomplishments

Take Action…

1. Look up the following passages and paraphrase each one.

   ☐ Psalm 146:5; Job 11:18; Psalm 25:3; Psalm 71:5; 1 Tim. 1:1; 1 Thess. 1:3; 1 Thess. 5:8; Heb. 6:19; 1 Peter 1:13; 1 John 3:1-3

Reflection

1. After reading today's devotion, I realize…
2. The key statements I need to remember and work on are…
3. The positive consequences of remembering and working on these statements are…

DAY 170 - 171

SELF-RESPECT

But because of his great love for us, God, who is rich in mercy, made us alive with Christ even when we were dead in transgressions—it is by grace you have been saved. (Ephesians 2:4-5)

Respect your efforts, respect yourself. Self-respect leads to self-discipline. When you have both firmly under your belt, that's real power.

~Clint Eastwood

Today we're going to look at the importance of self-respect. While you're on God's potter's wheel being re-shaped He is removing areas of shame and guilt. When He does this, you internalize His forgiveness. As a result of this correcting and reshaping, you regain your self-respect and develop a passion deep within your soul not to lose it again.

We learn self-respect from our parents because they are our first role models. They teach us our values and beliefs through their actions and words. What they role model and teach us becomes what we believe and value in life. As a result, we spend our adulthood working on what beliefs and values we should keep, and what we should remove. Believe it or not, if you're disrespecting yourself it might be because you saw these behaviors and attitudes from your parents. Take a look at your life, are you respecting yourself? What would others say? What does a person with self-respect look and act like?

A person with self-respect….

> Has integrity and dignity
> Has self-discipline
> Sees themself as special and unique because God created them
> Eliminates disrespectful behavior (swearing, lying, manipulating, etc.)
> Takes responsibility for their attitudes, feelings and behaviors
> Treats others the way they want to be treated
> Considers others' feelings and needs
> Receives God's forgiveness

➢Forgives self and others

➢Practices honesty

➢Finds principles to live by

➢Doesn't judge or criticize self and others

➢Takes time to get to know themselves

➢Takes care of their body

➢Admits wrongs

➢Works through failure and unfair treatment

➢Doesn't hurt themselves or sabotage themselves because they are hurt or didn't get what they want.

Consider this:

Today I want you to ask yourself the following questions.

    1. Do I:

        ☐Have integrity and dignity?

        ☐Have self-discipline?

        ☐See myself as special and unique because God created me?

        ☐Eliminate disrespectful behavior (swearing, lying, manipulating etc.)?

        ☐Take responsibility for my attitudes, feelings and behaviors?

        ☐Treat others the way I want to be treated?

        ☐Consider others' feelings and needs?

        ☐Receive God's forgiveness?

        ☐Forgive myself and others?

        ☐Practice honesty?

        ☐Find principles to live by?

        ☐Not judge or criticize myself and others?

        ☐Take time to get to know myself?

        ☐Take care of my body?

        ☐Admit wrongs?

        ☐Work through failure and unfair treatment?

    2. What do I need to work on? What can I do to have more self-respect?

    3. What did I learn from my parents regarding self-respect?

Take Action…

    1. Look up the following passages and paraphrase each one.

☐ Matt. 22:39; Mark 12:31; Matt. 7:12; Matt. 19:19; Rom. 12:3;
Eph. 5:29; Prov. 31:25; Phil. 3:4

Reflection

1. After reading today's devotion, I realize…
2. The key statements I need to remember and work on are…
3. The positive consequences of remembering and working on these
   statements are…

DAY 172

THE COURAGE TO … BE YOURSELF

*You made all the delicate, inner parts of my body and knit me together in my
mother's womb.*
*Thank you for making me so wonderfully complex! Your workmanship is
marvelous—how well I know it. **Psalm 139:13-14***

Today we're going to look at the importance of developing your own identity in
Christ.

OLD WAY OF THINKING

Tom's Story

I feel like I've been programmed by this world, my parents and church. I was
taught to be concerned about my image and what everybody thinks. It's like I
have this committee in my head. It's so unconscious that, at times I don't even
realize I'm doing it. I have this consuming sense of duty, compulsion, or
responsibility to succumb to what other people want to do, and to their beliefs
and values systems. I don't have my own set beliefs. I perform to be loved. I
often think if they really knew me, would they even like me? So I repress my
personality. I don't like to be criticized or corrected, so to avoid that I go along
with whatever and whoever. I feel loved at first but after a while I find myself
getting angry and resentful. It's hard to move forward in life when you don't
have an identity.

NEW WAY OF THINKING

PRINCIPLE

Today I want you to start allowing yourself to experience your feelings, needs, wants, desires, choices and decisions. It's going to be hard for you to be successful in the sanctification process if you're preoccupied with what others are thinking or doing. Limit your reactions to people, places and things. If you continue to care about what others think you will not fulfill your true purpose or calling. God has a plan and purpose for you. Make choices based on your goals and passions. Line your decisions up with God's Word. Develop your own opinions on issues and speak up. You matter, and so do your insights and contributions. Set boundaries. This is where you end and others begin. Remember, it's not a sin to have your own opinions, needs, desires and wants.

Remain teachable but at the same time, don't be afraid to say you don't agree. Try to formulate your own opinions first, and then seek out advice. Don't be afraid of failing or making a mistake. God forgives and besides, it's part of being human. We all fall short from time to time (like, every day, in one way or another!).

Take Action…

1. Look up the following passages and paraphrase each one.

    ☐   1 Chron. 28:20; Gen. 12:1-4; Heb. 11:8; Gen. 22:1-5; Heb. 11:17-19; 2 Cor. 12:10; Matt. 8:26; Matt. 14:30-31; 2 Tim. 1:6-8; James 1:6

Reflection

1. After reading today's devotion, I realize…
2. The key statements I need to remember and work on are…
3. The positive consequences of remembering and working on these statements will be…

DAY 173

CHRISTLIKENESS

This is my commandment, that you love one another as I have loved you.
(John 15:12)

Today I want you to read a resolution I wrote pertaining to being Christ like. After you read it feel free to write your own.

I'm going to observe myself and others without judgment and expectation. To me, judging is a form of control and I'm not in control, nor am I the boss. All I have to do is to take care of my soul and spirit. I don't need to take everybody's inventory. What do I gain from this? Yes I do have expectations and I will let them be known in the hopes that people will listen, but the reality of it is, we forget.

If my expectations aren't met I'm not going to become punishing or vindictive. I'm going to state what I want and need. Set a boundary if I need to. I'm going to do my best not to hold a grudge. All I know is that Jesus expects certain actions from me and I don't always follow through. He doesn't send down a lightning bolt to hurt me, He loves and convicts me. He will not condemn me, nor should I condemn others for not meeting my expectations.

Mercy and compassion is needed on a daily basis. I need to make it my goal each day to show mercy and compassion to myself and others. I will not take everything so personally, nor will I blow things out of proportion when things don't go my way.

Paul reminds me that God is to judge the living and the dead, and by His appearing and His kingdom: to preach the word; be ready in season and out of season; reprove, rebuke, and exhort, with complete patience and teaching (1 Timothy 4:1-2). Again I'm not to judge, my responsibility is to be patient and to teach others how to treat me.

Ask yourself:
1. Do I share my expectations with others?
2. How do I react when my expectations aren't being met?
3. I know I'm judging others when I...
4. Am I taking things personally?
5. How well do I live out Col. 3:12-17?

Take Action...

1. Look up the following passages and paraphrase each one.

☐ Rom. 2:1-3; Rom. 14:1-13; Col. 2:16; James 2:1-4; James 4:11-12

Reflection

1. After reading today's devotion, I realize...
2. The key statements I need to remember and work on are...
3. The positive consequences of remembering and working on these statements will be...

DAY 174-175

YOU'RE A WORK IN PROGRESS

And I am certain that God, who began the good work within you, will continue his work until it is finally finished on the day when Christ Jesus returns. (Philippians 1:6)

Today you're going to read a letter sharing how Jesus helped Peter see his worth. *Note: This letter is written from my interpretation of scripture.*

Dear_____

Put your name here

Don't learn the hard way like I did... trust me. I thought I had to be perfect. I lacked balance and temperance. Satan won many battles because I wasn't sober minded; I allowed my emotions to overtake me. I had a problem with controlling my anger. I would stuff, and then explode. I used to get really upset when justice wasn't being served or when I thought others were being treated unfairly. When people behaved inappropriately I used to try to fix them, or the situation. I had a habit of trying to correct and change people, places and things; this lead to a big fight when they tried to arrest Jesus. I cut a man's ear off. I used to get upset with myself, especially when I betrayed Jesus. It took me a while to get over it.

I used to think I was only a fisherman. Jesus taught me that I had to stop rejecting myself and that I was a work in progress. Your sanctification and recovery is a journey, not a destination. It's freeing to know that you don't have to be perfect, and make sure you remind Satan of that when he tries to devour you through perfection. Your self-worth and self-image shouldn't be based on being good or not failing. Other people's behaviors have nothing to do with your worth as a person. Keep in mind that you don't have to be a good boy or girl to receive His approval... Jesus loves you the way you are but refuses to leave you that way.

~ Peter, the Apostle (*1 Peter 5:8*)

Ask yourself:
   1. How does Satan try to devour me? How does my personality change?
   2. Do I feel responsible to change or correct a problem which is beyond my responsibility, ability, power or authority?
        a. What will it cost me if I don't change this?
        b. What will I gain if I do?
   3. When does my perfectionism kick up?
        a. What can I do to rid myself of the perfectionistic need to control every aspect of my life so that nothing goes wrong in it?
   4. What will I do when...
        a. Someone does the opposite of what I expect them to do?
        b. Someone lets me down?

Keep in mind:

Be well balanced (temperate, sober of mind), be vigilant and cautious at all times; for that enemy of yours, the devil, roams around like a lion roaring [¹in fierce hunger], seeking someone to seize upon and devour. *(1Peter 5:8)*

Practice:
   1. Self -Talk:
        a. I have faults and weaknesses and I want to change. God is working in me and through his Spirit I can stop being perfectionistic
        b. My mistakes and errors have nothing to do with my worth
        c. Everyone has faults, so I'm not a complete failure just because I am not perfect
   2. Owning your mistakes and failures
   3. Acceptance of others
   4. Giving another person the space to be him or herself
   5. Noticing when internal resistance comes up to do something pleasurable

Take Action...

1. Look up the following passages and paraphrase each one:

Psalm 13:5; Exod. 15:13; Psalm 51:1; Psalm 130:7-8; Isaiah 54:10; John 13:1; 1 John 4:9; Rom. 5:1; Rom. 14:3; Rom. 15:7; Matt. 10:40; Matt. 18:5; Matt. 25:40; Eph. 1:1; Phil. 1:1

Reflection

1. After reading today's devotion, I realize...
2. The key statements I need to remember and work on are...
3. The positive consequences of remembering and working on these statements will be...

DAY 176

YOU MEASURE UP

You are fearfully and wonderfully made. (Psalm 139)

Today we are going to look at the importance of knowing that you measure up and that you're just as good as anybody else. Part of the sanctification process is God showing you just how valuable you are as His child.

Stop Comparing...

Now that you know Jesus, you don't have to be concerned about measuring up to the world, or to others. That way of thinking needs to stop. In Christ, you can accept you for you. (Romans 15) You don't have to compare yourself to others.

Focus on who God made you to be. If your parents constantly compared you to a sibling or to another person, you can stop that mental habit today by lining your image up to God seeing that you were created in His image. You don't have to carry this feeling or belief into your adult life.

Risks...

In Christ mistakes and failures are forgiven. God knows you fall short. Maybe your parents frowned about failure; now, because of that, when you do fail you feel ashamed and guilt ridden so you don't take risks. The good news is that Jesus wants you to take risks; He wants you to get out of the boat.

Lighten up…

If you take yourself seriously I suggest you stop. You're made from the dust of the earth. The more pressure you put on yourself to perform or to be perfect, the more your chance of failure increases, and so do the chances of you walking away from God. God sees you differently than others see you. Make sure you are more concerned about His expectations than man's.

Take Action…

    1. Look up the following passages and paraphrase each one.
        ☐Psalm 139:13-18; Psalm 138:7; Jer. 1:5; Isaiah 43:1; Gal. 4:9; Rom.
           8:10; 2 Cor. 5:17; John 14:20; 2 Cor. 13:5; Gal. 2:20;
           Eph. 3:14-19; Col. 1:27

Reflection

    1. After reading today's devotion, I realize…
    2. The key statements I need to remember and work on are…
    3. The positive consequences of remembering and working on these
       statements will be…

DAY 177

YOUR UNITY WITH JESUS

But the person who is joined to the Lord is one spirit with him. (1 Cor. 6:17)

Today I want to drive home the truth that you no longer have to base your worth on man's approval.

Because you're united with Jesus, you don't have to seek out the security and approval of man. Your main focus should be on your relationship and unity with Jesus.

Keep in mind…

Because of this unity and connection I have with Jesus....

1. **I no longer:** Have to live by others' rules, standards and ideas of right and wrong
2. **I no longer:** Need to put myself under the control of others.... I will be spirit lead
3. **I no longer:** Have to be self-conscious, shy or insecure around people... because I'm not thinking about their opinion which weakens me
4. **I no longer:** Have to worry about the impression I'm making with others... I can be me
5. **I no longer:** Have to put other people's opinions above God's, or my own

Ask yourself:
1. Do I struggle with anything mentioned above? If so, what can I do to change my thinking?
2. How can this truth change my need for approval and acceptance?
3. How can this truth help me with the following habits and hang ups?

- Feelings of abandonment and loss
- The sense of something missing from life. Others have what I am missing.

4. What will it look like if you live out the fact that you're united with and connected to Jesus? Read the list below and check off what you think it will look like:
   - ☐ More honesty and less self-deception
   - ☐ You own all of your feelings and can look at your motives, contradictions, and emotional conflicts without denying or whitewashing them
   - ☐ You may not necessarily like what you discover, but you do not try to rationalize your emotions, nor do you try to hide them from yourself or others. You're not afraid to see yourself "warts and all."
   - ☐ You'll be willing to reveal highly personal and potentially shameful things about yourself because you're determined to understand the truth of your experience so that you can discover who you are and come to terms with your emotional history. This ability also enables you to endure suffering with a quiet strength. Your familiarity with your own darker nature makes it easier for you to process painful experiences that might overwhelm others

5. What has my need for approval (from man) cost me personally, relationally and spiritually?

Take Action…

    1. Look up the following passages and paraphrase each one.
          ☐Phil. 4:19; Rom. 1:25; Rom. 8:1-2; 2 Cor. 5:17,21
          ☐Matt. 16:24-26; Gal. 5:18; Rom. 6:6

Reflection

    1. After reading today's devotion, I realize…
    2. The key statements I need to remember and work on are…
    3. The positive consequences of remembering and working on these
       statements will be…

DAY 178-180

THE OLD LIFE IS GONE

This means that anyone who belongs to Christ has become a new person. The old life is gone; a new life has begun! (2 Corinthians 5:17)

Freedom from approval seeking…

Before you had a relationship with Jesus you might have been easily manipulated by people because you wanted their approval and/or you placed their opinion above God's and your own. You might have felt trapped by other people's agendas, activities, wants and needs to the point that you forgot to take care of yourself or to live your own life. You don't have to live this way anymore; the old is gone and your new life has begun.

The Good News

So now that you're a new person in Christ you no longer…

    1.   Need to feel threatened by people who love you conditionally. You know
          those people who *"love you if you"*…..
    2.   Need to look for or crave reassurance from a person to feel approved.
          You are approved and valued by Jesus.

3. Have to place a high priority on pleasing others rather than on pleasing God or yourself. But seek ye first the kingdom of God, and his righteousness and all these things shall be added unto you. Isn't that liberating?

4. Need to ignore your personal needs, wants and dreams because you need approval. Your life is just as important as anybody else's. You can make your relationships win/win, not win/lose. Stay balanced.

5. Need to put up with difficult, judgmental people who annoy you! Why? Because you don't need their approval. Set a boundary. If they have a problem with it then maybe they have the character issue, not you. Isn't that liberating? Keep your relationships two-way, not one way.

Ask yourself:

1. Where am I on the following continuums?

- Seeks God's Approval ---------------------------- Seeks Man's Approval
- Secure in Jesus ---------------------------- Needing security/approval from people
- I feel cherished---------------------------- I feel abandoned, alone and different

Scenario:

Billy only felt important when someone told him that he was important. If nobody validated him, he would feel like he didn't have a purpose or meaning. He was only happy when people were happy or pleased with him.

1. What advice would you give Billy?
2. What's causing him to think and behave this way?

Sara wasn't able to think straight when she worked with her boss. She would experience anxiety and, in some cases, panic. She was excessively concerned about how she would perform in front of her boss. She was also preoccupied with her looks and her hair.

Sara wants to be close to others so she starts to people please. She wants to be loved and express her feelings to others, and to be needed and appreciated, to get others to respond to her, to validate her.

1. What advice would you give to Sara?
2. What's causing her to think and behave this way?

Take Action…

1. Look up the following passages and paraphrase each one
   Isaiah 61:10; Gal. 5:18; Gal. 1:10; Eph. 4:17-24; Eph. 3:16-19
   2 Cor. 13:5; 2 Cor. 3:16-18; Gal. 4:19; Luke 10:19

Reflection

1. After reading today's devotion, I realize…
2. The key statements I need to remember and work on are…
3. The positive consequences of remembering and working on these statements will be…

REVIEW & REPAIR

Reshaping Your Soul

1. What did I learn this past month about myself, God and others?

2. What concepts or ideas stood out to me in the devotions? Why?

3. What adjustments do I need to make in my life?

4. What, if anything, needs to change about how I think, feel and act?

5. What changes have I made so far? What actions have I taken?

6. How are people reacting to my changes?

7. Steps I will continue to take are…

8. I'm committed to…

9. My victories this week were…

10. God please help me with…

DAY 181

WE ALL FALL SHORT OF GOD'S GLORY

For everyone has sinned; we all fall short of God's glorious standard.
(Rom. 3:23)

Stop Judging Yourself...

Paul tells us in Romans 3:23 that we're all going to make mistakes and fail from time to time, so you don't need to hide them anymore. Better yet, you can stop judging yourself for your sin. Learn to have mercy on yourself. Live in God's grace. If you conditionally love yourself, you're going to become stressed, depressed, anxious or angry.

Your worth isn't based on how many victories or losses you might have, it's based on the fact that you're valued, loved, and cherished by Jesus. If, as a child or teen, you were asked to be perfect, not expected to be successful, lived with high expectations, low expectations, loved only if you got an "A" or did the right thing, and not appreciated, it's going to be hard for you to take risks or even appreciate your accomplishments.

Jesus wants you to know that you're loved no matter what, and that you're capable of whatever God has called you to do. You can do all things through Him.

Keep in mind:

Mistakes...

1. Remind you that we're human.
2. Have nothing to do with your personal worth.
3. Are not meant to be carried around with you. Stop dragging baggage.
4. Make you better, and reliant on the Holy Spirit.
5. Cause you to seek Him for wisdom, knowledge and direction.
6. Make you seek out more information before you act.
7. Are not meant to be used by others to condemn or guilt you.
8. Aren't meant to cause you to live a life time of regret.
9. Show us what doesn't work and eventually lead us to what does work (but only if we let them)
10. Shape you into the person God wants you to become. That is, if you don't condemn yourself and fall into Satan's lies.
11. Occur because we live in a fallen world

12. Don't punish yourself if you make a mistake. Do the opposite... love yourself... and learn from it. Think about Peter when he denied Jesus three times. What was Jesus reaction?
13. Are meant to bond you to others. When you make a mistake confess it... admit and accept it. Find a better solution and seek God's forgiveness if it was caused by sin and disobedience. Seek counsel. Seek help if you keep making the same mistake.

Some famous people's attitudes about mistakes

1. Experience is simply the name we give our mistakes **(Oscar Wilde).**
2. I prefer you to make mistakes in kindness than work miracles in unkindness. **(Mother Teresa).**
3. Every great mistake has a halfway moment, a split second when it can be recalled and perhaps remedied **(Pearl Buck).**
4. The only real mistake is the one from which we learn nothing **(John Powel)**
5. Just because you make mistakes doesn't mean you are one **(Author Unknown).**
6. Truth will sooner come out of error than from confusion. **(Francis Bacon)**
7. Admit your errors before someone else exaggerates them **(Andrew V. Mason).**
8. Even the knowledge of my own fallibility cannot keep me from making mistakes. Only when I fall do I get up again **(Vincent van Gogh).**
9. Don't argue for other people's weaknesses. Don't argue for your own. When you make a mistake, admit it, correct it, and learn from it – immediately **(Stephen R. Covey)**

Take Action...

1. Look up the following passages and paraphrase each one.
   Prov. 28:13; 1 John 1:9; Luke 3:2; Acts 17:30; 2 Cor. 7:10;   1 Thess. 1:9; Psalm 130:8; Isaiah 40:2

Reflection

1. After reading today's devotion, I realize...
2. The key statements I need to remember and work on are...
3. The positive consequences of remembering and working on these statements will be...

DAY 182

JESUS HAS REDEEMED YOU

No condemnation in Jesus. (Rom. 8:1)

Today I want to talk to you about guilt. This emotion lets you know that you violated a value or belief. That's it – nothing more, nothing less. If you feel guilt or remorse that's a good thing as this means you have a conscience.

Guilt gives you an opportunity to make some changes in your character and personality. It also gives you an opportunity to revisit your values, standards and beliefs to make sure that they're yours and that they line up with God's Word. You might be living according to a parent's values or standards and not even know it. You might have some outdated rules you need to change.

Guilt is separate from your worth and identity as a person.

Keep in mind:

1. For all have sinned and fall short of the glory of God. (Rom. 3:23)
2. If we confess our sins, he is faithful and just to forgive us our sins and to cleanse us from all unrighteousness. (1 John 1:9)
3. Mistakes are part of life, everyone makes them, and everyone regrets them. But, some learn from them and some end up making them again. It's up to you to decide if you'll use your mistakes to your advantage. *Meredith Sapp*
4. It's regret, I think that really is the worst kind of pain, yeah guilt is bad, and sadness is bad, but regret is the sickly combination of both. — *Unknown*
5. "The only difference between me and you is you regret what you did, I regret what I didn't do."- *Cassi*
6. "Guilt is the price we pay willingly for doing what we are going to do anyway" *I. Holland*
7. Let go of the past and look forward to what lies ahead.

Take Action…

1. Look up the following passages and paraphrase each one.
   Rom. 5:1-2; Eph. 2:14-18; Col. 1:19-22; Heb. 2:17; Heb. 10:19-22; Matt. 26:27-28; Luke 24:46-47; Eph. 1:7; 1 John 1:9

Reflection

> 1. After reading today's devotion, I realize…
> 2. The key statements I need to remember and work on are…
> 3. The positive consequences of remembering and working on these statements will be…

DAY 183-184

GUILT IS OPTIONAL

There is no condemnation in Christ (Rom. 8:1)

God makes no mistakes…

Sometimes we equate our behaviors with our self-worth. We need to learn how to separate the two. Clark Moustakas said, "Accept everything about you."

Some people walk around focused on what's wrong with them and how they don't measure up. I think we need to see our differences as God's design. He didn't clone us. To prove it He gave us all unique finger prints which will stay the same no matter how old we are.

Acceptance…

Learn to accept yourself and others. When God made you He broke the mold. Be who God created you to be. This way you will live your life with purpose and meaning.

Let's take a look at some guidelines we can live by that will help us love ourselves through Jesus. Check off what you need to work on.

Guidelines to live by: Learning to love yourself through Jesus

☐Stop comparing yourself with other people. Try this for one week.
☐Stop criticizing yourself for one week.
☐Accept your defects. If you can fix them then do it.
☐Take responsibility for the things you don't like about yourself
☐Don't live life likes it's a competition

☐Don't be so worried about making a mistake or saying something wrong

☐Celebrate your uniqueness and differences

☐Focus and build on your strengths

☐Treat yourself like a close friend

☐Ask questions and seek knowledge

☐Stop blaming yourself for everything that goes wrong. Just own your part. That's all that God expects you to do

☐Control your inner critic. That voice that tells you everything that you and others are doing wrong. This voice comes from your perfectionist and idealistic side.

Take Action…

1. Look up the following passages and paraphrase each one.
   John 3:3-7; Rom. 12:1-2; Titus 3:3-7; 1 John 5:4-5; Rev. 2:4; Eph. 4:32; Matt. 18:23-35; Matt. 5:23-24; Lev. 4:20; Jer. 50:20; Psalm 103:12; Luke 23:34; Matt. 26:28; Psalm 51

Reflection

1. After reading today's devotion, I realize…
2. The key statements I need to remember and work on are…
3. The positive consequences of remembering and working on these statements will be…

DAY 185

LEARN HOW TO FORGIVE YOURSELF

My dear children, I am writing this to you so that you will not sin. But if anyone does sin, we have an advocate who pleads our case before the Father. He is Jesus Christ, the one who is truly righteous. (1 John 2:1)

Forgiving ourselves isn't always an easy thing to do. The more we understand God's forgiveness the easier it is to receive it for ourselves.

Joe's Story

Forgive Yourself...

Joe really wanted to change. He was eager to become the man God wanted him to be. But he kept getting stuck. Every time he would measure himself against God's word he felt depressed and insignificant. If he sinned, failed, or made a mistake he was crushed. He would condemn himself for days. He was trying to earn God's love. He didn't understand that he was designed to depend on God.

Joe was doing what many of us do. He was unconsciously comparing his relationship with his father to his relationship with God.

In order for Joe to receive any love or encouragement he would have to do something perfect, or be perfect. Mistakes and failure wasn't allowed in Joe's life. Weakness wasn't permitted, nor was showing any type of emotion. This made Joe hollow inside.

A Moment with Joe

Asking for help made me feel weak. I was taught that a man makes his own way. If I had a problem I would work it out myself.

I've learned through the years that forgiveness isn't about feelings, it's about obedience and choice. It's hard to fight off the human tendency to get even. When I get hurt I just want to hurt the other person back.

It takes a mature person to forgive because God has forgiven them. That doesn't come easy. True forgiveness is only possible when you understand the depth of God's forgiveness and Jesus' death on the cross.

Unforgiveness...

If I don't forgive, I'm the one who suffers. It's like drinking poison and expecting the other person to die. I've made a lot of bad decisions out of bitterness and resentment. I've learned to be honest with God and myself when I'm hurt. I don't hide it anymore. Hiding hurt and pain only makes me sick and more vulnerable to sin and separation from God. To me, it's not worth holding grudges because it messes with my anointing.

I look at it this way: when I make a choice to forgive and seek my Father's help and guidance, I'm only going to get better. God will deal with the person that hurt me. God's conviction is much more powerful and effective then my condemnation and criticism.

Baggage Dragging...

I had to learn not to drag my hurt and past around. I remember reading Phil 3:1... Forgetting the past and looking forward to what lies ahead... After I read this I realized that I had to stop rehashing what happen to me and what I did over and over again in my mind. I was keeping the past alive on purpose. The fact of the matter is, I was hurting myself... no one else.

What helped me was my friends and family. I was able to open my heart and be honest about my hurt and feelings. I found grace and forgiveness as well as acceptance and encouragement. Once I got the pain and hurt off my chest I had to stop rehearsing the issues over and over. I had to fight off the temptation of talking about what I forgave.

Ask Yourself:

1. Do I need to forgive someone?
2. Do I find myself rehearsing the past in my mind?
3. Do I continuously talk about the past?
4. Who can help you work through the forgiveness process?

Keep in mind:

1. If you want to forgive you need face the offender in order to deal with the offense.
2. If the person you need to forgive is deceased you might want to write a letter expressing your feelings and hurts.
3. If an offense is committed against you, admit that it happened. Don't deny it. See it for what it is.

Take Action...

1. Look up the following passages and paraphrase each one.

Psalm 51:1-5; Isaiah 6:1-5; Rom. 3:9,23; Psalm 51:7; Psalm 103:8-12; Psalm 130:3-4; Prov. 28:13; Isaiah 1:18; Acts 2:38; Heb. 9:12-22; Heb. 13:12; 1 Peter 1:18-19; Rev. 7:14

Reflection

1. After reading today's devotion, I realize…
2. The key statements I need to remember and work on are…
3. The positive consequences of remembering and working on these statements will be…

SANCTIFICATION

&

ADVERSITY

Dear brothers and sisters, when troubles come your way, consider it an opportunity for great joy. For you know that when your faith is tested, your endurance has a chance to grow. So let it grow, for when your endurance is fully developed, you will be perfect and complete, needing nothing.
(James 1:1-4)

DAY 186

WE HAVE A CHOICE

"We all grow up with the weight of history on us. Our ancestors dwell in the attics of our brains as they do in the spiraling chains of knowledge hidden in every cell of our bodies." ~ Shirley Abbott

Plans succeed through good counsel;
don't go to war without wise advice. (Proverbs 20:18)

Today I want to discuss how important it is for us to make right choices. I think you would agree that where we are in life today is a direct result of the choices we have made.

A key to staying strong is to remind ourselves that we have choices. Life doesn't just happen to us. This mentality will lead to defeat and depression. We have a choice as to how we respond to our circumstances. Every person has rights. We have the right to say yes or no, to change our minds and to share our opinions, etc. We are not victims - we are victorious because we belong to God. I can't stress it enough that we need to work through whatever stops God's pruning process. If you continue to make the same bad choices, there's a good chance you need healing from the wounds of your past that are lying dormant deep within your soul.

Optimism is so important to our success. Winston Churchill said it best, "*A pessimist sees the difficulty in every opportunity; an optimist sees the opportunity in every difficulty.*" We have a choice, let's choose hope and optimism. Even if our parents didn't encourage us growing up, we still need to encourage ourselves.

In every situation you encounter, you have a choice. Take the time to think it through. **Peacefulness follows any decision, even the wrong one (Rita Mae Brown). Make your choice based on your beliefs and values, no one else's. Dig into your inner strength that God has given you.**

Consider this…

1. God will give you what you need to face hardships and adversity. He has placed His resources within your heart and soul.

2. You're not alone, God is with you. He dwells within the people He has put in your life. Reach out and ask for help, prayer and love.

3. You might be pressed on every side, but we still have room to move. We are often in much trouble, but we need never give up. People make it hard for us, but we are not left alone. We are knocked down, but we are not destroyed (2 Corinthians 4:8-9, paraphrased).

4. Strength comes when you're weak. "That's why I take pleasure in my weaknesses and in the insults, hardships, persecutions, and troubles that I suffer for Christ. *For when I am weak, then I am strong.*" (2 Co 12:10)

Take Action...

1. Look up the following passages and paraphrase each one.
   Acts 1:8; Eph. 3:16,20; 2 Thess. 2:16-17; 1 Tim. 1:12; 2 Tim. 1:7; 1 Cor. 1:31; Gal. 6:14; Heb. 13:6; Zec. 4:6-7; John 14:1; Rom. 15:13

Reflection

1. After reading today's devotion, I realize...
2. The key statements I need to remember and work on are...
3. The positive consequences of remembering and working on these statements will be...

DAY 187

LIVING IN TODAY

Therefore do not worry about tomorrow, for tomorrow will worry about itself. Each day has enough trouble of its own. (Matt. 6:33)

Regardless of what's going on in my life or what goals I'm trying to achieve, I can keep an attitude of gratitude. I can be happy while I wait for my breakthrough. My happiness isn't just achieving my goals or passions.

Happiness and joy comes from being present with God and enjoying life in good times and bad.

Commitment...

We made a vow to God, for better or worse, in sickness and health, for richer or poorer. We need to be all in, committed to serving our creator and boss. One thing you need to stop doing is complaining about what God is or isn't doing for you or your situation. Be still and deal with what's on your plate. God will only give you what you can handle.

Offer up praise...

Sing God a song when you're hurt or defeated. Accept that life doesn't go your way every day. Enjoy it anyway. Live life on life's terms. Trying to control God or life is futile. Control you and only you.

You might have a problem to solve today; you might need to apologize for a behavior or attitude you had yesterday. Just do it. Fess up. Life is up and life is down. Life is a rollercoaster. If it wasn't wouldn't be boring? Let go of the idea that life has to be predictable and certain because it isn't and it never will be. The only thing we can predict is our response and even that's pushing it.

God doesn't want us to focus on our problems or our challenges, He wants us to focus on Him through our challenges and problems. Work through the emotions that come with disappointment and loss. God is in it and at the helm. Don't try to escape or avoid, face it head on. Be human and feel.

Keep your joy...

Keep your fruit of Joy. God tells us in James 1:2-4 to count it joy when life throws us curve balls and unexpected hardships and let downs. Keep your mind on what's right in your life and don't avoid what isn't. This will just keep you sick.

If you're waiting to become perfect or waiting to have the perfect job, spouse, grades, body or savings account to be happy, then you're missing the point and you're missing out on life. Nothing will ever be perfect. Only Jesus was perfect. Seeking perfection and ideals is like chasing the wind. Just be the best you can be, one day at a time.

Count it joy...

Praise God regardless of what your day brings you, and see troubles that come your way as an opportunity for great joy. I think we're better off when we make the decision to be happy and joyful. Whatever happens, let it. Keep your mind on your gratitude list and remember, this isn't home, and this too shall pass.

Keep in mind…

1. Face your problems head on. Don't turn your back on them, they have a purpose. God knows them and designed them for a purpose and reason.
2. See your problems through Jesus. Ask for guidance and direction.
3. If you can't rise above the problem, ask God to help you accept it and give you the strength to work through it. Keep serving the Lord and fulfilling your calling. Sow seeds of joy and love while God works behind the scenes.
4. Study God's word and ask the Holy Spirit for illumination and revelation.
5. God uses our problems to increase and deepen our faith. Their like presents that require His presence.
6. Sometimes God uses problems as way to work on our deeper issues. Go through the pain and rely on others for help when needed.
7. Don't fear setbacks or problems. See them as an opportunity to grow in Christ and character.
8. Keep your faith and stay engaged in your day to day responsibilities. Life shouldn't stop because you have some unsettled issues. God is a big God. Stay enthusiastic and expect God's favor.
9. Seek the lessens within the problem
10. Don't get stuck in the "Why ME's?!"
11. Read John 6: 33 and paraphrase it.
12. We make our life difficult when we try to avoid a problem. Make sure you take your thoughts captive and line them up with God's truth. Confess the fact that God gives us what we can handle through Him.
13. Try reverse psychology… Count it all joy. Use the problem to get you jazzed, pumped up and motivated so you will work on solving it. See the solution and wait on the Lord.
14. Connect to the pain and suffering the problem creates in your soul. When you do this you connect to Jesus and His suffering.
15. Satan will lie to you and try to get you to deny your feelings because he knows that when you accept and welcome your feelings, both negative and positive, they lose power over you. So let your emotions flow.
16. Avoid quick fixes. Get to the root. Look at it this way -- it does take more time eliminating the causes but once you get to the root and find solution, the problem is gone for good.

Take Action...

1. Look up the following passages and paraphrase each one.
    Luke 18:6-7; John 16:27; John 17:11,15; Rom. 8:32; 2 Cor. 1:3; Eph. 3:16; 1 Peter 4:14; Matt. 6:33; Luke 12:31; Jer. 17:7-8; Rom. 8:6; Psalm 55:22; Phil. 4:6-7

Reflection

1. After reading today's devotion, I realize...
2. The key statements I need to remember and work on are...
3. The positive consequences of remembering and working on these statements will be...

DAY 188-189

KEEP A POSITIVE MINDSET AND START EACH DAY CLEAN

For the rest, brethren, whatever is true, whatever is worthy of reverence and is honorable and seemly, whatever is just, whatever is pure, whatever is lovely and lovable, whatever is kind and winsome and gracious, if there is any virtue and excellence, if there is anything worthy of praise, think on and weigh and take account of these things [fix your minds on them]. (Phil. 4:8)

The fact of the matter is, everyday isn't going to be a great day. As you know, life has its ups and downs. I want to remind you today that you have the ability, through Christ, to count your adversity, hardship, bad choices, regrets, loss and pain, as joy (James 1). As God's child you can tap into an attitude of gratitude during the worst times of your life through the help of the Holy Spirit. Don't be mistaken, you're a human being and you **will** experience hurt and pain which still need to be grieved. But as you grieve you can still be joyful and grateful.

Read each of the following statements about your ability to ***Keep a Positive Mindset and Start each day Clean.*** Rate how true it is for you on a scale of 0 - 10. (*"0" meaning the statement is not at all true, "10" meaning the statement is totally true*) Place your answer on the line in front of each statement.

1.__ I am able to stay positive most of the day
2.__ I am able to keep my mind focused on the good things in my life
3.__ am able to look for the best in every situation
4.__ When things get tough and hard, I don't allow myself to get down and discouraged.
5.__ I remind myself that God is in control when I start to get out of control.
6.__ Throughout the day I engage my mind in thoughts of joy, peace, victory, abundance and blessings.
7.__ I start my day off with prayer and devotions.
8.__ I set out to make the best out of each day.
9.__ I stay happy even though I make mistakes, lose my cool or get frustrated
10.__ I accept myself as a human being (Knowing we all fall short)
11.__ I forgive myself for mistakes or failures
12.__ I get back on the wagon immediately after falling off
13.__ I accept that the ideal is only a guideline or goal to be worked toward, not to be achieved 100 percent
14.__ I set realistic and flexible time frames for the achievement of a goal
15.__ I operate out of patience and without the need to "get it done yesterday"
16.__ I'm easy on myself; setting unrealistic or unreasonable goals or deadlines sets me up for failure
17.__ I recognize that the human condition is one of failings, weakness, deviations, imperfections and mistakes; it is acceptable to be human
18.__ I recognize that one's backsliding does not mean the end of the world; it is OK to pick oneself up and start all over again
19.__ I stop my thoughts when I find my mentally scolding my for not being "good enough"
20.__ I visualize reality as it will be for a human rather than for a super human
21.__ I accept myself the way I am; I've let go of the ideas of how I should be
22.__ I enjoy success and achievement with a healthy self-pride, and eliminate the need for self-deprecation or false humility
23.__ I enjoy success without the need to second guess my ability to sustain the achievement
24.__ I reward myself for my progress to reinforce my efforts to change even when progress is slight or doesn't meet up to my idealistic expectations
25.__ I love myself; I believe that I deserve good things

26.___ I have eliminated unrealistic expectations and the idea that I am infallible

27.___ I visualize myself as "winning" even when it takes more energy, and more perseverance, than what I had planned

28.___ I let go of rigid, moralistic judgments of my performance and have an open, compassionate understanding for the hard times, obstacles and temptations

29.___ I'm flexible in setting goals and am willing to reassess my plan from time to time to keep things realistic

30.___ I'm open to the idea that I will be successful in my efforts to change, even if I am not "first," "the best," "the model," "the star pupil," "the exemplar" or "the finest"

31.___ I realize that the important thing is to be going in a positive direction

32.___ I don't let inconveniences frustrate me for too long

Reflection

1. After completing this assessment, I realize…

2. The key statements I need to remember and work on are…

3. What are the consequences of these problems for me?

4. To what extent am I satisfied or dissatisfied with myself?

DAY 190

SUFFERING IS OPTIONAL

"Never to suffer would never to have been blessed"

~ Edgar Allen Poe

For to this you have been called, because Christ also suffered for you, leaving you an example, so that you might follow in his steps. (1 Peter 2:21)

Bad things happen…

Everything happens for a reason. When something spontaneously changes in our life some of us have a tendency to overreact. Some of us deny it and then there's some that just deal with it.

Have you ever thought about why bad things happen to good people? Sometimes God allows us to go through change or suffering to get our attention because, for some reason, we got off track. I know that when I start to lean on my own understanding God does something to redirect me.

New beginnings can be painful, especially when something happens to you and you've done nothing to deserve it, or so we think. It leaves you hanging. You feel like you're on sinking sand.

The Rock...

So what do we need to do when this happens? Stand on the Rock. Lean on God and trust Him. He wants you to learn something. He never promised you a trouble-free life, in fact, He said you will have problems and adversities, "but I (Jesus) have overcome them" (John 16:33). What does your Higher Power say about suffering and new beginnings?

If you're going through a new beginning, trust God. Lean on him. Pray for strength and guidance. Look to others for support and encouragement.

Take Action...

1. Look up the following passages and paraphrase each one.
   Job 23:10; Psalm 119:67; Zec. 13:9; Heb. 12:10-11; 1 Peter 1:6-7; James 1:2-4; Eph. 5:25-27; Phil. 1:6; Jude 24-25; Rev. 21:2; Phil. 2:13; 2 Peter 1:3

Reflection

1. After reading today's devotion, I realize...
2. The key statements I need to remember and work on are...
3. The positive consequences of remembering and working on these statements will be...

DAY 191

BE RESILIENT

"Likewise the Spirit helps us in our weakness. For we do not know what to pray for as we ought, but the Spirit, himself, intercedes for us with groanings too deep for words . . . And we know that for those who love God, all things work together for good, for those who are called according to his purpose."
(Romans 8:26, 28)

Life isn't fair…

Let's face it, life isn't fair sometimes. We experience things that we think we don't deserve. Regardless of whether or not we deserve it, we need to learn to stretch. We need to take the punches and keep getting up. God uses these situations to sanctify us. We need to stay on the potter's wheel and trust that God knows what He's doing. God will use adversity as a tool to sanctify your soul.

God stretches us…

A great example of resiliency is Job. He lost everything but his faith (Job 42). He was stretched more than most people, why? Because of his strong faith in God. So if you're being stretched today, count it as joy. (James 1:2-4) Trust that God will see you through to the end.

Job turned his difficult, heart wrenching situation into spiritual gain and growth. Nothing mattered more to him than to be pleasing to God. God taught Job how to be optimistic and positive during severe suffering and trials. When challenges come, the best attitude to take is "Bring it on." The end result will be a deeper relationship with God, endurance (staying power and stamina) and Christ-like character.

Learn how to roll with the punches.

Consider this…

Affirmations for dealing with adversity and hardship:

- ☐ I've had many seasons of suffering in my life, but I'm able to learn and grow from them.
- ☐ I've dealt with my hardships and feel at peace.
- ☐ My character has grown in many different ways as a result of suffering and pain.
- ☐ I can accept why God has inflicted the adversity I've gone through in my life.
- ☐ I don't avoid my pain, nor do I deny it.

☐I talk about my tough times and struggles.

☐I don't bring more pain upon myself. I accept the hand God has dealt me and trust that he will see me through it. (Rom. 8:28).

☐Lately my hardships and adversities haven't been a direct result of my character defects.

☐I don't fall in to self-pity or become a martyr.

☐I believe that God only gives me what He knows I can handle.

Take Action...

1. Look up the following passages and paraphrase each one.
   ☐1 Cor. 10:13; 2 Cor. 3:18; 2 Cor. 9:10; Gal. 5:22-23; Phil. 1:6; Col. 2:19; James 1:17; James 4:6; Jude 24; Rom. 7:21-25; Rom. 8:37; Rom. 16:20

Reflection

1. After reading today's devotion, I realize...
2. The key statements I need to remember and work on are...
3. The positive consequences of remembering and working on these statements will be...

DAY 192

GOD KEEPS HIS PROMISES

God will make this happen, for he who calls you is faithful.
(1 Thessalonians 5:24)

How well do you do at keeping your promises? If I were to ask the people in your life how well you keep your promises, what would they say?

When I make a promise I know that my honor, integrity and image are at stake. I learned a long time ago that the way to get people to trust you is to keep your promises.

God's Promises...

God keeps His promises because He's trustworthy and good. His promises are messages to us so that we can hang onto them in good times and bad.

When I start to get disappointed and discouraged, I find myself saying ... "God what's going on ... Why aren't you doing something about this.... I need your help..... Don't forsake me.... Why are you doing this to me?"

Here's a list of 9 reasons why I think this happens:

1. I expect God to do what I think is right. I forget that He's in control and see's the big picture.
2. I forget that He has a purpose and plan for whatever I'm going through.
3. I forget that He wants to deepen my faith.
4. I think a particular promise is for me, but it was for that person at that time.
5. I add my own interpretation to God's promises.
6. I don't understand the promise.
7. I let my emotions rule me.
8. I live by my feelings and forget the TRUTH.
9. I don't remember or recall what God has already done for me.

So what about you, what causes you to get discouraged and weary? Can you praise God in the storms of life? Do you understand God's promises?

Take Action...

1. Look up the following passages and paraphrase each one.
   John 17:12,15; Rom. 8:35-39; Phil. 1:6; Heb. 7:25; Psalm 23:1,4; Phil. 4:19; Heb. 13:5-6; Psalm 118:6-7; Heb. 6:19; 1 Peter 1:3-5

Reflection

1. After reading today's devotion, I realize...
2. The key statements I need to remember and work on are...
3. The positive consequences of remembering and working on these statements will be...

DAY 193

TAKING LIFE FOR GRANTED

What's really important in life? Sitting on a beach? Looking at television eight hours a day? I think we have to appreciate that we're alive for only a limited period of time, and we'll spend most of our lives working. That being the case, I believe one of the most important priorities is to do whatever we do as well as we can. We should take pride in that.

~ Victor Kiam

There is nothing better for a person than that he should eat and drink and find enjoyment in his toil. This also, I saw, is from the hand of God. (Ecc. 2:24)

Live like you're dying...

I believe that it's important to live like you're dying and to appreciate the time we have on this earth. Personally, I'm trying to enjoy where I'm at in my life and love the people that God has put into my life. All I know is that I don't want regrets. At the end of the day I don't want to say "I should have..." or "If only I..."

One of the main reasons why I suggest that you live like this is because when you go through changes, transitions, or experience a loss, you can say "I enjoyed every minute of that time, position or person."

Our attitude needs to go something like this, "I want to be able to let go when I need to and be willing and able to wait for what God has for me next."

Losses...

The other thing we have to contend with when we lose something or someone, is the fact that we lose a piece of our confidence, identity, purpose, certainty and comfort. This is the hardest part of going through any transition and working out our salvation. God has a purpose for all that happens and we need to believe that, because if we don't, how can we appreciate our journey and write the story of our life?

Take Action...

1. Look up the following passages and paraphrase each one.
   ☐Heb. 5:8; James 1:2-4; Matt. 16:2-3; Luke 12:54-55; Matt. 6:28-31; Luke 12:27-29; Ecc. 3:12-14; Ecc. 12:13-14

Reflection

1. After reading today's devotion, I realize…
2. The key statements I need to remember and work on are…
3. The positive consequences of remembering and working on these statements will be…

DAY 194-195

RISE ABOVE YOUR CIRCUMSTANCES AND MAKE THINGS HAPPEN

We are afflicted in every way, but not crushed; perplexed, but not driven to despair; persecuted, but not forsaken; struck down, but not destroyed.
(2 Cor. 4:8-9)

Donald Trump Story

Persistence…

Donald Trump experienced hard times through no fault of his own. Back in 1990 real estate values dropped and he lost $1.7 billion dollars. As a result, he owed about $900 million dollars. One of his biggest fears was about to become a reality - bankruptcy. At this point in time, Donald Trump needed to make a decision. He needed to create a plan. This was a turning point in his life and career.

He had a lot on the line, especially his image, considering he was known to be one of the best businessmen alive. He had a choice either to give up or to face this challenge. It was reported that he lined up ninety banks from around the world to establish a support team which would allow him to open up new credit lines so he could get through this crisis.

Be proactive not reactive…

The point I want to make is that Donald Trump didn't react, but rather became proactive. He didn't waste his time saying, "why me?" nor did he have a pity party. He exercised his God-given ability to take control of a situation.

He used his gifts and talents, as well as his support system, to see him through the toughest time of his life. I'm sure he felt out of control and that he lost all ability to influence the situation, but because he is a self-disciplined person, he was able to take control and find solutions to these problems.

God equips us…

You can do the same when you exercise control over the very things which you can influence. Remember to accept the things you cannot change and change the things you can. God will always give you the wisdom and strength to influence the situation that He has called you to do deal with or face. Never quit. You're designed to overcome. Be a winner, not a whiner.

If you're in a crisis turn it into a victory. Use it as a testimony - that's what Donald Trump did. In 1997 he wrote a book called "*The Art of the Comeback*." Between this book and other business endeavors he was able to achieve a net worth of $2 billion dollars. Donald Trump once said passion is the key ingredient to achieving success, passion about who you are, who you are trying to become, and where you are going.

God gives you all you need to be passionate, to stay passionate and to achieve your dreams.

God's in control…

You can make things happen by playing the hand God has given you. Heb 3:6 reminds you that Christ, as the Son, is in charge of God's entire house. And *you* are God's house, if we keep our courage and remain confident in our hope in Christ (italics mine). So what does this mean? It means that you have control in negative circumstances. God is giving you the ability to be in control no matter what you're going through. Take a look at what Paul said in 2 Corinthians 1:9, "In fact, we expected to die. But as a result, we stopped relying on ourselves and learned to rely only on God, who raises the dead."

God has put you in control of your life; in essence you're the master of your own destiny. You set your life plan and follow it. The idea is to create a plan and make sure it lines up with God's will. When you're in Christ you have the fruit of self-control and you must use it in order to achieve the things that God wants you to accomplish.

You're not a victim nor will you ever be one. Things might happen to you, but always remember, God is in control. You have to learn not to handle things on your own. What you have to learn do is to humble yourself before God and ask

Him to see you through. Remove your defenses, stop living in denial, face life head on and always play the hand God has given you.

Take Action...

1. Look up the following passages and paraphrase each one.
   Romans 8:28; Hebrews 10:36; Romans 5:3-4; Galatians 6:9
   Revelation 2:13; James 1:2-3; 1 Timothy 4:16; James 5:11

Today I will practice positive thinking. When something negative happens I will focus on what I can influence. I will pray to God and reach out to the body of Christ.

Reflection

1. After reading today's devotion, I realize...
2. The key statements I need to remember and work on are...
3. The positive consequences of remembering and working on these statements will be...

SACTIFICATION

&

SPIRITUAL WARFARE

The thief's purpose is to steal and kill and destroy. My purpose is to give them a rich and satisfying life. (John 10:10)

Stay alert! Watch out for your great enemy, the devil. He prowls around like a roaring lion, looking for someone to devour. (1 Peter 5:8)

INTRODUCTION

For the next several weeks we're going to explore how Satan tries to oppose the person and purposes of God. Satan will do what he can to get us, or keep us, stuck in the sanctification process. He will use deceit, temptation and testing, to get us to separate from God through disobedience. The only power Satan has is in the lies he tells you. He will use lies to compete against the presence and purposes of God.

My goal in this section is to use a letter format to expose Satan's character, which is full of deceit, and to show you how he seeks to influence you so you can't work out your salvation and go from glory to glory in Christ. (2 Corinthians 3:18)

DAY 196

SATAN'S LIES

YOUR PROBLEMS ARE HUGE, JUST GIVE UP

You are of your father the devil, and your will is to do your father's desires. He was a murderer from the beginning, and has nothing to do with the truth, because there is no truth in him. When he lies, he speaks out of his own character, for he is a liar and the father of lies. (John 8:44)

Satan's lies…

The last thing Satan wants you to do is to love or accept yourself. He tries to get you to find fault with whatever you attempt to do. He wants you to feel hopeless, inferior, insecure, unsafe, unloved and broken.

Satan's tricks…

One of his techniques is to get you to be overly concerned with how you might appear to others. Sometimes he plays on how you were raised. For example, if you were raised in a home that was worried about how they appeared to others, you might grow up with the same worry. Some parents teach their children that image is more important than originality. Satan wants to get you distracted through vanity by getting you to focus on making a favorable impression and getting worked up imagining the critical opinions of others.

Jesus doesn't want you to waste your time on this. He wants you focus on Him and how He views you and loves you. His opinion should take top priority in your life. When you do this, you can't help but be loved by others. In fact, it will make you a better person. Most people I know, like to be around secure and positive people.

Today make sure you have your armor on. Satan can overpower you with his lies… don't under estimate his strength. (Mark 5:4; Acts 19:16)

Take Action…

> 1. Look up the following passages and paraphrase each one.
>   ☐Psalm 34:12-13; Eph. 4:25; Col. 3:9-10; 1 Tim. 2:14; Psalm 26:3;
>   Psalm 119:141-142; Dan. 9:13; John 17:17

Reflection

> 1. After reading today's devotion, I realize…
> 2. The key statements I need to remember and work on are…
> 3. The positive consequences of remembering and working on these
>   statements will be…

DAY 197

SATAN'S A CRITIC

*The thief's purpose is to steal and kill and destroy. My purpose is to give them a
rich and satisfying life. (John 10:10)*

Today you're going to read a letter reminding you how much Satan hates you and how he tries to destroy you by separating you from God. The goal of this letter is to make you aware of Satan's character so you can see him coming and be prepared. *Note: This letter is written from my interpretation of scripture.*

Dear_____ (insert your name here),

I'm a critic. I'm subtle and cunning, and deception is my strength. (Genesis 3:1-6; Matthew 4; Luke 4; 2 Corinthians 11:3, 14; Revelation 12:9; Revelation 20:3, 8)

I have a small still voice too, but it's destructive. I go where you go. I'm watching you. I roam around. You can consider me an ongoing negative commentary. I sound like pessimism, complaining, "poor me," condemnation and judgment. I like to make you think that these are your own thoughts and ideas. They like to call me the 'Accuser of the brethren.' (Zechariah 3:1; Revelation 12:10). If you want to see a fault with God, others and you, come to me. I will be more than happy to make it your focus. I will fix your thoughts on lies, negativity, worse case scenarios, sinful pleasures and dread.

The world calls my voice the inner critic. They minimize me and get you to think that it's just yourself talking. Guess what, it's me and my demons. We're the ones whispering. We like to use voices from your past whenever we can. My goal is to get you to set your standards so high that you can't reach them. If I can do that, eventually you'll get discouraged and quit trying. I like you to hear the negative voices from the past – the perfectionist mother or the condemning father. I think you're stupid and imperfect and I feel the need to remind you of that.

I want to afflict you, mentally and physically. (2 Corinthians 12:7; Luke 8:27, 35, 36; 22:31, 32; John 8:44; 10:10; 13:27; Acts 16:16; 19:16; 2 Corinthians 11:3; 1 Timothy 4:1) I roam around 24 hours a day. I chip away at your beliefs and values. I do everything I can to make you feel like you have no worth. Your sin and weaknesses will cause your demise because I consistently remind you of them and how you fall short of God's glory. Eventually will disconnect you from the Holy Spirit and get you to go back to believing and feeling that you are insignificant.

I will tell you to be careful when you try to get out of the boat. I did it to Peter and I can do it to you too. Why make any effort at all? If you haven't fallen into your sin or old behaviors for a while, I will remind you that those desires are still there. Your past determines your future and don't let anybody else tell you different. You're a disappointment. Jesus Himself will tell you that you're nothing without Him and apart from Him you can do nothing.

My main objective is to hinder the work and the Word of God. (Daniel 10:12,13; Mark 4:15; 1 Thess. 2:18)

~ Satan

Take Action...

    1. Look up the following passages and paraphrase each one.

        ☐Job 1:12-19; John 8:44; Psalm 91:9-10; Rom. 8:35-39; Heb. 12:28

Reflection

    1. After reading today's devotion, I realize...

    2. The key statements I need to remember and work on are...

    3. The positive consequences of remembering and working on these statements will be...

DAY 198-199

SATAN'S LIES

You're inferior and you don't have value

But I am afraid that as the serpent deceived Eve by his cunning, your thoughts will be led astray from a sincere and pure devotion to Christ. (2 Cor. 11:13)

You are loved and valued...

God says you're loved and valued. One way of getting yourself to feel inadequate or inferior is to compare yourself with others. When you do this somebody's going to come up short. If this is a habit for you I suggest that you ask the Holy Spirit to help you stop. The healthy form of comparison is to have Godly role models that you aspire to be like. If you're not quite there yet don't condemn yourself for it, just work hard to achieve it. Make sure you're being realistic with you observations of yourself and others. You might want to consult a friend who is honest and forthright. They can help you have clarity about yourself.

God designed you just as you are... mind, body and spirit. Satan, of course, wants you to dislike everything about yourself. The key is to see yourself as God your Father sees you.

Stop judging yourself...

If there's something you want to change about yourself, by all means change it, but don't judge or criticize yourself for needing to change it. As a child of God you shouldn't feel worthless or less than, because God says you are fearfully and wonderfully made (Psalm 139). God made you to His liking. You're designed to live out His purpose. Your personality, looks, gifts, talents and abilities are all part of you achieving His purpose and plan for your life. He pulls it all together.

Remember that God made you valuable and nobody is better than the next person. God loves us all equally. Practice liking who God made you to be, both inside and out.

Rebuke…

Rebuke Satan when he starts to whisper in your heart thoughts like, "Look at him/her, you're not even close… you don't fit in… keep your mouth shut, you'll sound stupid. … You're fat/ugly compared to him/her."

Take action…

1. Look up the following passages and paraphrase each one.
   □ 1 Sam. 16:6-7 See also 1 Kings 8:39; 2 Chron. 6:30; Psalm 139:1-2; 2 Tim. 2:15; 2 Peter 3:17; 2 Cor. 10:4; John 16:1-4; 1 Peter 4:12; Rom. 8:31; 1 Cor. 15:58; Phil. 1:27-28; 1 Peter 5:9; Rev. 1:9; Rev. 13:10; Rev. 14:12

Reflection

1. After reading today's devotion, I realize…
2. The key statements I need to remember and work on are…
3. The positive consequences of remembering and working on these statements will be…

DAY 200

SATAN LIES

The thief comes only to steal and kill and destroy. I came that they may have life and have it abundantly. (John 10:10)

Have you ever heard this whisper deep within your consciousness? *"There's something wrong with you."*

If you don't have a healthy view of yourself, chances are it's going to be hard for you to handle rejection from others, disapproval and unfair treatment. You might even personalize offenses or dirty looks more than you should. If someone treats you the way you feel about yourself, this only confirms what you feel.

You're self-worth isn't based on people liking you, or at least, it shouldn't be. Your worth doesn't come from man's approval; it's designed to come from God. A lot of people disliked Jesus but He didn't let that stop Him. He didn't change who He was to get anyone's approval. When people disliked Him He let them have their opinions. People liking Him didn't change Him either. His following didn't give him worth, the love He knew His Father had for Him gave Him worth.

Ask yourself:

> 1. I get my worth from…

Take action

> 1. Look up the following passages and paraphrase each one.

> > ☐Col. 3:12-14; James 2:8; Gen. 1:26-27; Col 3:1; Gal 1:10; Col. 3:23

Reflection

> 1. After reading today's devotion, I realize…
> 2. The key statements I need to remember and work on are…
> 3. The positive consequences of remembering and working on these statements will be…

DAY 201-202

SATAN'S LIES

"YOU SHOULD BE ASHAMED OF YOURSELF"

Now is the judgment of this world; now will the ruler of this world be cast out.
(John 12:31)

Regret-free living…

The last thing you want to do is to live in regret. Satan looks for opportunities to shame you, to guilt you and to condemn you. If Satan can get you to act in self-defeating ways he will, and he does it by reminding you of something you did in the past that God has already forgiven you for. If you allow him, he will try to get you to forget the reason why Christ died for you. Jesus said, 'Forgive them father for they know not what they do.' Satan says condemn them for what they do. He is punitive and punishing whereas Jesus is forgiving and convicting.

Jesus is about win/win … Satan's about lose/lose. He puts pressure on you to perform and to be perfect, which you cannot achieve. Satan tries to establish a push-pull relationship with you. He pulls you in through temptation and playing on your flesh and weakness, and when you give in he pushes you away by condemning, accusing, and ridiculing you for what you did.

Be careful of should's and ought's. Satan uses these two words to make you feel overwhelmed and pressured (anxious, worried, hassled, forced, stressed and burdened). The end result is self-destructive behavior leading to a shame based identity. If Satan can get you to shame yourself he will.

Negative self-talk…

Part of the sanctification process is to allow the Holy Spirit to help you identify what you tell yourself, or what messages you listen to, that cause you to live in shame, guilt and condemnation. If you don't go through this process it makes it nearly impossible to claim your image and in heritage in Christ.

Keep in mind:

1. Stop reliving regret
2. If someone brings up your past, remind them that you are forgiven
3. Use the past as a learning tool and as a testimony
4. Celebrate how God made you… not somebody else (Psalm 139)

Practice:

1. Not complaining about who you are, embrace it. If you need to make a change, do it.

2. Not comparing yourself with others.

Take action...

1. Look up the following passages and paraphrase each one.
   John 13:2; Acts 10:38-39; Eph. 4:25-28; Eph. 6:11-12; 2 Tim. 2:25-26;
   1 Peter 5:8-9; 1 John 3:8-9

Reflection

1. After reading today's devotion, I realize...
2. The key statements I need to remember and work on are...
3. The positive consequences of remembering and working on these
   statements will be...

DAY 203

SATAN'S LIES

" YOU'RE DIFFERENT, WHY DON'T YOU FIT IN?"

*But Peter said, "Ananias, why has Satan filled your heart to lie to the Holy
Spirit and to keep back for yourself part of the proceeds of the land? (Acts 5:3)*

You fit in...

It doesn't matter where you came from, the type of background you came from,
the color of your skin, or the social class you were raised in. You fit in. God
does not show favoritism. (Romans 2:11)

Just because you're not like another person doesn't make you unlikeable. God
gave each of us a personality. The challenge is embracing and accepting it.
Make sure you're laying it on the potter's wheel so that God can reshape your
soul and make you more like Christ.

If you're feeling miserable about who you are as a person, there's a good chance
that Satan's lying to you. He doesn't want you to like yourself.

Jesus wants you to stop worrying and being concerned about fitting in with
others. If you practice being like Jesus and accept the personality He gave you,

you shouldn't have any problems. Don't allow how other people behave toward you to affect your self-image. Learn to deal with judgmental people who only know how to accept or love others conditionally. Jesus wasn't accepted by everybody and He still isn't, so He knows how you feel.

Think about how He was treated before He was crucified. He was mocked, beaten and condemned. This didn't stop Him, nor did it change how He viewed Himself. If someone doesn't like you maybe **they** have the problem. Regardless, you have worth and no man can steal that away from you unless you hand it over to them.

Take action…

1. Look up the following passages and paraphrase each one.
   Rom. 12:1-2; Gal 2:20; Gal 1:10; Psalm 34:18; Psalm 27:10;
   Rom. 14:17-18

Reflection

1. After reading today's devotion, I realize…
2. The key statements I need to remember and work on are…
3. The positive consequences of remembering and working on these statements will be…

DAY 204

SATAN'S LIES

SATAN WHISPERS, *"YOU SHOULD KNOW IT ALL"*

We know that we are from God,
and the whole world lies in the power of the evil one. (1 John 5:19)

God says, 'My people perish for lack of knowledge.' (Hosea 4:6) Let's look at how Satan twists things.

God doesn't expect you to know it all or give the appearance that you do. He wants you to learn and study. He wants you to ask questions. Asking questions is how you learn. Satan knows how to make you feel guilty about not knowing "enough" about spiritual things. First, he tries to condemn you because you don't know, and at the same time tries to find a way to prevent you from asking questions by telling some lie to distort your thinking.

Satan might bring to mind a time you asked a question and someone laughed at you. It's a vicious cycle. The key is to learn how to line your thoughts up with God's way and His word. To do this you need to be aware of what you're thinking. Think about what you're thinking about. Don't pretend you know it all or pretend you have the answer. Just ask. You don't have to lose your self-worth because you don't have the answer or knowledge. See it out. Ask. Jesus tells us "you have not because you ask not" (Matt 7:7).

Don't fall into Satan's blame game when you don't know something. I had this client who would condemn and judge herself for not knowing a fact or something about her recovery, and she would isolate because she felt defective. She really believed that she had to understand everything as soon as it was presented to her. She wouldn't ask for any explanation or clarification because of her shame and high standards.

Digging deeper we discovered that her father taught her to fake it till she makes it and never let anybody know that she didn't have an answer. She equated wisdom and knowledge with image and worth.

Take action...

> 1. Look up the following passages and paraphrase each one.
>   ☐Phil. 4:19; Psalm 139:13-18; Rom. 5:8; John 11:35

Reflection

> 1. After reading today's devotion, I realize...
> 2. The key statements I need to remember and work on are...
> 3. The positive consequences of remembering and working on these statements will be...

DAY 205

YOU'RE NOT ANY BETTER

Because of the privilege and authority God has given me, I give each of you this warning: Don't think you are better than you really are. Be honest in your evaluation of yourselves, measuring yourselves by the faith God has given us.
(Rom. 12:3)

Ego...

We have a tendency to think our issues or hardships are unique. Sometimes we feel like nobody understands. The truth of the matter is, Jesus understands. He doesn't see your faults, shortcomings and sins as being any worse than the next person's. Learn to see your problems as normal and repairable. Break free from self-imposed drama and/or pity parties. Satan likes to stir up your ego to get you to think that you're too special to have a problem, and when you do have one, you think, "Oh dear God, why me?!"

See yourself as equal to all of God's children. God has given you the same needs and desires as your brothers and sisters in Christ. You have temptations just like anybody else. If you think yours are special or unusual then give 1 Corinthians 10:13 a read; the temptations in your life are no different from what others experience. And God is faithful. He will not allow the temptation to be more than you can stand. When you are tempted, He will show you a way out so that you can endure.

Take action...

1. Look up the following passages and paraphrase each one.
        □Mark 10:42-45; Rom. 11:20-21; 2 Cor. 10:13-16; 2 Cor. 12:5-6;
        Phil. 2:5-8; 1 Peter 5:5; John 8:7; Rom. 2:1-4; 1 Cor. 10:13

Reflection

1. After reading today's devotion, I realize...
2. The key statements I need to remember and work on are...
3. The positive consequences of remembering and working on these statements will be...

DAY 206-207

SATAN'S LIES

Therefore, if anyone is in Christ, he is a new creation. The old has passed away; behold, the new has come (2Co. 5:17)

NOBODY'S PERFECT

Satan whispers… *"Don't say the wrong thing, always be good, be perfect because Jesus was perfect…you're supposed to be Christ-like right?"* **But Jesus says we all fall short. (Rom. 3:23)**

Jesus knows you're not perfect. He knows that, despite your best efforts, you're going to break a commandment. This is why He died for you. Your love for Him will help you follow His ways.

Un-realistic standards…

When you received Jesus as your savior God started to work on any unrealistic rules or standards you might have learned from your parents, pastors, friends, teachers, family or caretakers. Also, we have the world around us that encourages competition and perfectionism, which are often socially and culturally accepted, if not required. You're barraged by media images insisting that your self-worth and acceptance from others comes when you have the perfect body, perfect job, and perfect car or home.

God doesn't want you to base your security and self-worth on following rules and religion. He wants you to rely on Him for grace and strength to follow His commands that will bring you love, peace and hope.

Stop being punitive…

This was what God told Jesus to work on with the Pharisees. They were punitive and lived by all these internalized rules and regulations. You don't need to follow a set of idealistic standards to feel good about whom you are. God's laws don't heal you just by intellectually following them. You need to believe them in your heart. In one of the seven woes Jesus said, "Woe to you, teachers of the law and Pharisees, you hypocrites! You are like whitewashed tombs, which look beautiful on the outside but on the inside are full of the bones of the dead and everything unclean. In the same way, on the outside you appear to people as righteous but on the inside you are full of hypocrisy and wickedness."

Rules don't change hearts…

If you just live by a set a rules and regulations and don't allow them to transform your heart you're not going to experience intimacy with God. You're just trying to control your sin, negative habits, hurts and hang-ups. Sanctification means giving God control to heal you from the inside out. This is what Jesus was trying to get the Pharisees to see.

Jesus doesn't want you to lower your standards He wants you to ask the Holy Spirit to help you. He wants you to become more tolerant and accepting of the imperfections of yourself and others. Satan will lie to you and tell you that you need to perform perfectly every day. He does this because he knows it's impossible. Satan wants you to feel guilt and doom each and every day.

Be flexible…

Learn to be more flexible and accepting of the fact that you're doing the best you can each day. Rely on the Holy Spirit to help you follow your Father's way of life and doing things. Live according to God's standards…nothing else. Have the courage to admit your mistakes and accept them as a learning tool. Just don't keep repeating them.

Learn from Paul – He was trying to live according to the law and his own strength:

> I've discovered this principle of life—that when I want to do what is right, I inevitably do what is wrong. I love God's law with all my heart. But there is another power[e] within me that is at war with my mind. This power makes me a slave to the sin that is still within me. Oh, what a miserable person I am! Who will free me from this life that is dominated by sin and death? Thank God! The answer is in Jesus Christ our Lord. So you see how it is: In my mind I really want to obey God's law, but because of my sinful nature I am a slave to sin. (Rom. 7)

Ask yourself:

1. What did learn from my caretakers about perfectionism?
2. Was I taught that it's acceptable to make a mistake?
3. Dad's thoughts on mistakes…
4. Mom's thoughts about mistakes….
5. What thoughts dominate me?
6. God's thoughts about mistakes…

Take Action...

1.Look up the following passages and paraphrase each one.
      ☐Matt. 4:1-3,10; Matt. 13:38; Rev. 12; Matt. 4:1-11
      ☐Matt. 13:38-39; Luke 8:10-13; Eph. 4:17-22
      ☐Matt. 5:27-28; Matt. 6:1-3; Rom. 6:12-15

Reflection

1.After reading today's devotion, I realize...
2.The key statements I need to remember and work on are...
3.The positive consequences of remembering and working on these statements will be...

DAY 208-210

RESIST YOUR TEMPTATIONS

No temptation has overtaken you that is not common to man. God is faithful, and he will not let you be tempted beyond your ability, but with the temptation he will also provide the way of escape, that you may be able to endure it. (1 Cor. 10:13)

Take your thoughts captive...

The prodigal son is a prime example of how Satan can put thoughts into our minds. He entertained what his life would look like if he were to have his inheritance early. He fantasized about the lifestyle he was being tempted to live. He saw the parties and fantasized about the women. He physically felt what that life would be like. Somehow he was able to convince his father to give him his share of the inheritance.

Prodigal Son...

The prodigal son was probably the life of the party. It appears that he wanted his life to be one big party. Maybe he was fun to be around. You can assume that his weaknesses were impulsivity, avoidance of pain, problems and responsibility. He enjoyed the pleasures of his senses and didn't believe in any form of self-denial.

He wanted to maintain his freedom and happiness, to avoid missing out on worthwhile experiences, and to keep himself excited and occupied. He definitely wanted to avoid being deprived.

Satan's manipulations...

Satan manipulated his mind (Prodigal) and personality to accomplish his purpose. I think he wanted to destroy the father and ruin his testimony, upset the older brother, create division between him and his father, and divide the family.

Once Satan gets into your thoughts he can control your life and choices. The prodigal son didn't take his thoughts captive. It wasn't until he was willing to face and accept his reality and pain that he was able to ask for forgiveness from God and then his father.

Keep this in mind...

For no temptation (no trial regarded as enticing to sin), [no matter how it comes or where it leads] has overtaken you and laid hold on you that is not common to man [that is, no temptation or trial has come to you that is beyond human resistance and that is not adjusted and[/] adapted and belonging to human experience, and such as man can bear]. But God is faithful [to His Word and to His compassionate nature], and He [can be trusted] not to let you be tempted and tried and assayed beyond your ability and strength of resistance and power to endure, but with the temptation He will [always] also provide the way out (the means of escape to[/] a landing place), that you may be capable and strong and powerful to bear up under it patiently.

Instructions: *Use this checklist to evaluate your ability to **deal with temptation**. Check off what you're currently doing.*

20 Essentials for Resisting Temptation

☐ You need to admit to God, yourself and one other person that you need to make a change and that you need help to do it.
☐ You need to want to change.
☐ Don't rely on the law because it doesn't empower you to manage and confront your impulses (temptations). Rely on the Holy Spirit who strengthens you and empowers you.

☐Admit powerlessness.

☐Stay connected to your support network through good and bad.

☐Receive forgiveness.

☐Repentance: In short, a man must be set free from the sin he *is*, which makes him do the sin he *does*. --George MacDonald

☐Remove blame from your vocabulary.

☐Know what triggers your temptations. What need is at the core of your temptation?

☐List (on paper) your willful sins.

☐Confess your sin and repent.

☐Make amends.

☐Know what's motivating your sin. James 1:14-16 says, 'Temptation comes from our own desires, which entice us and drag us away. These desires give birth to sinful actions. And when sin is allowed to grow, it gives birth to death. So don't be misled."

☐Practice the following spiritual disciplines: Confession, repentance, support, correction, feedback, prayer, worship and discipline.

☐Guard against anything that triggers your weaknesses, habits and hang-ups. Be aware of situations that can cause you to stumble into sin.

☐Don't try to meet your needs outside of God.

☐Stop judging others, and let go of the idea that you can control others.

☐Don't isolate from God when you're struggling.

☐Submit to God and resist the devil, then the devil will flee.

☐Eliminate self-sufficiency: be sufficient in Christ.

Reflection

1. After reading today's checklist I realize…

2. The key statements I need to remember and work on are…

3. What can I do to change the areas I need to work on?

4. What kind of support and accountability do I need?

5. The positive consequences of remembering and working on these statements are…

Ask yourself:

1. What temptations do you have a hard time resisting?

Ask the Holy Spirit to:

1. Help you be more obedient in the area of your weakness

2. Give you the desire to do what pleases God

3. Enable you to live God's way

4. Control your fears and impulses

Take Action…

1. Look up the following passages and paraphrase each one.
   ☐Rom. 8:31; Josh. 1:5; Rom. 8:37-39; Heb. 4:15-16
   ☐Heb. 13:5; 1 John 2:1; 1 John 4:4; Rev. 3:10

REVIEW & REPAIR

Reshaping Your Soul

1. What did I learn this past month about myself, God and others?

2. What concepts or ideas stood out to me in the devotions? Why?

3. What adjustments do I need to make in my life?

4. What needs to change, if anything, about how I think, feel, and act?

5. What changes have I made so far? What actions have I taken?

6. How are people reacting to my changes?

7. Steps I will continue to take are…

8. I'm committed to…

9. My victories this week were…

10.God please help me with…

SANCTIFICATION

&

RENEWING YOUR MIND

A Living Sacrifice to God

And so, dear brothers and sisters I plead with you to give your bodies to God because of all he has done for you. Let them be a living and holy sacrifice—the kind he will find acceptable. This is truly the way to worship him. Don't copy the behavior and customs of this world, but let God transform you into a new person by changing the way you think. Then you will learn to know God's will for you, which is good and pleasing and perfect.
(Romans 12:1-2)

DAY 211- 221

ALLOW GOD TO RESHAPE YOUR MIND

We destroy arguments and every lofty opinion raised against the knowledge of God, and take every thought captive to obey Christ. (2 Cor. 10:5)

Renewing your mind...

A major part of our renewal and reshaping process starts with the renewing of our minds. When Jesus entered your heart He started the process of reshaping how you think which, in turn, will change how you feel and act. He went to work on your beliefs and the values that you were basing your life and choices on prior to Him. Your self-image and identity were formed based on what you believe and think. Jesus wants to expose any lies, accusations and deceptions that you believe and teach you the truth about God, yourself and others.

Read these two passages confirming that God wants to give you a mental makeover because, before Him, your mind was full of darkness.

Don't copy the behavior and customs of this world, but let God transform you into a new person by changing the way you think. Then you will learn to know God's will for you, which is good and pleasing and perfect. (Romans 12: 1-2).

With the Lord's authority I say this: Live no longer as the Gentiles do, for they are hopelessly confused. [18] Their minds are full of darkness; they wander far from the life God gives because they have closed their minds and hardened their hearts against him. [19] They have no sense of shame. They live for lustful pleasure and eagerly practice every kind of impurity.

But that isn't what you learned about Christ. Since you have heard about Jesus and have learned the truth that comes from him, throw off your old sinful nature and your former way of life, which is corrupted by lust and deception. [23] Instead, let the Spirit renew your thoughts and attitudes. Put on your new nature, created to be like God—truly righteous and holy. (Eph. 4:17-24)

We want to conform to God's way of thinking and behaving but our old way of thinking has been an automatic response for a long time.

We come to Jesus with deep patterns of erroneous maladaptive thinking patterns. Dr. Young wrote two books called "Reinventing Your Life" and "Schema Therapy." Dr. Young explores unhealthy thinking patterns and beliefs that keep us in bondage or trapped in life. In his book, Schema Therapy, he created a list of life traps (or what I call strongholds) that cause us to live in bondage to lies, accusations and assumptions.

So for the next 10 days, or however long it takes, I want you to explore the list of life traps (Satan's schemas, or strongholds) and check off or circle the statements that you identify with or have experienced.

As you identify your strongholds make sure you look up the scriptures that will help you overcome each stronghold. The goal is to overcome the lie (stronghold) with God's truth. (Eph. 6: 13-17) Remember - you're a new creation!

Satan's Schemas		
DISCONNECTION & REJECTION		
(Expectation that one's needs for security, safety, stability, nurturance, empathy, sharing of feelings, acceptance and respect will not be met in a predictable manner. Typical family origin is detached, cold, rejecting, withholding, lonely, explosive, unpredictable, or abusive.)		
Strongholds	**Satan's Lie, Deceptions, Accusations**	**God's Truth**
ABANDONMENT / INSTABILITY	Perceived instability or unreliability of those available for support and connection. Involves the sense that significant others will not be able to continue providing emotional support, connection, strength, or practical protection because they are emotionally unstable and unpredictable (e.g., angry outbursts), unreliable, or erratically present; because they will die imminently; or because they will abandon the patient in favor of someone better.	1. Matt. 28:20 2. Rom. 11:2 3. Heb. 13:5 4. Isaiah 54:5 5. Psalm 5:3 6. Psalm 145:18 7. Deut. 3:22 8. Deut. 31:6
MISTRUST / ABUSE	The expectation that others will hurt, abuse, humiliate, cheat, lie, manipulate, or take advantage. Usually involves the perception that the harm is intentional or the result of unjustified and extreme negligence. May include the sense that one always ends up being cheated relative to others or "getting the short	1. Isaiah 54:17 2. 1 Peter 5:8-9 3. Deut. 20:30 4. 2 Tim. 2:24-26 5. Psalm 63:1 6. Isaiah 55:6 7. Psalm 3:3 8. Psalm 61:3

	end of the stick."	9. Deut. 33:27 10. Psalm 91: 7 11. 1 Sam. 2:9
EMOTIONAL DEPRIVATION	Expectation that one's desire for a normal degree of emotional support will not be adequately met by others. The three major forms of deprivation are: 　A. Deprivation of Nurturance: Absence of attention, affection, warmth, or companionship. 　B. Deprivation of Empathy: Absence of understanding, listening, self-disclosure, or mutual sharing of feelings from others. 　C. Deprivation of Protection: Absence of strength, direction, or guidance from others.	1. Rom. 8:35, 38-39 2. Matt. 5:6 3. Psalm 107: 5,9 3. John 4:13-14 4. Rom. 8:37 5. John 15:3,7
DEFECTIVENESS / SHAME	The feeling that one is defective, bad, unwanted, inferior, or invalid in important respects; or that one would be unlovable to significant others if exposed. May involve hypersensitivity to criticism, rejection and blame; self-consciousness, comparisons, and insecurity around others; or a sense of shame regarding one's perceived flaws. These flaws may be private (e.g., selfishness, angry impulses, unacceptable sexual desires) or public (e.g., undesirable physical appearance, social awkwardness).	1. Psalm 139 2. Rom. 8 3. Isaiah 61:1-4 4. Jer. 29:11-14 5. John 3:16-17 6. John 15:9 7. 1 Cor. 13 8. Col. 3:15 9. Psalm 119: 6,80 10. Rom. 10:11 11. 2 Tim. 2:15 12. Rom. 5:5
SOCIAL ISOLATION / ALIENATION	The feeling that one is isolated from the rest of the world, different from other people, and/or not part of any group or community.	1. Ecc. 4:9-12 2. 1 Cor. 12 3. 1 Cor. 13 4. Gal. 6 5. Matt. 22:37-39

IMPAIRED AUTONOMY & PERFORMANCE

(Expectations about oneself and the environment that interfere with one's perceived ability to separate, survive, function independently, or perform successfully. Typical family origin is enmeshed, undermining of child's confidence, overprotective, or failing to reinforce child for performing competently outside the family.)

DEPENDENCE / INCOMPETENCE	Belief that one is unable to handle one's everyday responsibilities in a competent manner, without considerable help from others (e.g., take care of oneself, solve daily problems, exercise good judgment, tackle new tasks, make good decisions). Often presents as helplessness.	1. Jer. 29:11 2. Phil. 3:16 3. Psalm 139 4. Phil. 3:13-14 5. Psalm 25:4-5 6. Matt. 6:6
VULNERABILITY TO HARM OR ILLNESS	Exaggerated fear that imminent catastrophe will strike at any time and that one will be unable to prevent it. Fears focus on one or more of the following: (A) Medical Catastrophes: e.g., heart attacks, AIDS; (B) Emotional Catastrophes: e.g., going crazy; (C): External Catastrophes: e.g., elevators collapsing, victimized by criminals, airplane crashes, earthquakes.	1. Matt. 6:25-34 2. Jer. 17:7-8 3. Psalm 37 4. Psalm 91 5. Matt. 5 6. Phil. 4 7. Isaiah 40
ENMESHMENT / UN DEVELOPED SELF	Excessive emotional involvement and closeness with one or more significant others (often parents), at the expense of full individualization or normal social development. Often involves the belief that at least one of the enmeshed individuals cannot survive or be happy without the constant support of the other. May also include feelings of being smothered by, or fused with, others OR insufficient individual identity. Often experienced as a feeling of emptiness and floundering, having no direction, or in extreme cases questioning one's existence.	1. Psalm 139 2. 2 Cor. 5:17 3. Eph. 1:4-5 4. James 2:5 5. 2 Cor. 7:1 6. John 1:12 7. Rom. 14:8 8. Mark 1:35 9. Psalm 19:1
FAILURE	The belief that one has failed, will inevitably fail, or is fundamentally inadequate relative to one's peers	1. Rom. 8:1 2. Rom. 3:23 3. Psalm 139

	in areas of achievement (school, career, sports, etc.). Often involves beliefs that one is stupid, inept, untalented, ignorant, lower in status, less successful than others, etc.	4. Rom. 8 5. Psalm 37:23 6. Lam. 3:22 7. Psalm 60:12 8. John 6:37

IMPAIRED LIMITS

(Deficiency in internal limits, responsibility to others, or long-term goal-orientation. Leads to difficulty respecting the rights of others, cooperating with others, making commitments, or setting and meeting realistic personal goals. Typical family origin is characterized by permissiveness, overindulgence, lack of direction, or a sense of superiority rather than appropriate confrontation, discipline, and limits in relation to taking responsibility, cooperating in a reciprocal manner, and setting goals. In some cases, child may not have been pushed to tolerate normal levels of discomfort, or may not have been given adequate supervision, direction, or guidance.)

ENTITLEMENT /GRANDIOSITY	The belief that one is superior to other people, entitled to special rights and privileges, or not bound by the rules of reciprocity that guide normal social interaction. Often involves insistence that one should be able to do or have whatever one wants, regardless of what is realistic, what others consider reasonable, or the cost to others; OR an exaggerated focus on superiority (e.g., being among the most successful, famous, wealthy) -- in order to achieve power or control (not primarily for attention or approval). Sometimes includes excessive competitiveness toward, or domination of, others: asserting one's power, forcing one's point of view, or controlling the behavior of others in line with one's own desires---without empathy or concern for others' needs or feelings.	1. Rom. 12:3 2. Phil. 2:3,21 3. James 3:14-16 4. Rom. 8 5. Psalm 139 6. Job 38-40 7. 2 Tim. 3:2 8. 2 Cor. 5:15 9. Isaiah 56:11 10. 1 Cor. 13:5 11. 1 Cor. 10:33
INSUFFICIENT SELF-CONTROL / SELF-DISCIPLINE	Pervasive difficulty or refusal to exercise sufficient self-control and the ability to handle frustration which interferes with achieving one's	1. 1 Cor. 10:13 2. James 1:12 3. Heb. 2:18 4. Rom. 7

	personal goals, or to restrain the excessive expression of one's emotions and impulses. In its milder form the patient presents with an exaggerated emphasis on discomfort-avoidance: avoiding pain, conflict, confrontation, responsibility; or overexertion---at the expense of personal fulfillment, commitment, or integrity.	5. Heb. 4:16

OTHER-DIRECTEDNESS		
(An excessive focus on the desires, feelings and responses of others at the expense of one's own needs -- in order to gain love and approval, maintain one's sense of connection, or avoid retaliation. Usually involves suppression and lack of awareness regarding one's own anger and natural inclinations. Typical family origin is based on conditional acceptance: children must suppress important aspects of themselves in order to gain love, attention, and approval. In many such families, the parents' emotional needs and desires -- or social acceptance and status -- are valued more than the unique needs and feelings of each child.)		

SUBJUGATION	Excessive surrendering of control to others because one feels coerced -- usually to avoid anger, retaliation, or abandonment. The two major forms of subjugation are:
	
	    A. Subjugation of needs: Suppression of one's preferences, decisions, and desires.
	    B. Subjugation of Emotions: Suppression of emotional expression, especially anger.
	
	    Usually involves the perception that one's own desires, opinions, and feelings are not valid or important to others. Frequently presents as excessive compliance, combined with hypersensitivity to feeling trapped. Generally leads to a buildup of anger, manifested in maladaptive symptoms (e.g., passive-aggressive behavior, uncontrolled outbursts of temper, psychosomatic symptoms, and
		1. Psalm 139
		2. Phil. 4:6
		3. Phil. 4:19
		4. Psalm 55:22
		5. Isaiah 26:3
		6. Psalm 62:6

	withdrawal of affection, "acting out", and substance abuse).	
SELF-SACRIFICE	Excessive focus on voluntarily meeting the needs of others in daily situations at the expense of one's own gratification. The most common reasons are: to prevent causing pain to others; to avoid guilt from feeling selfish; or to maintain the connection with others perceived as needy. Often results from an acute sensitivity to the pain of others. Sometimes leads to a sense that one's own needs are not being adequately met and, to resentment of those who are taken care of. (Overlaps with concept of codependency.)	1. Matt. 6:33 2. John 5:41-44 3. Rom. 12:1-2 4. Heb. 11:6 5. Col. 3:22-25
APPROVAL-SEEKING / REC OGNITION-SEEKING	Excessive emphasis on gaining approval, recognition, or attention from other people, or fitting in, at the expense of developing a secure and true sense of self. One's sense of self-esteem is dependent primarily on the reactions of others rather than on one's own natural inclinations. Sometimes includes an overemphasis on status, appearance, social acceptance, money, or achievement -- as means of gaining approval, admiration, or attention (not primarily for power or control). Frequently results in major life decisions that are inauthentic or unsatisfying; or in hypersensitivity to rejection.	1. Psalm 63:1 2. Psalm 139 3. James 4:8 4. Psalm 25:12-14 5. Psalm 62:8 6. Psalm 23 7. Phil. 2:4 8. Col. 3:22-25 9. John 7:18

OVERVIGILANCE & INHIBITION

(Excessive emphasis on suppressing one's spontaneous feelings, impulses, and choices OR on meeting rigid, internalized rules and expectations about performance and ethical behavior -- often at the expense of happiness, self-expression, relaxation, close relationships, or health. Typical family origin is grim, demanding, and sometimes punitive: performance, duty, perfectionism, following rules, hiding emotions, and avoiding mistakes predominate over pleasure, joy, and relaxation. There is usually an undercurrent of pessimism and worry---that things could fall apart if one fails to be vigilant and careful at all times.)

NEGATIVITY / PESSIMISM	A pervasive, lifelong focus on the negative aspects of life (pain, death, loss, disappointment, conflict, guilt, resentment, unsolved problems, potential mistakes, betrayal, things that could go wrong, etc.) while minimizing or neglecting the positive or optimistic aspects. Usually includes an exaggerated expectation-- in a wide range of work, financial, or interpersonal situations -- that things will eventually go seriously wrong, or that aspects of one's life that seem to be going well will ultimately fall apart. Usually involves an inordinate fear of making mistakes that might lead to: financial collapse, loss, humiliation, or being trapped in a bad situation. Because potential negative outcomes are exaggerated, these patients are frequently characterized by chronic worry, vigilance, complaining, or indecision.	1. Psalm 23:3 2. Isaiah 54:8 3. Psalm 32:7 4. Phil. 4: 6-8
EMOTIONAL INHIBITION	The excessive inhibition of spontaneous action, feeling, or communication -- usually to avoid disapproval by others, feelings of shame, or losing control of one's impulses. The most common areas of inhibition involve: (a) inhibition of anger & aggression; (b) inhibition of positive impulses (e.g., joy, affection, sexual excitement, play); (c) difficulty expressing vulnerability or communicating freely about one's feelings, needs, etc.; or (d) excessive emphasis on rationality while disregarding emotions.	1. John 8:16 2. John 6:15 3. Ecc. 4:9-12 4. Deut. 31:6 5. James 4:7 6. Isaiah 54:17

UNRELENTING STANDARDS / HYPERCRITICALNESS	The underlying belief that one must strive to meet very high internalized standards of behavior and performance, usually to avoid criticism. Typically results in feelings of pressure or difficulty slowing down; and in hypercriticalness toward oneself and others. Must involve significant impairment in: pleasure, relaxation, health, self-esteem, sense of accomplishment, or satisfying relationships. Unrelenting standards typically present as: (a) perfectionism, inordinate attention to detail, or an underestimate of how good one's own performance is relative to the norm; (b) rigid rules and "shoulds" in many areas of life, including unrealistically high moral, ethical, cultural, or religious precepts; or (c) preoccupation with time and efficiency, so that more can be accomplished.	1. Rom. 3:23 2. Rom. 8:1 3. Psalm 139 4. Psalm 27:10 5. Rom. 7 6. 1 John 3:21 7. John 3:17 8. Rom. 14:22 9. Rom. 2:1 10. Rom. 8 11. Eph. 2:8-9 12. Psalm 51:10 13. Isaiah 59:2 14. Psalm 118:1 15. Rom. 12
PUNITIVENESS	The belief that people should be harshly punished for making mistakes. Involves the tendency to be angry, intolerant, punitive, and impatient with those people (including oneself) who do not meet one's expectations or standards. Usually includes difficulty forgiving mistakes in oneself or others, because of a reluctance to consider extenuating circumstances, allow for human imperfection, or empathize with feelings.	*See unrelenting standards*

Source Dr. Young: Schema Therapy

Now that you're done identifying your strongholds, Satan's schemas or life traps, I want you to process the information. Answer these questions for each stronghold.

Ask yourself:

1. What triggers your stronghold?

2. Who, or what, causes it to increase?

3. What specific things do you do that keeps the stronghold going?

4. What specific things do others do to contribute to the stronghold?

5. What do you do that you don't want to do when you believe the stronghold?

6. What do you *not want to do* that you do when you're active in your stronghold? What character defects seem to exist as a result of your strongholds?

7. How do you feel about yourself when the stronghold takes place?

8. What have you tried to do to control the stronghold?

9. What has worked best? What has **not** worked?

10. When you can control the stronghold how do you feel?

11. When it's over, how do you feel? What do you think about?!

12. How can others help you control your strongholds?

13. What books, groups or other resources have helped you?

14. What are your concerns about the stronghold recurring?

15. What has the stronghold cost you spiritually, relationally, personally, vocationally, financially, socially and physically?

NO PAIN, NO GAIN

Now that you have completed your stronghold inventory I want you to identify the character defects that result from your distorted beliefs/strongholds. Read through the list and check off what applies to you.

☐**SELF-CENTERDNESS** - putting myself first: everything and everybody must suit me; I am the most important person in the world; playing God. I am the center of it all; it blocks relationships, promotes ego, creates selfishness and self-seeking; causes me to pray for selfish ends; being obsessed about my needs and getting in my own way.

☐**RESENTMENT**- to hold ill feelings against anyone; remembering how others have hurt me and desiring retribution and/or retaliation; judging others; wanting revenge; blaming others; nursing grudges.

☐**ANGER OR HATRED -** desiring harm for others; not wanting a good life for others; bitterness; refusing help from others; uncontrollable temper, justifying my "righteous" anger.

☐**PREJUDICE -** automatically pre-judging; others are inferior; being superior to others who are different; despising others of a different race, class, education, addiction, sobriety, etc. Condemning others for their wrongs; maintaining a closed mind.

☐**MURDER -** gossip, character assassination of others; wanting someone dead.

☐**CONCEIT -** insisting on things being done my way; critical of authority; always an "expert;" impatient with those who do not meet my high standards; expectations exceeding my actual abilities; thinking too highly of my will; giving God orders; putting intellect or vanity first; thinking my judgment is better than that of others.

☐**GREED -** coveting or desiring what belongs to others; not content with what I have; collecting more material things for happiness; basing success on material things; possessions becoming my god; unwilling to share with others; lack and limitation; blind ambition; stealing; envy; jealousy of people and things.

☐**LUST -** adultery; secret lust for someone else; mental whoring; using people sexually for happiness; using other people for gratification; envious of lovers. Thinking love is the same thing as sex; rape; sexual fantasizing.

☐**INDIFFERENCE -** not caring about other people; not caring about God; choosing to ignore God's will; being indifferent to the desires and feelings of others; no desire to understand; not carrying the message, not practicing His presence in my life; being negative and inconsiderate; taking thinks for granted; mediocre.

☐**PHONINESS -** false pride; lying; arrogant dishonesty; a false front; concerned about the impression I make to other people; pretending to be a great philosopher and moralist; trying to give away something I do not have (sobriety, program, spirituality, etc.) using alibis to evade responsibility; putting others down so I feel good; being controlled by the acquired false self.

☐**FEAR -** (CHIEF ACTIVATOR OF DEFECTS) dread; gloomy pessimism; lack of trust in God; separation from God; not living in the here and now; negative thought and attitudes; guilt of the past; not surrendering my life and will over to the care of God; relying on the thinker to solve problems it cannot handle; self-centered fear - primarily, fear that we would lose something we already possessed or would fail to get something we demanded; fear of people; rejection; not living the steps (to recovery).

☐**SELF-PITY-** feeling sorry for myself; wallowing in my sorrows; magnifying my troubles; thinking that I am different; blaming my problems on others; withdrawing from the world; feeling that no one understands or loves me; feeling hopeless; feeling that I am a victim of circumstances.

☐**OBSESSION TO DRINK OR USE -** refusing to ask God to remove the obsession to drink/use; failure to do the steps to recovery.

☐**SELF-SUFFICIENCY -** lack of faith; attempting to manage my life; relying on my will only; having undue confidence; being smug or overbearing; putting material things before spiritual things; not living steps 1, 2, and 3. "I'd rather do it myself attitude".

☐**DEFIANCE -** anger at God because He has failed to meet my demands; resisting people or God; non-conforming.

☐**INTELLECTUAL -** knowledge is all-powerful; intellect can replace God or play God. Controlling my life or others; deluding myself into thinking I have "it"; belief only in my own reasoning; the thinking mind being my master; being self-reliant to the extreme, (ego and conceit).

☐**SELF-RIGHTEOUS -** feeling superior to other people; phony form of respectability; putting my values and ideas first; my way is the only right way.

☐**SELF-DECEPTION -** believing my will is God's will; believing that false ideas of myself are true; being something I am not; not living in reality.

☐**SELF-WILL -** blocking the entry of God; in collision with something or someone, even with good motives; into myself totally - me, myself, and I

- regardless of the consequences.

☐**FALSE DEPENDENCE** - emotional dependence on other people; depending on a stronger person for protection and guidance; leaning on others; insisting on being overly dependent on others - "I can't do this myself" and making others responsible for our progress, depending on people rather than on God.

☐**FINANCIAL INSECURITY** - hoarding money; fear of losing a job; being extravagant in my finances; manipulating; gambling; placing money over God; lack and limitation; "they don't give me what I deserve!"

☐**DOMINATION** - demanding attention, protection, and love from others; attempting to control others, telling others how their lives should be lived; unreasonable demands on others, playing God, dominating those around me, forcing others to do my will.

☐**FALSE PRIDE** - blind to my liabilities; demands upon me or others that misuse my God-given-instincts; hiding defects while blaming others for them; not making amends or a list of people I have harmed; associated with fear; exaggerated self-importance; feeling superior; braggart, grandiose; trouble admitting any human weakness at all.

☐**SELF-JUSTIFICATION** - continually making excuses for my behavior.

☐**LACK OF TOLERANCE** - failing to practice unconditional love; intolerant of others; not allowing others to have different ways of thinking or living.

☐**EMOTIONAL INSECURITY** - personal relationships which bring continuous or recurring trouble; sexual situations that cause anxiety, bitterness, frustration or depression; inability to accept conditions which I cannot change; unworkable relations with other people; over-dependence on people is unsuccessful because all people are fallible; I cannot control my emotional nature; instincts and intuition gone wild.

☐**DISHONESTY** - not being honest with God, myself, or other people; lying; cheating; depriving others of, not only their worldly goods, but of their emotional security and peace of mind, justifying my behavior; using alibis and stealing trust.

☐**SELF-DESTRUCTION-** obsession for alcohol and/or drugs, self-harm and self-sabotage, sabotaging my recovery or anything good that comes into my life.

☐**SLOTH -** procrastination; laziness; continually putting off things that need to be done now; complacency.

☐**GLUTTONY -** excessive eating or drinking; taking our comfort to the extreme; compulsion to overindulge.

☐**RATIONALIZATION -** imagining that I had good motives and reasons when I really didn't.

☐**PERFECTIONISM -** unwilling to accept human mistakes - mine or those of others; I set unrealistic standards for myself and others, then become frustrated and resentful if they are not met; believing my standards are equal to God's.

☐**IMPATIENCE -** I want what I want, and I want it now. Not living in the here and now; my timetable - not God's timetable - inability to delay gratification.

Reshaping exercise:

For this exercise I want you to identify how your strongholds trigger your defects of character. This awareness will help you to not get stuck in the sanctification process. Use the scripture from the tables above to help you replace the flawed belief.

	Stronghold	*Character Defect*	*Give your best example of this specific stronghold/ flaw in your life*	*Gods Truth*
	For Example: *Unrelenting Standards*	*Impatience, Lack of tolerance, Anger*	*Yelling at my kids, raging in traffic, Discontent, unable to live in the moment*	Rom. 3:23
1				
2				

3			
4			
5			
6			
7			
8			
9			
10			
11			
12			
13			

Reflection

1. After reading today's devotion, I realize…
2. The key statements I need to remember and work on are…
3. The positive consequences of remembering and working on these statements will be…

Resource:

1. www.cyberrecovery.net/forums/

DAY 222-225

WE BECOME OUR THOUGHTS

For as he thinketh in his heart, so is he: Eat and drink, saith he to thee; but his heart is not with thee. (Proverbs 23:7)

God created us in a way that when we put our mind to something we can achieve whatever we set out to do. He tells us that *"As a man thinketh so he is."*

Our thoughts create our circumstances because they get buried deep in our subconscious. Why do you think God tells us we can do all things through Christ? He knows that when we focus our minds on what we can't do, can't have or don't have, we act out those thoughts. Remember, we come to Christ with negative beliefs about God, ourselves, others and the world. Part of working out our salvation is identifying our negative beliefs and replacing them with God's truth.

This is why Paul advises us to, "Fix [our] thoughts on what is true, and honorable, and right, and pure, and lovely, and admirable. Think about things that are excellent and worthy of praise." (Phil. 4:8).

In other words, focus your mind on happy, constructive and loving thoughts. I realized long ago that I become my thoughts. This simply means that you and I have the power to manage our thoughts and move in any direction that we want to.

Reshaping exercise…

1. For the next three days or more, I want you to listen to your self- talk, identify your negative beliefs and answer the following questions. Take time to read through the list below:

   a. Are my thoughts generally positive or negative?

   b. What questions do I ask myself?

   c. What negative attitudes are working against me?

Instructions: Check off the negative beliefs you struggle with.

Not good enough (incompetent)

- ☐ I am no good
- ☐ I can't get it right
- ☐ I can't make it work (klutz)
- ☐ I can't fix it
- ☐ I am not good enough
- ☐ I am unsuccessful
- ☐ I'm not valuable
- ☐ I am inferior
- ☐ I am nothing
- ☐ I am worthless
- ☐ I am invisible
- ☐ I am insignificant

Not good enough (unlovable)

- ☐ I am unlovable
- ☐ I am unacceptable
- ☐ I am plain and dull
- ☐ I am not special
- ☐ I don't matter
- ☐ I am unworthy
- ☐ I am not interesting enough

Don't know, wrong

- ☐ I don't know
- ☐ I get it wrong
- ☐ I am always wrong
- ☐ I can't understand
- ☐ I'm not understood
- ☐ I am in the wrong place
- ☐ I am no good
- ☐ I am a mistake

Powerless, one-below

- ☐ I can't do it
- ☐ I can't
- ☐ I am a victim
- ☐ I am weak
- ☐ I am powerless
- ☐ I am a failure
- ☐ I am ineffective
- ☐ I don't have any choice
- ☐ I am less than
- ☐ I am helpless
- ☐ I finish last
- ☐ I am always number two
- ☐ I am always one-below
- ☐ I can't stand up for myself
- ☐ I am inferior
- ☐ I am a loser
- ☐ I am inadequate
- ☐ I can't say 'no'
- ☐ I am useless
- ☐ I am crazy
- ☐ I have a mental problem
- ☐ I am out of control
- ☐ I can't make myself clear
- ☐ I am mistaken
- ☐ I am unbalanced
- ☐ I will fail
- ☐ I am a failure
- ☐ I don't deserve to be loved
- ☐ I don't deserve to be cared for
- ☐ I don't deserve anything
- ☐ There's something wrong with me

☐I'm not safe
☐I am afraid

In danger or not safe

☐I'm not safe
☐I am afraid
☐I am uncertain
☐I am vulnerable
☐I am helpless

Unwanted, different

☐I don't belong
☐I am unwanted
☐I am alone
☐I am unwelcome
☐I don't fit in anywhere
☐I don't exist
☐I'm nothing
☐I shouldn't be alive
☐I'm not anybody
☐I am left out
☐I am unsuitable
☐I am uninteresting
☐I am unimportant
☐I don't matter

Defective, imperfect, bad

☐It's my fault
☐I am guilty
☐I am bad
☐I am not whole
☐I am imperfect
☐I am unattractive
☐I am flawed
☐I am stupid
☐I am awkward
☐I am slow
☐I can't be me
☐I'm not true
☐I'm dirty
☐I am ugly
☐I am fat
☐I'm shameful
☐I am unclean

Other:

☐I am a klutz (awkward)

Resource: John Nutting 1996- 2000   GROWING AWARENESS PTY LTD -

Reshaping exercise...

Instruction: For each negative belief you checked off, place it on the line provided below and then work through the following questions. (Do this for each one)

NEGATIVE/DISEMPOWERING BELIEF: _____

1. How is this belief ridiculous or absurd? How does it oppose God's truth? What truth from God's word can you use to counter this lie?
2. Was the person I learned this belief from worth modeling in this area?
3. What will it ultimately cost me emotionally if I don't let go of this belief?
4. What will it ultimately cost me in my relationship with God if I don't let go of this belief?
5. What will it ultimately cost me in my relationships with others if I don't let go of this belief?
6. What will it ultimately cost me physically if I don't let go of this belief?
7. What will it ultimately cost me financially if I don't let go of this belief?
8. What will it cost my family/loved ones if I don't let go of this belief?

GOD'S TRUTH/EMPOWERING BELIEF:

EXAMPLE

NEGATIVE/DISEMPOWERING BELIEF: For instance: I'm no good!

GOD'S TRUTH/EMPOWERING BELIEF: "Therefore, accept each other just as Christ has accepted you so that God will be given glory." (Rom. 15:7) I'm loved and accepted by God.

SANCTIFICATION

&

THE HOLY SPIRIT

I am a special messenger from Christ Jesus to you Gentiles. I bring you the Good News so that I might present you as an acceptable offering to God, made holy by the Holy Spirit. (Romans 15:16)

INTRODUCTION

For the next several days you're going to read letters describing the personality of the Holy Spirit. I wrote them in this format to make it more personal and to help you understand the Spirit's role in the sanctification and healing process.

The letters will help you to understand that the Holy Spirit is a real person with His own personality and that He encourages, equips and empowers you to fulfill God's will and purpose for your life. Also, you will learn through reading these letters that the Holy Spirit will provide you with a sense of peace and contentment during the most challenging times in your life.

My hope is that these letters will help you to heal those areas of your soul that are hurting and under developed, as well as help you to develop a better understanding of your helper and comforter. When you rely on the Holy Spirit you will be able to work through any challenge placed before you. Remember, not by power, not by might, but by my spirit says the Lord. (Zech. 4:6)

Look up the following passages and paraphrase each one.

> ☐Luke 5:17; Luke 6:19; Luke 24:49; Acts 1:4; Acts 8:20; Acts 10:45; Acts 11:17; John 16:13; John 14:16-18; Acts 11:12; John 16:8-11; 1 Cor. 14:24-25; John 7:37-39; Acts 1:8; Acts 2:4; Acts 4:31; Rom. 5:5; Gal. 3:5; Heb. 2:4

DAY 226-227

LEARN HOW TO LIVE A SPIRIT FILLED LIFE

But the Helper, the Holy Spirit, whom the Father will send in my name, he will teach you all things and bring to your remembrance all that I have said to you. (John 14:26)

Collaborate with the Holy Spirit

Let's face it, personal growth and healing is impossible without the Holy Spirit. Jesus left the Holy Spirit to help us reconcile our issues and to sanctify us. His job is to draw you to God and to partner with you to live out your purpose. In order to be Christ-like you need to address any personality or character issues that prevent you from living as Christ lived.

The Holy Spirit was commissioned by God to make you more like Christ. Your veil was removed so that you can be a mirror that reflects the glory of the Lord, and as the spirit of Lord works within you, you'll become more and more like Him and reflect His glory even more. (2 Corinthians 3:18)

How often do you talk to the Holy Spirit? Do you ever contemplate decisions or choices you need to make? Do you keep in mind that the Holy Spirit was given to you to guide you?

Open your Bible and turn to Romans 8:5-14. Paul talks to us about how the sinful nature continues when we think about sinful things. And when your mind is controlled by the Holy Spirit, there is life and peace. So what do you have to do to experience peace and a new life? You have to fix your mind on God and remind yourself daily of God's laws and truths that give you freedom, and help you overcome your sinful desires.

God's promise...

When you focus on God's word and promises you'll be spirit led. The key though is to apply them to your life on a daily basis. Apply them to the choices and decisions you need to make by asking God for guidance and direction. It all starts with your mind and what you allow yourself to think and meditate on. You need to remember that you have no obligation whatsoever to do what your sinful nature urges you to do. But through the power of the Holy Spirit you can turn from it and its evil deeds and the result will be peace, success, and happiness.

It's hard to be spirit led when you're not allowing God to change your defects of character and the way you think. Think about it; are you trying to work out your own salvation? Do you need help specific help? If so, what kind of help do you need? Ask God for help today and watch the Holy Spirit work.

Ask yourself:

- God help me with...

- Father I keep struggling with...

- I'm having a problem applying the following truths to my life...

Take action...

1. Look up the following passages and paraphrase each one.
   ☐Acts 13:2; Acts 15:28; 2 Cor. 3:18 See also Rom. 15:16; 2
   Thess. 2:13; 1 Peter 1:2; 2 Cor. 3:17 See also Rom. 8:2,5-9;
   Rom. 8:10-11

Reflection

1. After reading today's devotion, I realize...
2. The key statements I need to remember and work on are...
3. The positive consequences of remembering and working on these statements will be...

DAY 228

A LETTER FROM THE HOLY SPIRIT

But the Helper, the Holy Spirit, whom the Father will send in my name, he will teach you all things and bring to your remembrance all that I have said to you.
(John 14:26)

RECEIVING THE HOLY SPIRIT'S GUIDANCE

Today you're going to read a letter sharing with you how the Holy Spirit guides you and directs your steps. *Note: This letter is written from my interpretation of scripture.*

Dear _____

Put your name here

I'm here to teach you all things and help you remember what Christ has said. I will never leave you. If you will let me, I will search your heart and show you what you need to change. I will guide you into all truth. I know life can be scary - I just want you to know that I'm here and I will not leave you. I can give you the ability to do things you need to do and I will impart to you the gifts you need to do God's will. If you give me a chance I will help you live your life and fulfill God's plan and purpose for you.

God speaks to me and I relay the message to you. If you let me fill you I will control you. I can help you do things that are so against your personality and character, the things that you wouldn't normally do or think of doing. The things that God asks you to do that don't come naturally to you.

I will give you the words to say and the wisdom and insight you need to solve your problems. I remind you of God's love when you feel broken. I'll remind you of your victory when you feel like you've lost. I want to be part of your life each and every day, for this is why I'm here. Jesus told you that He will never leave you nor forsake you. This is why you have me. You were designed to overcome but because of sin you've lost the ability to do it on your own so that's why you need me... your helper.

If you want to change your life I'm here to help you. God has called me to help you live like a Christian. When you let me dwell inside your soul you will experience love, joy, peace, patience, kindness, goodness, faithfulness, gentleness and self-control. These behaviors and attitudes are a gauge for you to see if you're in God's will. The idea is to make sure that you have nailed your passions and the desires of your sinful nature to the cross and crucified them there.

Falling short....

I have ability to impart knowledge of God's truth to you and show you the areas of your life where you're falling short. My goal is to correct you and to keep you on track. Now the difference is, I **convict** you, not condemn you.

If you ever feel condemnation, guilt or shame for your sins, brokenness, and character defects, it's not me talking to you. It can be your own voice, the voice of others or Satan's voice. My goal is to train you in righteousness and to help you become a righteous person in all areas of your life; relationally, emotionally, physically, professionally and financially. God wants to be involved in every area of your life.

Sorting through old beliefs

Paul wrote in Romans 12:2 don't copy the behavior and customs of this world, but let God transform you into a new person by changing the way you think. And you will know what God wants you to do, and you will know how good and pleasing His will really is. I'm here to help you do this. I will help you identify the lies and false beliefs you may have. Before you came to Christ you developed a set of beliefs and values. My job is to help you sort through the beliefs and values that you have to make sure that they line up with God's word and truth.

Empowerment...

I equipped Jesus for a task of great spiritual importance. God wanted Jesus to be set apart so I was invited into the heart of Jesus and His ministry so I could meet Him in His preaching, healing and deliverance. I gave Him the strength to fulfill His great commission. I gave Christ the courage it took for Him to die on the cross. I'm here to do the same for you.

The only way to experience regeneration, reconciliation, redemption and transformation is to allow me to dwell within you. Humans can only reproduce human life but I give new life from heaven.

~ the Holy Spirit

Take action...
    1. Look up the following passages and paraphrase each one.
        ☐Matt. 28:19; Eph. 4:4-6; John 13:16; Rom. 7:17
        ☐Rom. 8:26; John 14:17; Zech.4:6

Reflection

    1. After reading today's devotion, I realize...
    2. The key statements I need to remember and work on are...
    3. The positive consequences of remembering and working on these
       statements will be...

DAY 229

A LETTER FROM THE HOLY SPIRIT

And Peter said to them, "Repent and be baptized every one of you in the name of Jesus Christ for the forgiveness of your sins, and you will receive the gift of the Holy Spirit. (Acts 2:38)

CONFESSION

Today you're going to read a letter sharing with you the importance of confession, sanctification and healing. *Note: This letter is written from my interpretation of scripture.*

Dear_____

Put your name here

If you want to grow in Christ and experience freedom you need to practice confession. God needs to hear your pain and hurt. If you're broken, tell Him. Don't hide it anymore. He wants you to come out of darkness so you can experience His grace and truth. Remember, you're a child of light. Don't hide your feelings; don't repress them, let them out. Tell God exactly how you feel so that I can help you to feel better. I remind you of God's love and security. I remind you of how accepted you really are despite how you might be feeling.

Temptations...

If you're struggling with temptation and sin I will give you the strength to overcome but you need to confess it. I can't help until you do that. I will guide you in the way that you should go and it's your choice to repent. I will empower you and encourage you to take risks and to do things that God is calling you to do but you're just too afraid to do it. I will help you get out of the boat just like I did for Peter. I can help you walk on water but you have to keep your eyes on Jesus. I will stretch you to do things that you thought you could never do. For example, I helped Moses, Jeremiah, David and Job to overcome their fears and I empowered and equipped them to fulfill God's will.

Confession and truth...

David is a prime example of your need to practice confession. David couldn't live the life God designed him to live until he confessed his sins. I had to work within his conscience. His conscience was weighing him down. His conscience was bearing witness to my conviction and it allowed him to see and accept the sorrow he had deep within his heart because of his disobedience. David had to step out in faith. Your part is to have faith, and my responsibility is to give you the power to accomplish your goals and purpose. I make it possible for you to step out in faith and to perform.

~ the Holy Spirit

Take action...

1. Look up the following passages and paraphrase each one.

☐Gal. 5:22-23; Rom. 14:17; 2 Tim. 1:7; Psalm 32:8; Luke 12:12; Eze. 36:27; 1 Cor. 2:10, 11; Isaiah 40:13; Acts 15:28; Gen. 6:3; John 16:8-11; 2 Cor. 3:18; Psalm 104:30; Matt. 11:28-29; 2 Pet. 1:3-10

Reflection

1. After reading today's devotion, I realize…
2. The key statements I need to remember and work on are…
3. The positive consequences of remembering and working on these statements will be…

DAY 230

A LETTER FROM THE HOLY SPIRT

"I still have many things to say to you, but you cannot bear them now. When the Spirit of truth comes, he will guide you into all the truth, for he will not speak on his own authority, but whatever he hears he will speak, and he will declare to you the things that are to come. He will glorify me, for he will take what is mine and declare it to you. All that the Father has is mine; therefore I said that he will take what is mine and declare it to you. (John 16:12-15)

REPROGRAMMING, RENEWING & REBUILDING

Today you're going to read a letter reminding you of how the Holy Spirit helps in the renewing of your mind. *Note: This letter is written from my interpretation of scripture.*

Dear _____

Put your name here

When you received Christ, you received me. So what does that mean? It means I started to reprogram your mind. How do I do that? I start showing you your morals and the way you view yourself, God, people, places and things. I'll give you a better and deeper understanding of what is right and what is wrong (1 Corinthians 2:10-13). What's my method? The word of God so therefore the amount of time and commitment you have to getting to know God and His ways is extremely important. I use church, worship and prayer. I would like you to memorize verses so I can remind you of the truth when you need it for particular situations that you might be going through, or challenges that you might be facing.

Old man…

Just think back for a minute, do you remember all the things that you used to do (sins, bad habits and negative attitudes) before Christ and once you received Christ you found them to be repulsive? This is what I mean when I tell you that I will help you to reprogram your mind.

If you let me work within your conscience I will help you make wise choices, warn you against bad choices, help you evaluate situations or circumstances through God's eyes and not your own. I will prevent you from being judge and jury. I'm here for you to bounce off the choices and decisions you need to make each and every day. Let me repeat myself -- you need me for the rest of your life here on earth. Without me it's impossible to be successful and to perform as God has designed you to perform; just refer to Paul's struggle in Romans 7:14-25. He was trying to live a Christian life without me.

~ the Holy Spirit

Take action...

1. Look up the following passages and paraphrase each one.

　☐Rom. 8:4; Rom. 8:13; Eph. 5:18; John 15:26; Rom. 8:16;
　Gal. 4:6; Rom. 8:4,13; Gal. 5:16,25; John 14:16,26

Reflection

1. After reading today's devotion, I realize...
2. The key statements I need to remember and work on are...
3. The positive consequences of remembering and working on these statements will be...

DAY 231-232

MOTIVATION AND THE HOLY SPIRIT

"I still have many things to say to you, but you cannot bear them now. When the Spirit of truth comes, he will guide you into all the truth, for he will not speak on his own authority, but whatever he hears he will speak, and he will declare to you the things that are to come. He will glorify me, for he will take what is mine and declare it to you. All that the Father has is mine; therefore I said that he will take what is mine and declare it to you. (John 16:12-15)

Today you're going to read a letter explaining to you how the Holy Spirit empowers you to please God. *Note: This letter is written from my interpretation of scripture.*

Dear_____

     Put your name here

I'm the force within you that drives you to do something. The world defines this as motivation. I am the small still voice that pushes you to achieve important goals. I either nudge you in a certain direction or I encourage you to go a different direction. Sometimes I tell you to stop or to be still.

God created your subconscious mind. In your subconscious mind is where I encourage you and motivate you. I encourage you through your feelings. I use the emotion of pleasure to encourage you to move in the direction God is calling you. You're motivated by needs and wants. The more you get to know God, the more you understand what you need and want.

Awareness of God...

As you grow closer to God you will develop a better understanding of what your values are. God uses values to motivate you to serve him and to love others as well as yourself. As you allow me to help you renew your mind, you'll discover what is truly important. I will show you what your greatest abilities are, along with your greatest liabilities. If you want to set goals just ask God and He will let me know what they are and I will tell you.

Inspiration...

I will motivate you through ideas, wants, needs, feelings and conditions. I will help you take responsibility for your life situations. I will use motivation to help you take responsibility for yourself. If you get stuck it's probably because you're disconnected from God. If you ask Him why you're stuck He will tell me and I will show you. You just need to listen and be obedient. If you experience a setback remind yourself of your purpose. You will always have a plan and purpose until the day you die.

When you experience a setback I will help you to renew your motivation. I will bring back to your mind God's purpose for your life, in other words, your goals. The person you want to be. You're designed for excellence and for achievement. Sometimes you might set your goals too high and sometimes you might set them too low.

I was the voice talking to Jesus in the Garden of Gethsemane. I was reminding Him of His purpose and why His Father sent Him here. I talked to Him so He would have the confidence to work toward the goal and purpose God set out for Him.

                                                    ~ the Holy Spirit

Take action…

Look up the following passages and paraphrase each one.

> Rom. 8:4,13; Gal. 5:16,25; Acts 11:12; 16:6-7; 20:22-23;
> Rom. 8:14; Gal. 5:18; Eph. 1:16-17; 3:5; 2 Peter 1:21;
> 1 John 2:20, 27

Below is a checklist to help you to review your beliefs about the Holy Spirit. I can't stress enough the fact that without a personal relationship with the Holy Spirit sanctification and working out your salvation (inner healing) isn't possible.

HOLY SPIRIT

He will guide you into all truth. (John 13:16)

Instructions: Check off the statements that you can truly agree with. Complete the reflection questions after each section.

☐I believe that I need the Holy Spirit to live as a Christian

☐I need the Holy Spirit to strengthen me and guide me

☐I rely on the Holy Spirit to counsel me and to give me wisdom

☐I know His voice

☐I know when I feel convicted by the Holy Spirit

☐I understand His purpose and personality

☐I understand what it means to walk in the Spirit

☐The Holy Spirit is helping me work out my salvation

☐He guides me through God's Word

☐The Holy Spirit has given me strength in my body to do things I never thought I could

☐He reminds me of the truth when adversity and hardships occur

☐I feel His presence

☐I'm being sanctified by God's Spirit

☐I've been justified by God's Spirit

☐ Through my obedience to the word of God, I've been and continue to be sanctified by the Spirit (2 Thess. 2:13)

☐I yield my will to Him daily

☐I talk to the Holy Spirit daily

☐He reminds me of God's truth

☐He leads me to confess my pain and sins

☐He helps me to repent of my sins and bad habits

☐He helps me to feel, trust and share my life with others

☐He gives me discernment

☐I allow Him to correct me and change me

☐He's my counselor, psychologist and Life Coach

☐I believe He will never leave me

☐He comforts me when I'm in pain

☐He leads me to joy, peace and love

☐Without the Holy Spirit I can't love as God wants me to

Reflection

1. After reading today's checklist I realize…
2. The key statements I need to remember and work on are…
3. What can I do to change the areas I need to work on?
4. What kind of support and accountability do I need?

5. The positive consequences of remembering and working on these statements are…

Reflection

1. After reading today's devotion, I realize…
2. The key statements I need to remember and work on are…
3. The positive consequences of remembering and working on these statements will be…

HOW TO PUT AWAY

CHILDISH THINGS

ON

THE POTTER'S WHEEL

O LORD, you are our Father.
We are the clay, and you are the potter.
We all are formed by your hand. (Isaiah 64:8)

When I was a child, I spoke and thought and reasoned as a child. But when I
grew up, I put away childish things. (1 Cor. 13:11)

DAY 233-234
PUTTING AWAY CHILDISH THINGS

*The Spirit of the Sovereign LORD is on me, because the LORD has anointed me
to proclaim good news to the poor. He has sent me to bind up the
brokenhearted, to proclaim freedom for the captives
and release from darkness for the prisoners, to proclaim the year of the LORD's
favor and the day of vengeance of our God, to comfort all who mourn,
and provide for those who grieve in Zion— to bestow on them a crown of beauty
instead of ashes, the oil of joy, instead of mourning, and a garment of praise
instead of a spirit of despair. They will be called oaks of righteousness,
a planting of the LORD for the display of his splendor. (Isaiah 61:1-4)*

THE HEALING PROCESS

I think Isaiah 61:1-4 best describes what occurs on the potter's wheel, so today I
want you to focus on this passage and think about God's healing process and
what you need to do to receive God's healing.

Ask yourself:

1. What does healing mean to me?
2. Explain why I think healing is a choice. Why or why not?
3. What type of healing do I need? Write a letter to God.
5. Who's involved in my healing process?
6. What is within our power to be healed? What do I have influence over?

God's healing process includes the following principles and actions:

1. Telling the truth
2. Not hoping what is disturbing you will just go away
3. Accepting the fact that your brokenness will not get better on its own
4. Stop turning away from a hurtful situation that has occurred in the
   present or the past because it might disturb your happiness today
5. Realizing that your problems almost always get worse because they are
   allowed to become entrenched, and grow without opposition
6. Overcoming your fears about speaking candidly about your hurts
   because you fear being rejected
7. You stop concealing what you really feel or believe
8. You stop hiding your true feelings in order to overcome your loneliness
   and suffering.

God's principle of healing and getting over hurts so you can lead a productive, joyful, abundant life (Isaiah 61:1-4; Matt. 18:15-17; Lev. 19:17):

1. Respect yourself
2. Face the truth, even if it hurts.
3. Identify your feelings
4. Express them to the person who inspired them
5. Be prompt. Don't wait for ideal conditions
6. Be simple. Long explanations are not necessary
7. If the person hears you, you have succeeded
8. If he refuses to hear you, understand who you're dealing with
9. Be willing to accept the situation as it is
10. Let go of your hurts and forgive
11. Move on

Take action…

   1. Look up the following passages and paraphrase each one.
      ☐Phil. 2:12-13; 2 Peter 1:3-11; John 15:10; John 14:21

Reflection

   1. After reading today's devotion, I realize…
   2. The key statements I need to remember and work on are…
   3. The positive consequences of remembering and working on these
      statements will be…

DAY 235-236

PUTTING AWAY CHILDISH THINGS

Do not be afraid; you will not be put to shame.
Do not fear disgrace; you will not be humiliated.
You will forget the shame of your youth. (Isaiah 54:4)

"When the solution is simple, God is answering."
~ Albert Einstein

WORKING THROUGH YOUR BROKENNESS

Healing your brokenness is a process and it takes time. The key is to stay on the potter's wheel long enough to heal. Often times we get off the wheel and get stuck in the sanctification process. In my experience, God will not let His children progress in their salvation until they work through issues He's calling them to deal with.

Take some time today and read through the strategies and principles God uses to reshape your soul. See which ones you're currently doing. Find ways to apply and practice the principles that you're not currently applying to your brokenness.

1. **Admit your pain:** In order to change, it's important to admit and accept that you're hurt. You can't change or grow when you're feeling down and ashamed. I remind myself of a Chinese proverb I once read, "A diamond with a flaw is worth more than a pebble without imperfections."

2. **Be humble and prayerful**: Start to pray as soon as you notice you're feeling down, anxious, disappointed, worried, depressed or hurt. Pray for wisdom, help, support, direction, strength and courage. Jesus will not let you down. Read God's word. Especially the red letters (Jesus's words).

3. **Lean on your support:** It's important to reach out to people you trust. Share what's going on in your life. Don't be a Lone Ranger or a porcupine. Be open to any advice and feedback they might give you and try to apply it to your life. Think about where you would be if you had (or had not) followed advice that was given to you five years ago.

4. **Values**: Lean on what you value and believe in. Use your values as a roadmap for your life. I personally rely on God's word to help me go through my tough times.

5. **Be optimistic:** Learn to see your troubles and adversities as an opportunity to grow closer to God and others. I like what Anne Bradstreet said, "If we had no winter, the spring would not be so pleasant, if we didn't sometimes taste adversity, prosperity would not be so welcome."

6. **Spirituality:** "Keep the faith." I personally believe and accept that, because God loves us, He's going to create times and opportunities for us to grow in character and personality. John Neal once said, "A certain amount of opposition is of great help to a man. Kites rise against, not with the wind." Like the old English proverb says, "A smooth sea never made a skilled mariner."

7. **Nobody's perfect:** St. Augustine said, "This is the very perfection of man, to find out his own imperfections." It is so important to accept your defects of character. Don't beat yourself up for mistakes or standards you can't meet. What kind of perfectionist are you? Do you struggle to live up to the high standards of others and appear to be at risk of self-critical depression? Do you outwardly expect perfection from others and as a result have failed relationships? Are you a people pleaser? Do you try to live up to the ideals of others?
   a. Reassess your expectations and standards.
   b. Be the best you can be but don't fall apart when you don't achieve the goal. I like what Mickey Rooney said, "You always pass failure on the way to success."

  c.Live by your own set of standards. Failure doesn't mean you should punish yourself. If you fail, it has nothing to do with who you are as a person. You're still lovable and special. You're a miracle. When you fail, get up and start again. I love Sylvester Stallone's line in Rocky Balboa. "Life's not about getting hit, it's about getting back up."

  d.If you're comparing yourself or your life to others, I suggest you stop. This only adds to the pain you're already feeling. Take a look at what they have and make a plan to achieve it yourself.

8. **You're Human**. Remind yourself that you're human every chance you get. Read this awesome list of '**Ten Rules for Being Human' written by Cherie Carter-Scott** as often as you need to. Think about what you need to improve on and the results you will experience if you do so.

10 Rules for Being Human

1. You will receive a body. You may like it or hate it, but it's yours to keep for the entire period.

2. You will learn lessons. You are enrolled in a full-time informal school called, "life."

3. There are no mistakes, only lessons. Growth is a process of trial, error, and experimentation. The "failed" experiments are as much a part of the process as the experiments that ultimately "work."

4. Lessons are repeated until they are learned. A lesson will be presented to you in various forms until you have learned it. When you have learned it, you can go on to the next lesson.

5. Learning lessons does not end. There's no part of life that doesn't contain its lessons. If you're alive, that means there are still lessons to be learned.

6. "There" is no better a place than "here." When your "there" has become a "here", you will simply obtain another "there" that will again look better than "here."

7. Other people are merely mirrors of you. You cannot love or hate something about another person unless it reflects to you something you love or hate about yourself.

8. What you make of your life is up to you. You have all the tools and resources you need. What you do with them is up to you. The choice is yours.

9. Your answers lie within you. The answers to life's questions lie within you. All you need to do is look, listen, and trust.

10. You will forget all this.

Take action…

1. Look up the following passages and paraphrase each one.

☐ John 1:12; Matt.18:3; John 14:21; 1 Cor. 3:16; Luke 11:13; Luke 10:19 Rom. 5:5; 1 Cor. 6:17; Luke 10:19; Col. 2:13-15; Matt. 16:24-25; Col.1:10-11; Prov. 24:10; 1 John 4:4, 1 Cor. 10:13

Reflection

1. After reading today's devotion, I realize…
2. The key statements I need to remember and work on are…
3. The positive consequences of remembering and working on these statements will be…

REVIEW & REPAIR

Reshaping Your Soul

1. What did I learn this past month about myself, God and others?

2. What concepts or ideas stood out to me in the devotions? Why?

3. What adjustments do I need to make in my life?

4. What needs to change, if anything, about how I think, feel and act?

5. What changes have I made so far? What actions have I taken?

6. How are people reacting to my changes?

7. Steps I will continue to take are…

8. I'm committed to…

9. My victories this week were…

10. God please help me with…

DAY 237-241

PUTTING AWAY CHILDISH THINGS

Then Jesus said to him, "Get up! Pick up your mat and walk." (John 5:8)

PICK UP YOUR MAT

Living in the past...

God doesn't want you to waste time living in the past, hating your past or wishing you had a different life. Don't stay paralyzed by your bad choices, circumstances and excuses. You have a bright future and a new life to live.

- What's preventing me from picking up my mat? Do I waste time living in the past? If so, what can I do to change it?
- List attitudes and beliefs that prevent you from asking God for help.

Responsibility...

When it comes to taking responsibility for your issues and problems, God will show you what to take responsibility for.

Consider this...

- Change will occur when you see the need. When you accept the reasons why you need to change, your excuses stop making sense to you.
- Like the man by the pool in Bethesda, you can't wait for a miracle to save you. You need to collaborate with God and eliminate the excuses that keep you stuck and broken. (John 5:8)
- List excuses that you use that prevent you from healing and living a new life.

Spiritual and emotional growth...

Growth will occur when you understand and confess the need to change.
- List what needs to change in my life and the reasons why it needs to change
- Seeing the truth about your life and taking responsibility for it is the key to spiritual and emotional healing. It's God's prescription for Christlikeness.
    1. What would my life look like if I took responsibility for the areas of my life that I listed above?

Now I want you to read through the checklist below so you can see if you're ready for change and healing.

SIGNS OF WANTING TO GET WELL

Then Jesus said to him, "Get up! Pick up your mat and walk." At once the man was cured; he picked up his mat and walked. (John 5:8-9)

Instructions: Check off the statements that you can truly agree with. Complete the reflection questions.

☐I believe that, apart from God, I can do nothing.

☐I believe I need to meet God halfway so I can grow and heal

☐Faith without works is dead

☐I believe I need to reconcile with God

☐I need to confess my sins, faults, hurts, hang-ups, and bad habits

☐I need to give myself healing time

☐It's okay if I make mistakes while I'm learning new things about God and life

☐My sanctification doesn't have to be perfect

☐I realize that I am who I am because of the DNA from my family, the circumstances I experienced and the choices I made. So I need to put forth and effort to change

☐I need to eliminate my excuses

☐Letting go of certain defects, sins, and bad habits scares me

☐I don't fear what I need

☐Taking ownership of my soul is important to me

☐I try to learn something new everyday

☐I ask God to show me the areas I need to grow in my life

☐I try to keep my heart open and vulnerable with God and others

☐I read books to help me keep growing

☐I take risks in the areas I need to grow in

☐I'm open to feedback from people I trust and whom God puts in my path

☐I try to be interdependent- trusting God and others, and the Spirit in me

☐I don't fear failure or rejection. I know who I belong to

☐I want to get well

☐I want to be Christ-like

☐I set goals and make plans for my life

☐I know my weaknesses and shortcomings

☐God is the power greater than myself

☐I ask God to remove my shortcomings

☐I know why I rebel against God's commands and ways

☐I get angry with God but I talk to Him about it

☐Surrender is key for me

☐I know God's voice

☐My defenses are down

☐I know and use the gifts, talents and abilities God has given me

☐I know what drives me

☐I know my passions

☐I know I'm a work in progress

☐I don't compare my sanctification to that of others

☐I fellowship with other believers

☐I believe God honors His promises

☐I practice spiritual disciplines: confession, repentance, prayer, worship, fellowship, serving and studying God's word

☐I line my beliefs and values up with God's Word

☐I strive for spiritual gains

☐I walk what I talk

☐I'm patient with God

☐I attend Bible studies, conferences, trainings, groups, workshops and seminars that will increase my knowledge of God, others and myself

☐I seek first the Kingdom

☐I follow Jesus' two greatest commands: Love God with all my heart, soul, mind and strength, and love others as I love myself

Take action...

1. Look up the following passages and paraphrase each one.

☐   Phil. 2:13; 2 Peter 1:3; John 1:16; John 4:14; John 15:2,5; 1 Cor. 10:13; Phil. 2:12; 2 Peter 1:5-9; Rom. 6:19; 2 Cor. 7:1; Gal. 5:16,25; Eph. 5:25-27; Phil. 1:6; Jude 24-25; Rev. 21:2

Reflection

1. After reading today's checklist I realize...
2. The key statements I need to remember and work on are...
3. What can I do to change the areas I need to work on?
4. What kind of support and accountability do I need?
5. The positive consequences of remembering and working on these statements are...

DAY 242-252

PUTTING AWAY CHILDISH THINGS

Remember not the former things,
nor consider the things of old. (Isaiah 43:18)

EXPLORE YOUR PAST

Based on my experience, it's only a matter of time before God wants you to
explore your past. Why, you might say? I believe based on my personal
experience that He wants you to develop your testimony, or the story of your life.

I've heard many testimonies and they always seem to include what their life was
like before they received Christ. A lot of the testimonies address childhood,
adolescence and adulthood in some cases adult life. I believe that part of the
sanctification process is to allow God to explore how you got where you are and
why you think and behave like you do.

I believe God wants you to know the truth so you can break free from any guilt,
shame or condemnation. Remember, in our formative years our self-image is
developed based on our interactions with our families and our experiences as
well as perceptions. For the next 10 days I want you to ask the Holy Spirit to
help you put together a timeline of your life so you can have a better
understanding of yourself, defining moments and critical people in your life.
This exercise will help you gain a better understanding of who you are and how
you got that way. **Please take your time. It's so important to complete if you
want to get the most out of this book. Record your answers in your journal.**

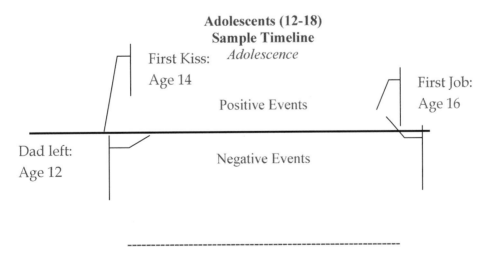

Adolescents (12-18)
Sample Timeline
Adolescence

First Kiss:
Age 14

Positive Events

First Job:
Age 16

Dad left:
Age 12

Negative Events

Childhood (3-12)

Ask yourself:

1. What was my childhood like?
2. Happy times in my childhood:
3. Saddest times in my childhood:
4. Achievements in childhood:
5. Failures in childhood:
6. Hurts in childhood:
7. Broken trust:
8. Losses:
9. Let downs and disappointments:
10. Bad memories:
11. Abuse:
12. Bad choices:
13. Emotions commonly felt:
14. Family life:
15. Spiritual Life:
16. Positive events:
17. Negative events:
18. People in my life:
19. Emotions commonly felt:

Adolescence (12-18)

Ask yourself:
1. What were my adolescent years like?
2. Happy times in my adolescence:
3. Saddest times in my adolescence:
4. Achievements in adolescence:
5. Failures in adolescence:
6. Hurts in adolescence:
7. Losses:
8. Broken trust:
9. Let downs and disappointments:
10. Bad memories:
11. Abuse:
12. Family life:
13. People in my life:
14. Spiritual Life:
15. Positive events:
16. Negative events:
17. People in my life:
18. Emotions commonly felt:

Young adulthood (18-35)

Ask yourself:

1. What were my young adulthood years like?
2. Happy times in my young adulthood:
3. Saddest times in my young adulthood:
4. Achievements in young adulthood:
5. Failures in young adulthood:
6. Hurts in young adulthood:
7. Broken trust:
8. Regrets:
9. Let downs and disappointments:
10. Bad memories:
11. Abuse:
12. Losses:
13. Family life:
14. Spiritual life:
15. Positive events:
16. Negative events:
17. People in my life:
18. Emotions commonly felt:

Middle Adulthood (35 to 65)

1. What was my middle adulthood like?
2. Happy times in my middle adulthood:
3. Saddest times in my middle adulthood:
4. Achievements in middle adulthood:
5. Failures in middle adulthood:
6. Hurts in middle adulthood:
7. Broken trust:
8. Regrets:
9. Let downs and disappointments:
10. Bad memories:
11. Losses:
12. Abuse:
13. Family life:
14. Spiritual Life:
15. Positive events:
16. Negative events:
17. People in my life:
18. Emotions commonly felt:

Late Adulthood (55 or 65 to Death)

1. What was my late adulthood like?
2. Happy times in my late adulthood:
3. Saddest times in my late adulthood:
4. Achievements in late adulthood:
5. Failures in late adulthood:
6. Hurts in late adulthood:
7. Broken trust:
8. Regrets:
9. Let downs and disappointments:
10. Bad memories:
11. Losses:
12. Abuse:
13. Family life:
14. Spiritual Life:
15. Positive events:
16. Negative events:
17. People in my life:
18. Emotions commonly felt:

Keep in mind:

1. Jesus came so you can live in the light not the darkness.
2. To break free from the past you need to know your past.
3. You're not a victim of your past but you will be if you don't expose it and get real about it. You need to explore the lies that you believe, in order to change.
4. As a Christian you now have the power to break free from the strongholds in your mind.

Take Action...

1. Look up the following passages and paraphrase each one.
Matt. 6:14-15; Col. 3:13; James 1:21; Phil. 4:8; Psalm 23:1-6; Eph. 5:14-16; Heb. 7:22-25; Matt. 16:24-25; Col.1:10-11; Prov. 24:10; 1 John 3:8

Reflection

1. After reading what I wrote, I realize...
2. The key statements, situations, memories, emotions, and loses I need explore and work on are...
3. The positive consequences of remembering and working on these statements are...

DAY 253-263

PUTTING AWAY CHILDISH THINGS

Nevertheless, I tell you the truth: it is to your advantage that I go away, for if I do not go away, the Helper will not come to you. But if I go, I will send him to you. And when he comes, he will convict the world concerning sin and righteousness and judgment: concerning sin, because they do not believe in me; concerning righteousness, because I go to the Father, and you will see me no longer; concerning judgment, because the ruler of this world is judged. I still have many things to say to you, but you cannot bear them now. **When the Spirit of truth comes, he will guide you into all the truth, for he will not speak on his own authority, but whatever he hears he will speak, and he will declare to you the things that are to come.** *He will glorify me, for he will take what is mine and declare it to you. All that the Father has is mine; therefore I said that he will take what is mine and declare it to you. (John 16:7-15)*

GET REAL ABOUT YOUR LIFE

Life Coach…

The Holy Spirit is your life coach, your strategist and your counselor. He was given to you to help you get real about your life. Getting real means:

1. Taking an honest inventory of your life to explore why you are the way you are.

The Holy Spirit was given to you to help you take an honest look at your life, character and personality. He will help you see the areas of your life that need healing and freedom. He will show you where you're broken. He is here to walk you through your recovery and sanctification process.

When I received Christ I realized after a while that I had some work to do. Once I started to understand my new identity in Christ and what I had inherited, God started to reshape my soul. It was as if He was telling me, "It's time to get real." As I dug deeper I realized that I was trapped and shackled by certain emotions. I didn't know why until I started to look at my childhood and how I was raised. At first I thought that I didn't have to deal with that because I was a new creation, but I was wrong. Jesus wanted to show me why and how I became the person I was, and why He died for me, and He wants to do the same for you.

God has shown me that we are all, in one way or another, affected by our families and the way we were raised.

Keep in mind:

1. As children, we learn important skills like communication (how to communicate our feelings, needs, wants, likes, dislikes and personality), and trust within the family dynamic. It's all too common that most families fail at providing and teaching these essential life skills to their children. This creates generational curses and dysfunctional patterns of relating to others which often carry over into adulthood.
2. If you weren't taught these skills there's a good chance that you will end up repressing or suppressing your emotions, be aggressive or passive instead of being assertive, and grow up having issues of trust with God, with others and, in some cases, being unable to trust even yourself.

For the next 10 days, or for however long it takes, I want you to work on the following questions. Be sure to ask the Holy Spirit to guide you and to reveal things you need to know and let go of.

Ask yourself:

1. What, if anything, is hurting me, upsetting me or frustrating me on a continuous basis?
2. Things I like about my mother and father are:
3. Things I disliked about my father and mother:
4. I learned the following things about communication from my mother and father:
5. I wish my mother and father would have:
6. Growing up, I think I needed more of:
7. I learned the following things about trust from my mother and father:
8. I learned the following things about trust from my family:
9. I love my mother and father because:
10. My mother and father taught me the following values:
11. My mother and father believed in:
12. Things my mother and father never taught me are:
13. I resent my mother and father because:
14. I'm a lot like my father in the following ways:
15. I'm a lot like my mother in the following ways:
16. Beliefs I need to change are (refer back to New Life/ New Design):
17. My mother and father viewed God in the following ways:
18. I learned the following things about relationships from my mother and father:
19. Mom why did you:
20. Dad why did you:
21. Mom and Dad, thank you for:
22. Things I wish I hadn't seen or experienced:
23. My relationship with my siblings:

Healing exercise:

- Based on your answers write a letter to your Mom and Dad or caretakers but don't send it. See if there's anything you might need to let go of. Share it with a friend, mentor, sponsor, or counselor. The goal is to ask Jesus to set you free from your past hurts, habits, and hang-ups.

Take action…

1. Look up the following passages and paraphrase each one.
   - ☐Luke 9:23-24; Rom. 6:11; Eph. 4:22-24; Heb. 5:14-15; James 1:17; Col. 1:10-11; Col. 1:27; Matt. 4:4; Jer. 2:13; John 15:8-12; James 1:22-25; Rom. 12:10-11; Gal. 6:1; Rom. 5:3-5; James 1:19-20; Col. 3:13

Reflection

1. After reading today's devotion, I realize…
2. The key statements I need to remember and work on are…
3. The positive consequences of remembering and working on these statements are…

DAY 264-266

PUTTING AWAY CHILDISH THINGS

Blessed are the peacemakers, for they shall be called sons of God. (Matt. 5:9)

"There is no detachment where there is no pain. And there is no pain endured without hatred or lying unless detachment is present too."

~ *Simone Weil*

MAKING PEACE WITH YOUR PAST

Growing up is hard when you have parents who didn't grow up themselves. Some parents have unresolved childhood issues that never received attention and they come out when they have their own children. As we get older we realize how emotionally immature our parents really are.

Part of overcoming our childhood wounds and making peace with our parents is taking the time to identify and understand their hurts, habits and hang-ups, and not trying to fix them or deny them. Remember, our parents fall short too. (Rom. 3:23) Our parents were our role models so there's a good chance that some of their immaturities and sins rubbed off on us.

Here's a list of hurts, habits and hang-ups. Read through them and check off what you identify with. Circle if it was your mom or dad.

My parents…

- ☐Lack assertiveness – Mom or Dad
- ☐Repress their emotions - Mom or Dad
- ☐Are/were dishonest - Mom or Dad
- ☐Are/were passive aggressive - Mom or Dad
- ☐Abused me - Mom or Dad
- ☐Deny/denied their weaknesses– Mom or Dad
- ☐Lack social skills– Mom or Dad
- ☐Lack boundaries and share their problems with anyone and everyone – Mom or Dad
- ☐Were more of a friend to me than a parent– Mom or Dad
- ☐Don't listen– Mom or Dad
- ☐Don't take care of themselves– Mom or Dad
- ☐Have a victim mentality– Mom or Dad
- ☐Vented their problems to me when I was a child– Mom or Dad
- ☐Shared their hurt and sadness with me when I was a child– Mom or Dad
- ☐Lack of friends– Mom or Dad
- ☐Lack of support– Mom or Dad
- ☐Try to make me feel sorry for them– Mom or Dad
- ☐Are reactive not proactive– Mom or Dad
- ☐Seem hopeless and helpless– Mom or Dad
- ☐Refuse to act like an adult– Mom or Dad
- ☐Pretend they have it together – Mom or Dad
- ☐Let others use them– Mom or Dad
- ☐Are rude– Mom or Dad
- ☐Impatient– Mom or Dad

☐Don't admit they need help– Mom or Dad

☐Don't trust– Mom or Dad

☐Don't talk– Mom or Dad

☐Suffer from addictions and/or mental health issues– Mom or Dad

☐Lack spirituality– Mom or Dad

☐Pushing/pushed religion on me– Mom or Dad

Take action…

1. Look up the following passages and paraphrase each one.

☐Psalm 107:20; Acts 17:28; Gal. 2:20; Col. 1:10-11; Col. 1:27

☐Col. 3:5-15; 2 Tim. 2:19-26; Col. 2:11-13; Phil. 2:12-18

☐Matt. 5:4

Reflection

1. After reading today's devotion, I realize…
2. The key statements I need to remember and work on are…
3. The positive consequences of remembering and working on these statements are…

DAY 267- 270

PUTTING AWAY CHILDISH THINGS

I tell you the truth, anyone who doesn't receive the Kingdom of God like a child will never enter it." Then he took the children in his arms and placed his hands on their heads and blessed them. (Mark 10:15-16)

"Home is not where you live, but where they understand you"
~ Christian Morganstern

ABBA FATHER

I'm not sure what kind of home you were raised in but, believe it or not, it matters. Our family can leave a mark on our souls and spirits. If mom and dad do their job as a parent, the child has a good chance at becoming a productive adult. If mom and dad, or just mom or just dad, neglects their responsibilities the child can grow up and become a menace to society, homeless, addicted to drugs or alcohol, a workaholic, performance based, abusive or mentally ill.

How do we know if mom and dad did a good job? How do we know if we need re-parenting? What are the signs? Here is a checklist to look at to see if you need to work on your inner child or adult child-like behaviors. Part of working out your salvation is allowing God to re-parent you. (Galatians 4:6)

You might need re-parenting if you…

☐Struggle with self-esteem or self-confidence

☐Feel unworthy

☐Struggle with guilt and shame

☐Grew up in a home where one of your parents showed favoritism to your siblings

☐Judge yourself without mercy

☐Withhold your emotions

☐Struggle letting go of the past

☐Lack tolerance of your faults and flaws

☐Feel guilt for making mistakes and/or failing

☐Lack self-forgiveness

☐Are resentful and bitter

☐Have few or no friends

☐Fear rejection and disapproval

☐Lack the ability to affirm yourself

☐Are an approval seeker, a people pleaser

☐Avoid conflicts

☐Try to get people to care for you in ways that fill voids of the past

☐Lack the ability to affirm yourself, be your own cheerleader so to speak

☐Lack purpose or direction

☐Find yourself feeling hostility and bitter much of the time

☐Are holding grudges against people in your past

☐Lack self-control and the ability to set limits

☐Impulsive

☐Have trouble with receiving feedback or criticism

☐Struggle with depression, addictions, anger issues or anxiety issues

☐Find yourself continuously getting involved in unhealthy relationships

☐Fear being abandoned

☐Are a perfectionist and never feel good enough

☐Lacked a parental role model
☐Were abused physically, emotionally, verbally, spiritually or sexually
☐Were neglected

Well, how did you do? Does it look like you need to be re-parented and overcome some childlike behaviors? Often times if people are raised in a dysfunctional family they withdraw or isolate from people. Dealing with people in authority becomes a challenge. Some individuals become people pleasers because they're trying to hide, or protect themselves from getting hurt again.

Alison Stormwolf said, "All healing starts in the mind." I want to encourage you to stay committed to this healing process as you are learning how to identify unresolved issues developed from your family of origin. A key to inner healing is recognizing your family patterns as they occur in your present relationships.

Do you have things left unsaid inside of you?" If so, learn how to identify your feeling and express them. Stop denying your feelings. God wants you to "speak the truth in love." If your parents taught you to be emotionally dishonest, stop.

Affects from living in dysfunctional families...

People raised with family dysfunction report a variety of long-term effects. The following questions may help you assess your own situation. Answering "Yes" to these may indicate some effects from family dysfunction. Most people could likely identify with some of them. If you find yourself answering "Yes" to over half of them, you likely have some long-term effects of living in a dysfunctional family. (Source: Toxic Families- Susan Forward)

1. Do you find yourself needing approval from others to feel good about yourself? Yes_____ No_____
2. Do you agree to do more for others than you can comfortably accomplish? Yes_____ No_____
3. Are you perfectionistic? Yes_____ No_____
4. Do you tend to avoid or ignore responsibilities? Yes_____ No_____
5. Do you find it difficult to identify what you're feeling? Yes_____ No_____
6. Do you find it difficult to express feelings? Yes_____ No_____
7. Do you tend to think in all-or-nothing terms? Yes_____ No_____
8. Do you often feel lonely even in the presence of others? Yes_____ No_____
9. Is it difficult for you to ask for what you need from others? Yes_____ No_____
10. Is it difficult for you to maintain intimate relationships? Yes_____ No_____
11. Do you find it difficult to trust others? Yes_____ No_____

12. Do you tend to hang on to hurtful or destructive relationships?
    Yes_____ No_____
13. Are you more aware of others' needs and feelings than your own?
    Yes_____ No_____
14. Do you find it particularly difficult to deal with anger or criticism?
    Yes_____ No_____
15. Is it hard for you to relax and enjoy yourself? Yes_____ No_____
16. Do you find yourself feeling like a "fake" in your academic or
    professional life? Yes_____ No_____
17. Do you find yourself waiting for disaster to strike even when things
    are going well in your life?
    Yes_____ No_____
18. Do you find yourself having difficulty with authority figures?
    Yes_____ No_____

Take action…

1. Look up the following passages and paraphrase each one.

    ☐Mark 14:36; Rom. 8:15; Matt. 1:23; Ecc. 12:13-14; 1 Peter 1:17 1
    John 4:11,19; Heb. 12:5-10; Phil. 2:12-13; John 17:23-24;
    John 20:17; Rom. 15:7

Process your Responses

1. Review your yes responses.
   a. What do you think?
   b. How do they make you feel?
   c. What can you do to improve these areas?
   d. What might prevent you?
   e. How will your life and relationships improve if you work on
      improving these areas?

Reflection

1. After reading today's devotion, I realize…
2. The key statements I need to remember and work on are…
3. The positive consequences of remembering and working on these
   statements will be…

REVIEW & REPAIR

Reshaping Your Soul

1. What did I learn this past month about myself, God and others?

2. What concepts or ideas stood out to me in the devotions? Why?

3. What adjustments do I need to make in my life?

4. What needs to change, if anything, about how I think, feel and act?

5. What changes have I made so far? What actions have I taken?

6. How are people reacting to my changes?

7. Steps I will continue to take are…

8. I'm committed to…

9. My victories this week were…

10. God please help me with…

DAY 271

PUTTING AWAY CHILDISH THINGS

*Yet, O LORD, you are **our Father**. We are the clay, you are the potter; we are all the work of your hand." (Isaiah 64:8 NIV)*

FAMILY RULES

Today I want you to look at the family rules you might have come to Christ with. Now that you have been made new and are alive in Christ you need to start letting go of those customs and traditions you were raised in. (Romans 12:1-2) Let's take a look at a list of unhealthy rules to live by because they will prevent you from working out your salvation and finishing strong. Read through the list and check off what applies to you currently.

George A. Boyd, a family expert, believes that dysfunctional families operate under the following rules and ideals:

- ☐ Don't talk about problems
- ☐ Don't express feelings openly or honestly
- ☐ Communicate indirectly, through acting out or sulking, or via another family member
- ☐ Have unrealistic expectations about what the Dependent will do for you
- ☐ Don't be selfish, think of the other person first
- ☐ Don't take your parents as an example, "do as I say, not as I do"
- ☐ Don't have fun
- ☐ Don't rock the boat, keep the status quo
- ☐ Don't talk about sex
- ☐ Don't challenge your parent's religious beliefs or these family rules

Keep in mind...

1. It's important to know that healthy relationships and families are created by talking about feelings and life experiences. Honesty creates intimacy with God and others. The key here is to make sure you have a healthy view of God.

2. Love and connection is built on healthy, honest communication and problem solving together. God is Abba Father and He wants you to learn how to communicate with boldness, confidence and assertiveness. Satan knows that if we deceive ourselves and others we will sabotage our life and relationships. God, on the other hand, wants His children to speak the truth in love.

3. God wants you to talk to Him because He wants to validate you and give you the attention you need. His attention is unconditional and He wants you to talk with Him no matter what's going on in your life. He will talk to you in good times and He will talk with you in bad times. He always wants to be part of your life.

Take Action...

1. Look up the following passages and paraphrase each one.

☐Heb. 4:16; Eph. 4:25-26, 29-32; Psalm 116:1-5; 1 Cor. 13:6-7;
Prov. 18:15; Matt. 9:36; Psalm 38:9; John 3:10; John 4:2;
Luke 15:7,10; 2 Cor. 1:3; Psalm 145:8-9

Reflection

1. After reading today's devotion, I realize…
2. The key statements I need to remember and work on are…
3. The positive consequences of remembering and working on these statements will be…

DAY 272-274

PUTTING AWAY CHILDISH THINGS

For the word of God is living and active, sharper than any two-edged sword, piercing to the division of soul and of spirit, of joints and of marrow, and discerning the thoughts and intentions of the heart. (Heb. 4:12)

FAMILY RULES Part 2

What happens to a person if they were raised under these family rules? How do they affect us mentally and relationally?

Today I want you to read through the checklist below so you can identify possible reason why you might be stuck in the sanctification process.

Dr. Kizziar believes that people who are raised under these rules have…

☐ Difficulty in accurately identifying and expressing feelings
☐ Problems in forming and maintaining close, intimate relationships
☐ Higher than normal prevalence of marrying a person from another dysfunctional family, or a person with active alcoholism or addiction
☐ Perfectionism, having unrealistic expectations of self and others, and being too hard on oneself
☐ Rigidity in behavior and attitudes, having an unwillingness to change
☐ Having a resistance to adapting to change, and fearful of taking risks
☐ Feeling over-identified or responsible for others' feelings or behavior
☐ Having a constant need for approval or attention from others to feel good about themselves

☐Awkwardness in making decisions, feel terrified of making mistakes, and may defer decision-making to others

☐Feeling powerless and ineffective, like whatever they do does not make a difference

☐Exaggerated feelings of shame and worthlessness, and low self-esteem

☐Avoiding conflict at any price, and will often repress their own feelings and opinions to keep the peace

☐Apprehension over abandonment by others

☐Acting belligerently and aggressively to keep others at a distance

☐Tendencies to be impatient and over-controlling

☐A hard time taking care of themselves because of their absorption in the needs and concerns of other people, and acting like martyrs, living for others instead of for oneself

☐Dread expressing own anger, and will do anything to avoid provoking another person. The particular expression of these traits by each individual is often a function of the type of family in which a child grows up.

Ask yourself…

Today I want you to …

1. Read the list and identify what applies to you.
2. Pick each statement you identify with and write as much as you can about it. Let it all out. If you have to, take your time to reflect and think. Ask for help if you need to.

Identify the area of your life that this affects you most. Then I want you set some goals to overcome your issues.

1. Area of my life…
2. My goal is….
3. Actions I need to take are…
4. Possible obstacles are…
5. I will overcome these obstacles by …
6. My life will improve in the following ways if I make the following changes…
7. If I don't make these changes my life will…

Take action…

1. Look up the following passages and paraphrase each one.

☐Isaiah 43:18-19; 1 Cor. 12:14-18,20-26; Psalm 55:1-8;
Eph. 4:31-32; Gal. 6:14; Phil. 4:8; Psalm 23:1-6; Psalm 23:3;
Isaiah 49:13; Neh. 9:17; Psalm 119:77; Psalm 34:18

Reflection

1. After reading today's devotion, I realize…
2. The key statements I need to remember and work on are…
3. The positive consequences of remembering and working on these
    statements will be…

DAY 275-279

PUTTING AWAY CHILDISH THINGS

'Man shall not live by bread alone, but by every word that
proceeds from the mouth of God.' (Matt. 4:4)

There are two great rules of life; the one general and the other particular. The first is that everyone can, in the end, get what he wants, if he only tries. That is the general rule. The particular rule is that every individual is, more or less, an exception to the rule. ~Samuel Butler

SURVIVE OR THRIVE

I think God wants us to do more than survive. I think He wants us to thrive. I think the only way we can thrive is if we stay on God's potter wheel no matter what. (Isaiah 64:8)

If we are going to more than survive we need change how we think, how we feel, and how we act. We need to take a look at our attitudes, beliefs, and values. We need to look at each area of our life and see what's working and what's not.

Like any other game, life has a set of rules. No matter what area of your life, you have a set of rules and standards to live by. Sometimes we don't even realize the self-imposed rules we place on ourselves, or we live by other people's rules (parents, partner, co-worker) that just aren't working.

In order to thrive you need to take a look at the rules you're currently living by and to see if they line up with God's truth and way of life.

Ask yourself...

Complete the sentences at least 6 times.

What rules do you have for...?

☐**Being Happy**: I can be happy if...
☐**Having peace**: I can have peace if...
☐**Becoming successful**: I'm successful if I...
☐**Having fun:** I can have fun when...
☐**Enjoying life**: I can enjoy life when...
☐**Trusting others**: I can trust you if...
☐**Being vulnerable**: I'll be vulnerable if...
☐**Relationships:** I will have a relationship with you if...
☐**Connecting to others**: If I'm going to connect with others...
☐**Asking for Help**: I'll ask for help when...

Are your rules setting you up for God's peace, success, joy and love?"

Take Action...

   1. Look up the following passages and paraphrase each one.
    ☐ 1 Peter 1:13-14; Rom. 12:3; 1 Cor. 1:26; 1 Cor. 3:18;
       1 Cor. 10:12; 1 Cor. 14:20,37; 2 Cor. 11:5-6; Gal. 6:3; Phil. 2:3;
       1 Tim. 4:4; Deut. 6:6; Eze. 11:19; Rom. 12:2; 2 Cor. 4:6;
       Eph. 4:23; Phil. 4:8-9; Heb. 8:10; Jer. 31:33; Deut. 6:6-7;
       Deut. 11:18; Josh. 1:8; Psalm 119:15,23,78,97

Reflection

   1. After reading today's devotion, I realize...
   2. The key statements I need to remember and work on are...
   3. The positive consequences of remembering and working on these
      statements will be

DAY 280

PUTTING AWAY CHILDISH THINGS

Blessed are the peacemakers, for they shall be called sons of God. (Matt. 5:9)

"Hanging onto resentment is letting someone you despise live rent-free in your head." ~Ann Landers

VICTOR OR VICTIM

This passage is telling us that we need to forgive and let go. We need to deal with and confront our demons. We have to get real and face what's hurting us so that we can heal and grow in character, becoming more like Christ.

We need to change our old patterns, bad habits, and get rid of our hang-ups. These negative ways of acting are often developed because we didn't take responsibility for the broken heart caused by loss or our childhood. I want you to truly take the time to put closure on yesterday, live for today and plan for tomorrow. Your past doesn't determine your future.

If you want to be a victor:

- ☐ Be determined to be an effective person
- ☐ Forgive yourself and others
- ☐ Receive forgiveness from God
- ☐ Resolve your guilt and shame
- ☐ Stop with the self-destructive behaviors
- ☐ Pay attention to your negative self-talk
- ☐ Take risks
- ☐ Admit your pain
- ☐ Admit you made mistakes
- ☐ Move on
- ☐ Develop spirituality
- ☐ Work out your anger and bitterness
- ☐ Be vulnerable
- ☐ Don't let people rent space in your head
- ☐ Don't dwell on the past - resolve it
- ☐ Allow your past to teach you what not to do, or what to do differently
- ☐ Accept what you can't change and change what you can
- ☐ Pray for others, your enemies, and yourself. Seek God's perfect will.

☐Start trusting yourself (your feelings, wants, needs, likes, dislikes, opinions, ideas, thoughts, values, beliefs and choices)

☐Trust others….safe people

Well, what do you think? What do you need to do to live your life? Take a look at the check list – what do you need to focus on the most? What are you already working on?

Take action…

1. Look up the following passages and paraphrase each one.

☐Rom. 7:8,24; 2 Cor. 8:12; James 1:22-25; John 7:17; Matt. 12:10-13; Eph. 3:3-4; Phil. 3:13-14; John 6:28-29; Psalm 103:12; Eph. 4:22-24; Matt. 5:5; Matt. 5:6; Matt. 5:7; Matt. 5:8; Matt. 5:9; Matt. 5:10; Matt. 5:11; Matt. 5:21-26; Matt. 5:38-48; Matt. 6:1-18; Gal. 1:10

Reflection

1. After reading today's devotion, I realize…
2. The key statements I need to remember and work on are…
3. The positive consequences of remembering and working on these statements will be…

DAY 281-286

PUTTING AWAY CHILDISH THINGS

Set your minds on things above, not on earthly things. (Col. 3:2)

NEW LIFE ~ NEW RULES ~ NEW ROLES

God expects you to live by His rules and to change your image. I know this takes time and a lot of hard work. Like I said early on, salvation and sanctification mean change and transition. Take some time today and read through what's occurring in your soul and what God is doing on His potter's wheel.

New Life...

Because of your new life in Christ:

- You can talk to God about your needs and problems. (Phil. 4:6-7)
- You don't have to be perfect. (Rom. 3:23)
- You let go of your mistakes, failures, regrets, sin, shame and guilt. (Rom. 8:1)
- You can learn to trust again. (Psalm 71:5)
- You can be weak. (2 Cor. 12:10)
- You can say no to evil and selfishness.
- You have the right to communicate with God and others. (Eph. 4:15, Heb. 4:16)
- You can be angry and confront your issues with others. (Eph. 4:26-27)
- You can enjoy life. (John 1:16)
- You no longer need to conform to the traditions of this world. (Rom. 12:1-2) Break the habit of conforming to rules and beliefs that don't line up with God's ways.
- Your needs are important.
- You are loved equally by God. (Gal. 3:23)

New Roles...

Before you came to Christ you were raised under a family system in which you took on certain roles according to your family dynamics. Today we're going to explore these dysfunctional roles and explore what God's word has to say about them. Your job is to identify what role you played in your family.

You no longer have to ...
- **Be a hero:** Provided self-esteem for the family, often the oldest. Carries guilt, inadequacy, hurt and frustration.
  - God has specific dreams and plans for your life
  - God has given you a separate identity from the others
  - You have a place in God's family (Eph. 4:4)
  - You can relax and live in the moment (Matt. 11:28)
  - You're good enough (Psalm 139)
  - If you fail you're still loved (Rom. 8)
- **Be the scapegoat (victim or fall guy):** Acts out the family dysfunction and takes the blame for the family. Carries hurt, anger, shame and fear.
  - God loves you as you are

- Stop reacting to conflicts
- You're a new person now (Col. 3)
- You're not a victim but a victor
- Study Rom. 8:28
- Take responsibility for your life
- Stop seeing yourself as the prodigal son. Come to your senses. God awaits you at the end of the driveway (Luke 15).
- God sees you as special and loved. He will never leave you or forsake you (Psalm 27:10)
- You're part of God's family now. (Rom. 12) You no longer need to feel abandoned
- God has given you the fruit of self-control so you can stop self-destructing
- God says, "For I know the plans I have for you," says the LORD. "They are plans for good and not for disaster, to give you a future and a hope. [12] In those days when you pray, I will listen. [13] If you look for me wholeheartedly, you will find me. [14] I will be found by you," says the LORD. "I will end your captivity and restore your fortunes. I will gather you out of the nations where I sent you and will bring you home again to your own land."(Jer. 29:11-15). You no longer need to see yourself as an underachiever.
- You might think you lack direction but God says, "Trust in the LORD with all your heart; do not depend on your own understanding. Seek his will in all you do, and he will show you which path to take." (Proverbs 3:5-6)

o **Be the lost child: Deals with the family dysfunction by escaping.** Carries hurt, sadness, fearful, feels worthless.
  - God knows the number of hairs on your head
  - God will give you direction (Prov. 3:5-6)
  - Stop withdrawing from God for He is near
  - Connect to others stop, withdrawing into your own world
  - Set goals (2 Tim. 3:17)
  - Take time to seek God's direction and will (Psalm 25:4-5; James 1:5)
  - You're responsible for your purpose in life (Jer. 29:11)
  - Ask questions (Matt. 7:7-8)

o **Be the mascot: Provides humor to relieve family stress and tension.** Carries insecurity, fear, guilt, confusion, loneliness.

- ▪Stop using humor to mask your pain. God will heal your hurt (Isaiah 61:1-4)
- ▪Seek Gods direction (the Lord's Prayer)
- ▪Put away childish things (1 Cor. 13)
- ▪Take responsibility for your soul (Gal. 6:5)
- ▪God will help you to focus and He will give you direction (John 16:13)

o**Be a people pleaser: Feels responsible for other people's happiness.** Performance based love and acceptance mentality. Carries low self-esteem, inferiority, shame, and feels flawed.

- ▪Let Jesus love you
- ▪Stop feeling guilty when others try to love you
- ▪Learn to receive from others
- ▪Let go of guilt, it's normal to have needs and wants
- ▪Your main purpose in life is to love God and serve him
    - ✓For am I now seeking the approval of man, or of God? Or am I trying to please man? If I were still trying to please man, I would not be a servant of Christ. (Gal. 1:10)
    - ✓Whatever you do, work heartily, as for the Lord and not for men. (Col. 3:23)
    - ✓Slaves, obey in everything those who are your earthly masters, not by way of eye-service, as people-pleasers, but with sincerity of heart, fearing the Lord. (Col. 3:22)
    - ✓There is neither Jew nor Greek, there is neither slave nor free, there is no male and female, for you are all one in Christ Jesus. (Gal. 3:23)
    - ✓On the contrary, we speak as those approved by God to be entrusted with the gospel. We are not trying to please people but God, who tests our hearts. (1 Thess. 2:4)

Take action...

1. Look up the following passages and paraphrase each one.
   ☐Col. 1:10; Rom. 12:10-11; Gal. 6:5,10; Prov. 14:12; Isaiah 55:8-11; Rom. 12:1-2

Reflection

1. After reading today's devotion, I realize…
2. The key statements I need to remember and work on are…
3. The positive consequences of remembering and working on these statements will be…

DAY 287-289

PUTTING AWAY CHILDISH THINGS

Strive for peace with everyone, and for the holiness without which no one will see the Lord. (Heb. 12:14)

WHY DO I NEED TO FORGIVE?

Let's face it; it happens to all of us. We're humans and we hurt each other, especially the ones we love the most.

What will you say if a child asks you this question? Why do I have to forgive people when they hurt me?

Ask yourself the following questions. Finish the sentence several times.

1. If I don't forgive:

2. Forgiveness allows me to:

11 consequences of being unforgiving

Unforgiving people…

1. Become vengeful
2. Separate from God, others, your soul
3. Hard hearted and abusive
4. Distant and uninvolved
5. Defensive and suspicious
6. Anxious and fearful
7. Judgmental and critical
8. Bitter
9. Addicted to drugs or alcohol

10. Depressed
11. Hostile

Consider this...

1. "I have found the paradox, that if you love until it hurts, there can be no more hurt, only more love." (Mother Teresa)
2. Love is an act of endless forgiveness, a tender look which becomes a habit. (Peter Ustinov)
3. Hate leaves ugly scars, love leaves beautiful ones. (Mignon McLaughlin, *The Second Neurotic's Notebook*, 1966)
4. The past is behind us, love is in front and all around us. (Terri Guillemets)

Keep in mind...

1. He who covers and forgives an offense seeks love, but he who repeats or harps on a matter separates even close friends. **Proverbs 17:9**
2. For if you forgive men when they sin against you, your heavenly Father will also forgive you. But if you do not forgive men their sins, your Father will not forgive your sins. **Matthew 6:14-15 NIV**
3. Then Peter came to Jesus and asked, "Lord, how many times shall I forgive my brother when he sins against me? Up to seven times?" Jesus answered, "I tell you, not seven times, but seventy-seven times." **Matthew 18: 21-22 NIV**
4. When they came to a place called the Skull, there they crucified him, along with the criminals – one on his right, the other on his left, Jesus said, "Father, forgive them, for they do not know what they are doing." **Luke 23:33-34 NIV**
5. When they kept on questioning him, he straightened up and said to them, "If any one of you is without sin, let him be the first to throw a stone at her." **John 8:7 NIV**
6. On the contrary: "If your enemy is hungry, feed him; if he is thirsty, give him something to drink. In doing this, you will heap burning coals on his head."
7. We are blessed to have God's word to guide our lives and our actions. Let us go forth and live by His words about forgiveness. **Romans 12:20 NIV**

Reshaping exercise....

Read through the list below and check off the consequences you're currently experiencing because you're hurt and unforgiving. Remember unforgiveness keeps you stuck in the sanctification process. ***"Leave your sacrifice there at the***

altar. Go and be reconciled to that person. Then come and offer your sacrifice to God. (Matthew 5:24)

Let's think about this, what do we gain from bitterness and hatred?

☐A vengeful spirit

☐Depression

☐Hostility

☐Aggression

☐Lack of trust

☐Anxiety and stress

☐Stubbornness and pride

☐Defensiveness

☐Fear of rejection and failure

☐Anger outbursts

☐Strained relationships

☐Irreconcilable differences

☐Emotional suppression and repression

☐Regret, shame and remorse

☐Poor choices and decisions

☐Poor communication

☐Critical and judgmental spirit

☐Isolation and withdrawal from relationships

If you hate a person, you hate something in him that is part of yourself. What isn't part of ourselves doesn't disturb us. (Hermann Hesse, *Demian)* We need to realize that bitterness and resentments causes us to stay in our pain and our past. We tend to cut people off in the present and lose interest in forming new relationships. We also can disconnect ourselves from God. What about you?

Are you hanging onto resentments? If you have bitterness is it affecting your life in any way? Can you identify with any of the consequences of bitterness and hatred? What can you do to let go of your pain so you can heal your brokenness?

Take action…

1. Look up the following passages and paraphrase each one.

☐Psalm 66:18-19; Luke 11:4-5; Psalm 139:23-24; James 1:13-15
1 Peter 5:8-9; 1 Peter 1:5; Prov. 8:13; Rom. 12:9

Reflection

1. After reading today's devotion, I realize…
2. The key statements I need to remember and work on are…
3. The positive consequences of remembering and working on these
    statements will be…

DAY 290-295

PUTTING AWAY CHILDISH THINGS

*"Be kind to one another, tender-hearted, forgiving each other, just as God in
Christ also has forgiven you."*
(Ephesians 4:32)

FORGIVE SO YOU CAN HEAL AND TRANSFORM YOUR LIFE

I've learned that unforgiveness will keep me from bouncing back and living my
life every day. It also prevents me from becoming the person God designed me
to be. Satan knows that if he can keep us angry and bitter there's not much we
can do for God.

Forgiving is divine…

I had to come to terms with the fact that when I forgive someone I'm not saying
that what they did to me is okay, I'm saying Lord help me, heal me of my hurt
and disappointment so I can move on with my life.

I ask God to deal with it. I also confess the fact that we all fall short of the glory
of God. (Romans 3:23) Who am I to hold a grudge? I'm no better. My hands
are dirty.

When something happens to me, I remind myself that God saw it before it
happened. Everything under the sun has a purpose. I just deal with it as it
comes. The fact of the matter is, hurt is right around the corner, but we can't let
that stop us from loving others. You've got to learn to love…the world you're
living in. (Bon Jovi)

For me to forgive, I need God's help. I can't do it alone. So I ask God to help
me and to work through me. I forgive so I don't get sick. Regardless of what the

other person thinks and feels about what they did to me, it's my pain and my responsibility.

Forgiveness sets you free...

You will set yourself free from all you thought they did to you. They need not ask for forgiveness in order to be forgiven. They might even believe that there is nothing for which they need to be forgiven. That is fine. Do not concern yourself with how they choose to experience reality, for it has no effect on you unless you allow it to. For something or someone to affect you, you must first allow it to affect you. (James Blanchard Cisneros)

"If you forgive those who sin against you, your heavenly Father will forgive you. But if you refuse to forgive others, your Father will not forgive your sins. (Matthew 6:14-15)

Instructions: Use this checklist to evaluate your beliefs or rules about **forgiveness**. Check off what applies to you.

FORGIVENESS

28 Rules to Live By...

☐Express yourself
☐Keep short accounts
☐Don't keep records of wrongs
☐Resentments hurt you so let them go
☐Forgive because God has forgiven you
☐List the lessons you're learning from the negative situation
☐Unforgiveness makes you sick, both mentally and physically
☐List the benefits of forgiveness
☐List the benefits of unforgiveness
☐Forgiveness takes away our excuse to sin and to justify our bad habits and hang-ups
☐Stop reliving the hurt, let it go
☐Know the part you played in the situation and make a plan so it doesn't happen again
☐Practice empathy for the person who offended you
☐Forgiving someone brings you peace and happiness
☐Forgiving someone makes you stronger and pleasing to God
☐Forgiving others builds your character and makes you a better person
☐Forgive even if they don't apologize
☐Stop trying to satisfy your need for justice and vindication. Vengeance belongs to God (Rom. 12).
☐Forgive because it breaks the cycle of sin, violence, upsets Satan, brings unity, and honors God

☐Practice compassion, tolerance and mercy (Col. 3)

☐We all fall short, even you

☐We all need mercy and compassion

☐Repay evil with good (Rom. 12)

☐We all make mistakes, so forgive

☐We all need forgiveness, so give and receive it

☐Live in the here and now. Let the past go and look forward what lies ahead

☐By remembering that, it will free me from the burden of the stress I feel, also, if I can't forgive then how can I expect to ever be forgiven? -*Leslie Brown*

☐Understand this: whether you like it or not, over time, you will stop feeling the pain, so why hold on to something that's going to away anyway? -*Nirav KAKU*

Take action…

1. Look up the following passages and paraphrase each one.

> ☐Matt. 6:12,14-15; Luke 23:34; Matt. 18:21-22
>
> ☐Eph. 4:32; Col. 3:12-13; Prov. 20:22
>
> ☐Lev. 19:18; Gen. 50:19-20; 1 John 1:8-9

Reflection

1. After reading today's checklist I realize…
2. The key statements I need to remember and work on are…
3. What can I do to change the areas I need to work on?
4. What kind of support and accountability do I need?
5. The positive consequences of remembering and working on these statements are…

DAY 296

PUTTING AWAY CHILDISH THINGS

Forgiving is love's toughest work, and love's biggest risk. If you twist it into something it was never meant to be, it can make you a doormat or an insufferable manipulator. Forgiving seems almost unnatural. Our sense of fairness tells us people should pay for the wrong they do. But forgiving is love's power to break nature's rule. ~Lewis B. Smedes

Let all bitterness and wrath and anger and clamor and slander be put away from you, along with all malice. (Eph. 4:31)

LIGHTEN YOUR LOAD

Lessons in forgiveness...

The greatest lesson I've learned was the one about forgiveness. I used to think it was an emotion. Guess what, it's not. Like happiness, it's a choice. I had to make a decision to let go of the people who hurt me so I can heal and grow. My heart was too heavy to touch the sky. My unforgiveness dragged me down. For me to get on with my life I needed to let go and let God.

I need to learn how to be a forgiving person because, by nature, I'm not. I can be very punitive at times. I used to get so mad at the people who hurt me because I would wait for them to say they were sorry. Then it dawned on me, "What will I do if they never apologize?" So I realized that I needed to forgive all who have offended me - not for them, but for myself. (Harriet Nelson)

I was tired of crying, I needed to get on with my life and dreams. I had to release them so I could teach the wind to fly. I gave them to God. He does a better job at convicting than I do because I condemn. I'm learning to apply the advice of Robert Fulghum, he said, "Peace is not something you wish for; it's something you make, something you do, something you are, something you give away."

So you heard my story. What's yours? Are you a forgiving person?

Consider this...

Read the following statements and check off what applies to you.

A forgiving person...

- ☐ Believes they can't force another person to be aware of their feelings
- ☐ Accepts that they can't make an individual accept responsibility for wrongdoings

☐Knows that they are limited in their ability to apply consequences that might cause the wrongdoer to think about his or her actions

☐Accepts that they can share their needs with God, but then they have to recognize that they can't dictate anything to Him. After all, He's God and they're not.

☐Realizes that they are limited in their ability to sway others' opinions so they will support their needs and views

☐Knows that communication abilities are limited. They hinge on the willingness of others to hear and absorb

Insights

1. What did you learn about yourself?
2. What can you start applying to your life? How will it help?
3. If you start accepting your limits, letting God be in charge of your antagonist, what would be the result?
4. What can I do to stop struggling with the things I can't change?
5. How can I handle life's unfairness better?

Take action…

1. Look up the following passages and paraphrase each one.
    ☐Matt. 5:44; Matt. 5:24; Matt. 5:44-45; Mark 11:25; Luke 6:35-38,42; Col. 3:13; Heb. 10:16-23

Reflection

1. After reading today's devotion, I realize…
2. The key statements I need to remember and work on are…
3. The positive consequences of remembering and working on these statements will be…

DAY 297- 298

PUTTING AWAY CHILDISH THINGS

Blessed is the one whose transgressions are forgiven,
whose sins are covered. Blessed is the one

whose sin the LORD does not count against them
and in whose spirit is no deceit. (Psalm 32:1-2)

ADMITTING THE TRUTH WILL MAKE YOU EMOTIONALLY HEALTHY

Today I want you to make sure that you're not living in deceit or wearing a mask. God wants us to share everything with him because He's our Daddy.

Why do you hold back from expressing your emotions? Covering up your pain will not bring you the deeper healing God desires for you. What do you do when you can't express your emotions? We don't always have that opportunity because if you do, it can make matters worse.

Feeling numb…

When you can't express your emotions you need to learn how to pray and talk to your Father. David would constantly pray and sing to the father when he was hurt, angry, ashamed, happy and bitter. He dealt with his emotions because he knew that, if he didn't, those emotions would work against him.

You need to deal with your emotions as they happen instead of postponing it. Emotional problems occur because we postpone the expression of our hurt. If you pray to God, His spirit will help you process the hurt, especially if nobody else is available.

David is a prime example of what not to do. He held in his pain and his sin for way too long and it made his life miserable. He was so weighed down with regret. (Psalm 51:32)

Negative emotions…

The worst thing we can do is to hold in negative emotions because it affects our brain chemistry, leads to bad choices and can lead to depression. Also, our personalities change for the worse when we repress our emotions and stress. David's focus was on the external. He utilized his intuition. He was internally focused to where he dealt with things according to how he felt about them, or how they fit in with his personal value system.

When David disconnected from God you can see how he isolated himself, possibly believing that God, and the world, was against him and therefore isolating himself which caused mood swings and deep sadness and unhappiness.

For I am conscious of my transgressions and I acknowledge them; my sin is ever before me… David

Here you see how God was convicting David. He was helping David to see his transgression so he can change his mind and attitude. David was storing his hurt and anger. He was trying to make sense of his feelings and how he was going to go about dealing with it. Like most people, David was insecure and feared rejection from God and feared revealing his vulnerability and losing face (his image).

He knew in his heart what he was doing and I believe it really troubled him that he was hurting God too. David realized that if he concealed his transgressions he would not prosper, but if he confessed and forsook {them} he would find compassion.

I want you to start looking at how you deal with your emotions. You can't control your emotions but you can manage them. People can't control you. If they do its only because you let them. God has given you the ability to replace your emotions with values and beliefs. Your emotions don't have to drive you down a negative path anymore.

Ask yourself:

1. Am I holding in any pain? Hurt? Anger?
2. I'm mad at…
3. I hate…
4. Help me…
5. Stop…
6. _____ frustrates me
7. Values I need to do better at following are….

Ask the Holy Spirit to:

1. Show you any unresolved hurt, anger, loss or pain.
2. Give you courage and direction to help you process.
3. Heal you and to fill the voids.
4. Help you to renew your mind.

Take action…

1. Look up the following passages and paraphrase each one

   ☐Isaiah 59:14-15; Amos 5:10; John 8:45-46; Eph. 4:25;
   Lev 19:11; Psalm 34:13; Col. 3:9-10; John 4:23-24; Ro 1:18;
   1 Cor 5:8

Reflection

1. After reading today's devotion, I realize…

2. The key statements I need to remember and work on are…

3. The positive consequences of remembering and working on these statements will be…

DAY 299-300

PUTTING AWAY CHILDISH THINGS

Therefore, confess your sins to one another and pray for one another, that you may be healed. The prayer of a righteous person has great power as it is working. (James 5:16)

EMOTIONS THAT TRAP YOU

Feel your life…

Jesus was given many opportunities to feel fear, anger, shame and guilt, and I'm sure you have too. Jesus didn't allow himself to get trapped in negative emotions. He felt them, but He lined His thoughts up with God's truth and moved on. Jesus went to His father with His hurt and pain. Father why have you forsaken me?

When you gave your life to Christ you said, "Father set me free from the negative emotions that trap me. Set me free from the strongholds that I created."

So today, let's take a look at some negative emotions that could be shackling you, or keeping you from working out your salvation. Take your time with this. Pray through each question. Invite the Holy Spirit in; let Him guide your pen and heart. Be specific. Bring to mind people, events, places and things connecting these emotions. Ask God to free you and to give you a godly perspective on your pain.

Ask yourself:

1. My fears are:
2. My hurts are:
3. I'm resentful over:
4. I'm ashamed of:
5. I hate:
6. I'm still prideful (false pride) over:

7. I feel guilty about:
8. I can't let go of:
9. I regret:
10. I frustrated over:

Keep in mind...

1. Communicate how you feel to God and to others
2. Speak the truth in love
3. Don't let the sun go down on your anger
4. Blessed are those who mourn
5. Journal your feelings and thoughts. Share them with a mentor, friend, counselor
6. Forgive when the Holy Spirit is telling you to
7. What Jesus said; Come to me all you are heavy laden…. I will give you rest
8. Jesus doesn't want your negative emotions to rob you of the abundant life He wants to give you

Take action...

1. Look up the following passages and paraphrase each one.
   Col. 3:15; Gal. 6:9; John 10:10; Prov. 4:23; Isaiah 9:6
   Eph. 2:13-14,17; Heb. 10:38; Rom. 8:29; Heb.4:9-10;
   Matt. 12:33-37; Ps. 119:165; John 14:23-24; Prov. 3:1-2;
   James 3:6; James 1:5

Reflection

1. After reading today's devotion, I realize…
2. The key statements I need to remember and work on are…
3. The positive consequences of remembering and working on these statements will be…

REVIEW & REPAIR

Reshaping Your Soul

1. What did I learn this past month about myself, God and others?

2. What concepts or ideas stood out to me in the devotions? Why?

3. What adjustments do I need to make in my life?

4. What needs to change, if anything, about how I think, feel and act?

5. What changes have I made so far? What actions have I taken?

6. How are people reacting to my changes?

7. Steps I will continue to take are...

8. I'm committed to...

9. My victories this week were...

10. God please help me with...

DAY 301

PUTTING AWAY CHILDISH THINGS

Be constantly renewed in the spirit of your mind [having a fresh mental and spiritual attitude], ²⁴And put on the new nature (the regenerate self) created in God's image, [Godlike] in true righteousness and holiness.
Therefore, rejecting all falsity and being done now with it, let everyone express the truth with his neighbor, for we are all parts of one body and members one of another. (Eph. 4:23-25)

INTERNAL RULES WE LIVE BY

Today I want you to think about the rules you have when it comes to expressing how you feel. The list I provided is healthy beliefs about emotions.

God wants us to **express** our emotions not to live by them. Our feelings are signals. They point to the issues we need to deal with. The key thing I want you to remember is that feelings aren't facts and we need to line up what we feel and think with God's truth. In my experience, both personally and professionally, we get stuck in the sanctification process because we repress what we truly feel and then act out as a result of it.

Rules for Expressing Emotion

Instructions: Check off the statements that best describes your personal *Rules about Expressing Emotions.*

☐It is healthy to feel your feelings.

☐There is no such thing as a right or wrong feeling.

☐All feelings are OK.

☐It is OK to feel what I am feeling now.

☐No one can take what I am currently feeling away from me.

☐I have a right to feel my feelings.

☐No one can judge me wrong for feeling the feelings I experience in my life.

☐It is OK to have negative feelings and to identify and express them freely.

☐I am feeling feelings every second of my waking hours.

☐Identifying and expressing my feelings makes me a real and authentic human being.

☐No one can deny me my feelings.

☐No one can tell me how I should be feeling.

☐No one has the right to make me feel bad or guilty for the feelings I am feeling.

☐I am more alive and vigorous when I am in touch with my feelings.

☐I have a right to have my feelings be visible, seen and heard by others.

☐I will no longer hide my feelings and emotions from myself and the others in my life.

☐I deserve to give and receive honest feedback about my feelings toward persons, places, things and events in my life.

☐I deserve to have my feelings listened to by others.

☐I choose to feel my feelings, be they positive or negative, so that I cease being numb to my life.

☐I have the right to experience the grief and mourning emotions which I will feel as I face the losses in my life.

☐I will heal and grow as I become more in touch with my feelings.

☐I will "grow down" more as I open myself up to get in touch with my feelings

Take action...

1. Look up the following passages and paraphrase each one.

☐James 4:17; Eph. 4:29; Rom. 2:6-9; 2 Cor. 10:3-5; Gal. 5:22-23; Col. 3:10; 1 Cor. 11:28-31

Reflection

1. After completing this assessment, I realize…
2. The key statements I need to remember and work on are…
3. What are the consequences of these problems for me?

DAY 302-304

PUTTING AWAY CHILDISH THINGS

Come to me, all who labor and are heavy laden, and I will give you rest. Take my yoke upon you, and learn from me, for I am gentle and lowly in heart, and you will find rest for your souls. For my yoke is easy, and my burden is light."
(Matt. 11:28-30)

"A work of art which did not begin in emotion is not art." ~ Paul Cezanne

COMMUNICATING YOUR FEELINGS

Gina's Story

Gina felt safe to express her anger and fear to Tommy. For her relationship to grow and to heal she needed to find a way to tell Tommy that she was scared, hurt and confused. "Let's not forget that the little emotions are the great captains of our lives and we obey them without realizing it." ~Vincent Van Gogh

We all need to learn how to communicate our feelings to one another because it's what makes relationships honest and strong. When we communicate, we are expressing our emotions. When we don't know what we're feeling our communication leads to misunderstandings.

Thoughts and feelings…

We need to realize that there is a difference between thoughts and feelings. Our thoughts consist of our beliefs, perceptions, values, convictions and opinions. Our feelings/emotions are sensations, moods, personality, and temperament. We need to express more than our thoughts or convictions, we need to express the feelings behind the thoughts. If not, they get buried and we don't want that. We need to get our thoughts and feelings working together in unison. For instance, when I think this _____ I feel this_____. When I feel _____, I act like this

_____.

Let's remind ourselves that joy and intimacy come when we take the time to feel. The last thing we need is to be out of touch with our soul and spirit. Feelings are much like waves, we can't stop them from coming but we can choose which one to surf. ~Jonatan Mårtensson.

Here's a list of positive and negative emotions. Please take some time to review. Refer to them daily so you can learn how to communicate what you need, want and feel. If you don't know what some of the feelings mean, please take the time to look them up. Good luck.

Positive Emotions

Adequate	Awe	Assured	Able
Capable	Certain	Charmed	Cheerful
Comfortable	Compassion	Courageous	Confidence
Determined	Delighted	Eager	Energetic
Enthusiastic	Excited	Exhilarated	Expectant
Elation	Empathy	Excellent	Fascinated
Glad	Good	Great	Grateful
Glorious	Glamorous	Graceful	Happy
Hopeful	Humorous	Inspired	Interested
Joyful	Magnificent	Lust	Love
Pleasure	Playfulness	Peaceful	Pleasant
Powerful	Pride	Positive	Relaxed
Relieved	Satisfied	Surprised	Sympathy
Stable	Sublime	Superior	Thrilled

Negative Emotions

Annoyed	Anxious	Apprehensive	Agonize

Anger	Anxiety	Apathy	Bored
Burdened	Cautious	Competitive	Concerned
Confused	Contempt	Depressed	Destructive
Disgusted	Distracted	Doubtful	Disappointed
Exasperated	Exhausted	Embarrassment	Envy
Frustrated	Fear	Guilty	Greed
Grief	Harassed	Hesitant	Hostile
Ignored	Impatient	Indifferent	Intimidated
Isolated	Irritated	Jealous	Jumpy
Lonely	Mad	Manipulated	Miserable
Obnoxious	Overwhelmed	Panic	Pressured
Remorse	Revenge	Shame	Sad
Scared	Shocked	Suspicious	Stress
Tired	Uncomfortable	Uneasy	Used
Wary	Weary	Wasteful	

Take action…

1. Look up the following passages and paraphrase each one.
   Col. 3:13; Heb. 12:15; James 4:6; James 1:19; 1 John 1:9
   Prov. 12:22; Heb. 13:18; Phil. 2:2-8; James 2:12-13; Eph 4:25

Reflection

1. After reading today's devotion, I realize…
2. The key statements I need to remember and work on are…
3. The positive consequences of remembering and working on these statements will be…

DAY 305-306

PUTTING AWAY CHILDISH THINGS

We must no longer be children, tossed to and fro and blown about by every wind of doctrine, by people's trickery, by their craftiness in deceitful scheming. But speaking the truth in love, we must grow up in every way into him who is the head, into Christ. (Ephesians 4:14-15 NRSV)

OBSTACLES TO EXPRESSING FEELINGS

When it comes to expressing feelings many people have a difficult time. However, effective communication, including appropriate ways to express feelings, fosters intimacy with others and can help build a strong sense of self. (Gen. 1:27)

When we lack the skills or knowledge to effectively express our feelings we can create "blocks" which can hurt or hinder how we relate to others. These "blocks" can create the opposite effect of intimacy, which can lead to a variety of problems in our relationships. The following illustrates ten blocks to expressing feelings effectively:

- **Mind reading.** You expect others to know how you feel and what you want without taking responsibility for expressing yourself directly.
- **Fear.** Your fear of rejection and disapproval is so great that you abandon yourself and swallow your feelings.
- **Conflict avoidance.** You avoid conflict or uncomfortable feelings at all costs.
- **Passive-aggressive.** Instead of sharing your feelings openly and honestly, you use covert tactics to communicate your displeasure.
- **Hopelessness.** You believe the situation will never change so why try? This creates a self-fulfilling prophecy.
- **Martyrdom.** You don't want to admit your feelings because you don't want to give anyone the satisfaction of knowing they've upset you. You suffer silently with great pride.
- **Low self-esteem.** You believe that you don't have a right to express your feelings or to ask others for what you want. At the expense of self, you focus on pleasing others instead.

☐ **Feeling defective.** You believe that you shouldn't have irrational feelings like anger, jealousy, anxiety, or depression, as that would indicate that you are flawed or "un-together."

☐ **Volcano.** You believe that once you start expressing your feelings the hot lava will begin to flow and no one will be able to stop it! All will be destroyed.

☐ **Miranda Warning.** You don't want to express your feelings because you are afraid they will be used against you.

Source: Unknown

Take Action…

1. Look up the following passages and paraphrase each one.
   ☐Prov. 16:13; Prov. 12:17; James 3:5-6
   ☐Psalm 25:4; Rom. 8:1; Col. 2:8; Prov. 26:24-26
   ☐2 Tim. 1:7; Psalm 56:3-4; Isaiah 41:10

Reflection

1. After reading today's devotion, I realize…
2. The key statements I need to remember and work on are…
3. The positive consequences of remembering and working on these statements are…

DAY 307-309

PUTTING AWAY CHILDISH THINGS

I have been forgotten like one who is dead; I have become like a broken vessel (Psalm 31:12)

So if the Son sets you free, you will be free indeed (John 8:36)

Nobody can hurt me without my permission.
~Mohandas Gandhi

FACING YOUR HURT

Today I want you to see how free you are emotionally so I created a checklist you can use to evaluate yourself. The statements you don't check off are the beliefs and actions you need to work on. I also created a checklist for you to refer to that evaluates your ability to manage negative emotions.

When we're in bondage emotionally we get stuck in God's sanctification process. God want your soul, which is your mind, will and emotions. He wants you to tell Him the truth about how you feel. He's your daddy. You can approach Him boldly with confidence.

People who are **Emotionally Free**:

☐ Pay attention to their negative feelings and allow themselves to feel them

☐ Stop lying to themselves

☐ Trust God to give them the courage to feel and express their hurt and pain

☐ Express their hurt in a way that will be heard

☐ Take responsibility for their pain because they realize that they have to deal with it in the end.

☐ Practice self-awareness by journaling their emotions so they can make sense out of them

☐ Explore the meaning behind their emotions. They look at the thought and beliefs that drive their emotions and reactions. The key is to disempower the dysfunctional beliefs that ruin our lives and relationships

☐ Explore the value in the emotion. They don't judge them or criticize them, they feel them and let them pass

☐ Are able to tell the person in a peaceful way that they are hurt, because they have processed the emotion already.

☐ Don't concern themselves with the other person's response or reaction to their hurt

☐ Don't allow themselves to fear rejection

☐ Know the difference between present hurt and past hurt

☐ Express their needs and wants and lets go

☐ Accept that their feelings are a reaction to their perceptions and beliefs as well as to the environment not lining up

The knowledge of Christ's love for us should cause us to love Him in such a way that it is demonstrated in our attitude, conduct, and commitment to serve God.

Spiritual maturity is marked by spiritual knowledge being put into action.
~ Edward Bedore

Instructions: *Use this checklist to evaluate your ability to* **<u>manage negative emotions</u>**. *Check off what applies to you.*

Managing Negative Emotions…

☐If I'm angry I'm going to process it and express it in a healthy way.

☐It's not healthy for me to conceal my negative emotions, so I identify them and process them.

☐I don't ignore my anger anymore.

☐I ask God to reveal to me any buried anger I might have.

☐I address any resentment I might have and offer forgiveness to that person.

☐I listen to my feelings of sadness.
> oIf I don't my heart will harden.
> oI will look at any loss I might have experienced.
> oIt's important that I share my sadness and losses with others.

☐I face my fears … I take the time to see if they're real or imagined.

☐I don't allow my fears to cause me to isolate and withdraw from God and people.

☐I'm aware of the fears that immobilize me.

☐I know the fears I need to work on.

Take action…

1. Look up the following passages and paraphrase each one.
   > ☐Gal. 5:22-23; Prov. 25:28; Eph. 4:26; Eph. 5:18; Col. 3:8
   > 1 Tim. 2:8; James 1:19-20; Prov. 3:5-7; 1 John 4:18; Phil. 4:6
   > Gal. 5:1; John 8:36; Gal. 4:6; Rev. 1:8; John 1:12

Reflection

1. After reading today's checklist I realize…
2. The key statements I need to remember and work on are…
3. What can I do to change the areas I need to work on?
4. What kind of support and accountability do I need?
5. The positive consequences of remembering and working on these statements are…

DAY 310-311

PUTTING AWAY CHILDISH THINGS

*Many of us come to Christ with emotional pain and distress. Many are broken and wounded. The good news is that we don't have to hide our pain anymore because Jesus was... sent to comfort the **brokenhearted** and to proclaim that captives will be released and prisoners will be freed.* [2] *He has sent me to tell those who mourn that the time of the LORD's favor has come, and with it, the day of God's anger against their enemies.* [3] *To all who mourn in Israel, he will give a crown **of beauty for ashes**, a joyous blessing instead of mourning, festive praise instead of despair. In their righteousness, they will be like great oaks that the LORD has planted for his own glory. (Isaiah 61:1-3)*

STOP PUNISHING YOURSELF

God designed hurt to limit your pain. These emotions will help you to avoid negative situations and bad choices. Life lessons and our testimony come from our hurt. In order for God to heal you emotionally you need to feel and experience your emotions (hurt, anger, sadness, disappointment etc.). Confess your hurt and pain when you experience it. Don't hold it in. Be honest and confess it to God and to a safe person. Jesus promises you that you will be comforted when you mourn (Matt. 5).

If we don't mourn we allow our emotions to rule over us. Satan wants your life to be either controlled by emotion, or for you to be emotionless. Either way, you determine how you're going to experience your feelings.

Make sure that you're not allowing your emotions to control you, because if you do, you're going to behave in ways that oppose your beliefs and values. The end result is self-punishment and self-sabotage. Part of working out your salvation is healing your damage emotions.

Be proactive, not reactive. You control your emotional state. Remember, when you're in the Spirit, you have the fruit of self-control (Gal. 5).

Take action…

1. Look up the following passages and paraphrase each one.

   ☐Phil. 1:6; Jude 24-25; Phil. 2:13; John 7:24; Rom. 14:1-13;
   2 Peter 1:3-4; Eph. 4:17-22; Matt. 5:27-28; Matt 6:1-3;

Gal. 5:19-21; Eph. 5:22-24; Rom. 10:10; Prov. 15:23; Heb. 4:16
James 4:6-8

Reflection

1. After reading today's devotion, I realize…
2. The key statements I need to remember and work on are…
3. The positive consequences of remembering and working on these statements will be…

DAY 312-315

PUTTING AWAY CHILDISH THINGS

"Being confident of this very thing, that he who began a good work in you will perfect it until the day of Jesus Christ." (Philippians 1:6)

*Then the man and his wife heard the sound of the LORD God as he was walking in the garden in the cool of the day, and they hid from the LORD God among the trees of the garden. ⁹ But the LORD God called to the man, "**Where are you?**" He answered, "I heard you in the garden, and **I was afraid** because I was naked; **so I hid."** (Gen. 3:8-10)*

HARMFUL HIDING

Today I want you to look at some possible ways you might hide from God. Hiding from God only keeps us stuck in the sanctification process. Also I want to mention that if you're hiding from God your perception of Him might be flawed.

In order to heal and grow spiritually and emotionally you need to do the following things:

1. **Stop hiding your real self from God and others**. You need to stop pretending to be somebody you're not in order to receive God's grace and healing. Complete the following sentences and record your responses.

☐I pretend to be…

☐Most people don't know that I…

☐I have a hard time accepting the following things about myself, others, God…

☐I give the impression of…

☐The mask I wear is…

☐On the surface I am…

☐The game I play is…

☐I hide behind…

☐The clothes I wear indicate…

☐The car I drive shows that…

☐My job or profession shows others that…

☐The real me hides under…

☐How long have I been pretending?

☐How often do I pretend?

☐I seem to pretend when…

☐The following people who trigger my need to pretend are…

2. **Developmental Stages:** We need to work through our developmental stage between the ages of 3 to 6 years. This is when we learn how to integrate the good with the bad.

   a. How you feel about yourself and your body and how you deal with and respect the positive and negative qualities in yourself and others are related to how you experienced these issues when you were between the ages of three and six.

   b. This period is when you began to learn the difference between good and bad behavior. When you were good (acting like the adults in your life expected and wanted you to act), you were rewarded with love, acceptance and attention. When you were bad (acting in ways that were unacceptable to these adults) you were punished or loved conditionally causing you to feel insignificant and/or unacceptable.

   c. The rewards may have been in the form of praise or you may have been given special food, toys or outings. Punishment may have been emotional: you may have been humiliated, teased, or your parents may have ignored you. Or it may have been physical: you were spanked, slapped, or sent to your room. Fearing the punishments and desiring the rewards, you quickly learned what was acceptable and what was not.

   d. 3 to 6 was a very tender time. It was when the foundation for self-worth was being laid. If you were taught that you are basically good, but that sometimes you did bad things, you probably would have developed a solid foundation on which to build your self-worth. You would, as an adult, be able to make mistakes without feeling that you are bad, the way a child would.

e.On the other hand, if as a child you were constantly told how bad you are, your self-worth would have suffered terribly. You might well have grown up believing that you always would be bad. As an adult, he would most likely fear making a mistake because each mistake would further confirm these feelings and this lack of self-worth. They feel shame when you feel you're not good enough, or are unworthy of love. I believe we develop shame in response to fear. You fear that you will be abandoned because you are unlovable.

3. Integrate the real self with the ideal self

•Deep down inside, we all realize difference between our ideal self, the perfect self we would like to be, and are real self, the one that truly is. If these two battle each other, we will be in constant conflict. The real self is, in Paul's words, unspiritual, sold as a slave to sin (Romans 7:14).

☐Identify some of your areas of weakness. Where do you fail? Where do you sin? (2 Cor. 7:10; 2 Cor.12:7-10)
☐Where are you broken? Where are you immature and emotionally underdeveloped? Where have you been injured? (Psalm 55:4-8)

4. Receive Christ's acceptance of you (Romans 15:7)

a.Acceptance is a state of receiving someone else relationship. To be accepted is to have all of your parts, good and bad, received by another without condemnation. It is closely related to grace, undeserved merit. Acceptance is the result of the working of grace.

☐Who in your life has offered you the gift of acceptance, receiving all of your parts, good and bad, without condemnation? (Rom. 14:12-13; Prov. 28:13-14)
☐Who in your life has been encouraged by your acceptance of his or her parts, good and bad? (Rom. 15:7)
☐Where are you getting total acceptance in your life now? If you can't identify any sources of acceptance, why not? What's getting in the way? What will you do to find acceptance – and when will you take the first step?

Consequences of hiding:

☐Hiding harms us when it means avoiding the good things God has for us

☐Hiding is self-protection, but it protects us from the very grace and truth we need

☐Hiding is caused by destructive and unsafe relationships which affect a person from being open and vulnerable

☐Hiding causes a person to isolate. Isolation prevents a person from growing. The results of isolation are losing grace (unconditional relationship) and truth (reality that we need).

☐Hiding causes a person to withdraw his/her need for bonding and attachment.

Source: Adapted- Hiding from Love: Dr. John Townsend

Take action…

1. Look up the following passages and paraphrase each one.
   ☐ Eph. 4:22-24; Psalm 6:6-7; Psalm 12:5; Psalm 16:4a
   ☐ Heb. 3:13; Rom. 1:20-32; Phil. 3:13; Prov. 1:7

Reflection

1. After reading today's devotion, I realize…
2. The key statements I need to remember and work on are…
3. The positive consequences of remembering and working on these statements are…

DAY 316-317

PUTTING AWAY CHILDISH THINGS

Therefore, if anyone is in Christ, he is a new creation. The old has passed away; behold, the new has come. (2 Cor. 5:17)

THE ONLY WAY OUT IS THROUGH

Let's start out with this truth today.

Therefore, if anyone is in Christ, he is a new creation. The old has passed away; behold, the new has come. All this is from God, who through Christ reconciled us to himself and gave us the ministry of reconciliation; Brothers, I do not consider that I have made it my own. But one thing I do: forgetting what lies behind and straining forward to what lies ahead, I press on toward the goal for the prize of the upward call of God in Christ Jesus…(Phil 3:13-14; 2 Cor. 5:17-18)

Break down or break through…

God uses brokenness to transform you. Satan uses it to keep you stuck. He wants you to stay stuck in the past and hardships. God uses them to break your self-will. Satan wants you to focus on the pain and loss. God wants you to surrender your will.

God wants you to be aware and accept that you're fractured without Him. Jesus said, "apart from me you can do nothing." When you accept that you need Him you will be shown love, support, grace and truth. Don't just admit your brokenness from your head, admit it from your heart, too.

O people of Zion, who live in Jerusalem, you will weep no more.
He will be gracious if you ask for help. He will surely respond to the sound of
your cries. (Isaiah 30:19)

Stop feeling broken and hurt all the time…

I had to learn a long time ago that if I continue to take things personally I wouldn't get far in life, and I would probably fail at accomplishing my goals. When we take a person's negative attitude or behaviors personally we're left feeling rejected, and in some cases feeling abandoned. Taking things personally disempowers us. The fact of the matter is, not everybody's going to approve of us. God uses broken things. It takes soil to produce a crop, broken clouds to give rain, broken grain to give bread, broken bread to give strength. It is the broken alabaster box that gives forth perfume... it is Peter, weeping bitterly, who returns to greater power than ever.

If you want to stop feeling broken...

1. Face your fears of being rejected
2. Stop avoiding rejection and failure
3. Take a look at your expectations of others. Are they to high? Are you expecting too much? Do you feel entitled to another person's love, approval and acceptance?

4. Learn to say no to others (without feeling guilt)

5. Stop settling for less

6. Develop a better opinion of yourself

7. Stop expecting others and yourself to be perfect

8. Stop trying to be all things for people

9. Stop procrastinating

10. Stop thinking everything's about you

11. Get out of the past. It's over. Learn from it, get over it and move forward

12. See yourself as equal to others

13. Make sure your opinion is your own

14. Never allow another person's opinion to be more important than yours

15. Believe in yourself and never quit

16. Watch your standards, don't set them to high

Take action…

1. Look up the following passages and paraphrase each one.

☐Rom. 6:4; Col. 3:10; Luke 5:37-38; 1 Cor. 10:6,11; Heb. 12:16; 1 Peter 3:5-6; 1 John 3:12; Psalm 78:11

Reflection

1. After reading today's devotion, I realize…

2. The key statements I need to remember and work on are…

3. The positive consequences of remembering and working on these statements will be…

DAY 318-319

PUTTING AWAY CHILDISH THINGS
Do not be anxious about anything. (Phil. 4:6)

GOT ANXIETY?

It's important to make sure that you're not feeding your anxiety, worry or stress. The affirmations below will help you break patterns that create your panic and anxiety. Read through them and repeat them throughout the day, but most importantly, apply them.

1. Today I will not be preoccupied with everyone else's needs; I'm going to consider my needs and desires too. I will find balance.
2. If I have a need, want, or desire, I will communicate it in a calm, peaceful way. I will make sure that my tones aren't aggressive, timid or coercive.
3. I have the right to share my ideas, suggestions, or perceptions with others. I will take the time to ask if they're interested in hearing them, instead of being pushy or compelled to share them.
4. I realize that things can't always be in their rightful place so therefore I will do my best not to insist that they are.
5. Being timid and shy can send others a negative message. I will display confidence and courage. I have no reason to be insecure.

Ask yourself:

1. How do I feed my anxiety? What can I do to stop?
2. What choices am I making on a daily basis that can be contributing to my loss of peace?
3. Jesus said be anxious for nothing.... what am I anxious about?
4. What or who am I preoccupied with?
5. I lose my peace when I...
6. Am I praying enough? Do I trust God enough?
7. How is Satan deceiving me?

Take action...

1. Look up the following passages and paraphrase each one.

   ☐Isaiah 26:3; Matt. 6:33; Luke 12:31; Jer. 17:7-8; Rom. 8:6
       Isaiah 49:13; 2 Cor. 1:3-4; Isaiah 43:1-13; Matt. 6:25-34
       Phil. 4:4-7; 1 Peter 5:7

Keep in mind:

1. Accept what you can't change and change what you can.
2. Don't be a fixer, enabler, rescuer, or a change agent. Just share a burden and don't take it on. The Holy Spirit is the change agent, not you.

Reflection

1. After reading today's devotion, I realize…
2. The key statements I need to remember and work on are…
3. The positive consequences of remembering and working on these statements will be…

DAY 320-323

PUTTING AWAY CHILDISH THINGS

Going a little farther, he fell with his face to the ground and prayed, "My Father, if it is possible, may this cup be taken from me. Yet not as I will, but as you will.
(Luke 22:39)

GRIPPED BY FEAR

Jesus in the Garden of Gethsemane…

I think Jesus was gripped by fear when it came time to realize and follow through on the purpose and mission His Father gave Him.

I believe His face was gripped with terror while He sweated drops of blood, pleading with God to change His mind. His muscles were probably tight, skin flushed, and I'm sure His voice trembled.

Jesus didn't deny His fear, He admitted it and accepted it. As a result, He was able to see His situation through the eyes of faith.

Fear Driven People

Jesus is a great example for fear driven people to follow because they give the appearance that things are peaceful and stable but deep inside they're petrified, frightened and guarded. As a result of this denial they don't give themselves a chance to develop their faith muscles. What does a fear driven person look like? See if any of these statements apply to you.

A fear driven person…

1. Hasn't developed faith in the area(s) they experience fear in.
2. Is flooded with pessimistic thoughts and attitudes about their ability to cope and overcome adversity and/or setbacks.
3. Has a hard time accepting things that are beyond their control and understanding.
4. Believes that they can't reveal their fear or lack of faith to others because they have to appear strong and in control at all times.
5. Doesn't confess their fear to God. They live behind their defenses instead.
6. Catastrophize's a situation and spends a lot of time worrying.
7. Says "I can't deal with this."
8. Is defensive when in arguments and disagreements.
9. Second guesses themselves.
10. Likes to keep things predictable.
11. Is usually a people pleaser.
12. Personalizes almost everything.

Ask yourself:

1. Am I driven by fear? What fear drives me the most? What does God's Word say about this fear? What are God's promises?
2. Do I spend too much time obsessing about solutions to problems that can't be readily solved?
3. Am I overly concerned with what people think of me? How does this make me lose my faith?

Keep in mind:

1. Jesus knows exactly what fear feels like. He will meet you where you're at. Confess your troubled heart to Him.
2. You need to take risks.
3. Keep your eyes on Jesus, if you don't, you will sink.
4. Be hopeful for the future.
5. Speak positive. Think positive.

Let go of:

1. The belief that you or others can't change.
2. Complaining about the injustices of life.
3. Your stubbornness
4. Bitterness and extend forgiveness.

Take action:

1. *Accept your Anxiety:* If you don't, it will increase and get worse. Call it out and manage it. Jesus was aware of what He was

thinking, feeling, and how He was behaving. This gives you the ability to manage the situation you're in. This will break the cycle of anxiety.

2. ***Share your Anxiety:*** Confess your fears to God and at least one other person. (Ecc. 4:9-12)
3. Behave and act like Jesus. Imitate Him.
4. Claim and apply: Isaiah 40:28-31; Matt. 11:28-30; 2 Cor. 4:16-18; Phil. 4:12-13; Luke 16:25; Phil. 2:1

DAY 324-334

PUTTING AWAY CHILDISH THINGS

For I the Lord your God hold your right hand; I am the Lord, Who says to you, Fear not; I will help you! (Isaiah 41:13)

IDENTIFY THE FEARS THAT PREVENT YOU FROM LIVING YOUR NEW LIFE IN CHRIST

For the next 10 days I want you to explore the fear(s) you might have that are causing you to get stuck in your sanctification process. Take your time and work through the checklist I provided.

Letting Go… God asks us to change certain things about our character and personality. Is God asking you to change a character/personality trait but you're refusing? If so, what is it? What are you afraid of?

Common Fears…Here's a list of common fears that prevent people from changing. Check off what applies to you. What can you do to overcome these fears? What does God say about these fears? What promises are you standing on?

1. **Fear of Failure**: When you overcome your fear of failure you are also overcoming:
   a. Perfectionism
   b. Codependency
   c. Addiction(s)

    d. Depression

    e. Worry

    f. Anxiety

    g. Procrastination

    h. Anger, bitterness

    i. Lack of motivation

    j. fear

    k. When Satan lies to you and uses the fear of failure to prevent you from changing or taking a risk, remind him of the following truths…

        i. Greater is who that's in me than he who is in the world

        ii. Failure doesn't determine my worth

        iii. There's no condemnation for those who are in Christ (Rom. 8:1)

        iv. You have value regardless of what you do or accomplish

        v. You don't have to perform to be love and accepted by God or man

        vi. God is and will equip you for what He's called you to do or change (Phil. 1:6)

        vii. We all fall short of God's glory and God still loves you regardless (Rom. 3:23)

        viii. You are forgiven (Rom. 4:6-8)

        ix. God doesn't love you for your good works, He just loves you.

        x. When people work, their pay is not given as a gift, but as something earned. "But people cannot do any work that will make them right with God. So they must trust in him, who makes even evil people right in his sight. Then God accepts their faith, and that makes them right with him. David said the same thing. He said that people are truly blessed when God, without paying attention to their deeds, makes people right with himself." (Rom. 4:5-6)

2. **Fear of rejection/disapproval**: when you're dealing with the fear of rejection you're also dealing with:

    a. Anger and bitterness

    b. Fear and anxiety

    c. Lack of vision and goals

    d. Perfectionism

    e. Codependency

f.Depression

g.Lack of risk taking

h.Isolation

i.Withdrawing

j.Hiding

k.Passivity

l. Aggression

    i.When Satan lies to you and uses the fear of rejection/disapproval to prevent you from changing or taking a risk remind him of the following truths...

        ☐Rom. 8:31-39 (paraphrase)

        ☐Col. 1:21-22 (paraphrase)

        ☐Psalm 27:10 (paraphrase)

        ☐1 Peter 5:7 (paraphrase)

        ☐Psalm 16:8 (paraphrase)

        ☐2 Cor. 4:7-9 (paraphrase)

        ☐Matt. 6:33 (paraphrase)

        ☐Acts 5:29 (paraphrase)

        ☐Col. 3:23-24 (paraphrase)

3. Fear of success

a.When Satan lies to you and uses the fear of success to prevent you from changing or taking a risk, remind him of the following truths:

    ☐Psalm 1:1-3 (paraphrase)

    ☐Psalm 37:5 (paraphrase)

    ☐Jer. 29:11-13 (paraphrase)

    ☐Prov. 22:4 (paraphrase)

    ☐Matt. 6:33 (paraphrase)

    ☐Rom. 8:16-18 (paraphrase)

    ☐Job 36:11 (paraphrase)

b.Remind yourself of the following quotes:

    ☐Success usually comes to those who are too busy to be looking for it. (Henry David Thoreau)

    ☐It takes 20 years to become an overnight success. (Eddie Cantor)

    ☐There are no secrets to success. It is the result of preparation, hard work, and learning from failure. (Colin Powell)

4. Fear of Change

a. When Satan lies to you and uses the fear of change to prevent you from changing or taking a risk, remind him of the following truths:

- ☐ Psalm 55:19 (paraphrase)
- ☐ 2 Tim. 2:7 (paraphrase)
- ☐ 2 Cor. 5:17 (paraphrase)
- ☐ Rom. 12:2 (paraphrase)
- ☐ Matt. 18:3 (paraphrase)
- ☐ Eph. 2:10 (paraphrase)
- ☐ Phil. 1:6 (paraphrase)

b. Remind yourself of the following quotes:

1. Everyone wants to change, but change demands desire and discipline before it becomes delightful. There is always the agony of choice before the promise of change. (Larry Lea)

2. If you feel stuck, bring your whole self to Christ, not just the problem, but you. Ask God to change your heart. Commit yourself to pray to that end. It's God's heart to give good gifts to His children. (Sheila Walsh)

5. Fear of confrontation

a. When Satan lies to you and uses the fear of confrontation to prevent you from changing or taking a risk, remind him of the following truths:

- ☐ Prov. 15:1 (paraphrase)
- ☐ Matt. 18:15-20 (paraphrase)
- ☐ Eph. 4:15 (paraphrase)
- ☐ Psalm 133:1; Josh. 7:19; Matt. 5:25 (paraphrase)
- ☐ Prov. 26:5 (paraphrase)
- ☐ Matt. 18:15; 1 Tim. 5:20 (paraphrase)
- ☐ Matt. 5:24 (paraphrase)

6. Fear of competition

a. When Satan lies to you and uses the fear of competition to prevent you from changing or taking a risk, remind him of the following truths:

- ☐ Col. 3:23 (paraphrase)
- ☐ Phil. 2:3-4 (paraphrase)
- ☐ 1 Cor. 9:24 (paraphrase)
- ☐ Phil. 4:13 (paraphrase)

☐John 15:13 (paraphrase)

☐Luke 1:37 (paraphrase)

☐Gal. 6:14 (paraphrase)

7. Fear of intimacy and closeness

a. When Satan lies to you and uses the fear of competition to prevent you from changing or taking a risk, remind him of the following truths:

☐ Ecc. 4:9-10 (paraphrase)

☐1 Cor. 13 - Love (paraphrase)

☐Heb. 10:4 (paraphrase)

☐1Peter 4:10 (paraphrase)

☐Eph. 4:2 (paraphrase)

☐James 5:16 (paraphrase)

☐Gal. 6:2 (paraphrase)

☐Rom. 12:14,15 (paraphrase)

☐Rom. 12:5 (paraphrase)

☐1 Thess. 5:11 (paraphrase)

8. Fear of making a mistake or being wrong

a. When Satan lies to you and uses the fear of making a mistake or being wrong to prevent you from changing or taking a risk, remind him of the following truths:

☐ Rom. 3:23 (paraphrase)

☐ Rom. 8:1 (paraphrase)

☐ Isaiah 41:10 (paraphrase)

☐ Col. 3:12-15 (paraphrase)

☐ Psalm 37:24 (paraphrase)

☐ Eph. 5:8 (paraphrase)

☐ Jer. 29:11-14 (paraphrase)

Resolution...

1. I will face my fears now that I believe and trust God with my Mind, Will and Emotions.

Reflection

1. After reading today's devotion, I realize...

2. The key statements I need to remember and work on are...

3. The positive consequences of remembering and working on these statements will be...

REVIEW & REPAIR

Reshaping Your Soul

1. What did I learn this past month about myself, God and others?

2. What concepts or ideas stood out to me in the devotions? Why?

3. What adjustments do I need to make in my life?

4. What, if anything, needs to change about how I think, feel and act?

5. What changes have I made so far? What actions have I taken?

6. How are people reacting to my changes?

7. Steps I will continue to take are…

8. I'm committed to…

9. My victories this week were…

10. God please help me with…

DAY 335-337

PUTTING AWAY CHILDISH THINGS

Refrain from anger, and forsake wrath!
Fret not yourself; it tends only to evil. (Psalm 37:8)

ADMIT YOUR ANGER

Today I want you to think about how well you express your anger. Most people don't like to acknowledge their anger or to let others know when they're angry.

Apparently Paul had some experience with anger. He wrote, "Don't sin by letting anger control you...Don't let the sun go down while you are still angry." I think the key to living out this verse is not to fear anger. If you're angry, be angry! Jesus lived out this verse. I can't imagine how many times He must have gotten angry at His disciples, especially when they fell asleep in the garden of Gethsemane.

If you bottle up your anger or hold it back, you become a pressure cooker. If and when you explode, you make your worst fears come true. Your anger can't stay contained too long because it eventually leaks out in passive aggressive ways, or even worse, it can turn into depression because anger turned inward eventually turns into depression.

Reasons why I think anger isn't a bad thing...

1. Anger is a natural reaction or result from being hurt. Our needs, wants or expectations go unnoticed or ignored. Sometimes they are flat out rejected or dismissed. Sometimes people insult us, take advantage of us or make fun of us. God gave us this emotion of anger for self-preservation purposes.
2. Everybody was given this emotion so don't be afraid of it. You're not bad for having it.
3. Expressing your anger prevents you from becoming a defensive person. When you don't express it, it steals your energy, joy and peace. Repressed anger will only divert you from goal setting and living out your purpose for God.
4. It's a secondary emotion...an indicator. It lets you know you're hurt.

Ask yourself:

1. Am I angry about anything?
2. Am I hurt, disappointed?
3. Do I have peace in my heart?
4. Do I have old anger (grudges, resentments)? If so, why?
5. How have I sinned as a result of my anger?
6. Has my anger affected my relationships (with people, with God)?

Ask God:

1. To show you if you have old anger.
2. To help you express your anger in a way that honors Him.
3. To help you become aware of your anger.

4. To give you the courage to admit to being hurt.

Take action…

1. Look up the following passages and paraphrase each one.

☐1 Peter 1:13-16; Eph. 2:10; Phil. 3:13-14; Psalm 140:9-10
Rom. 12:20-21; Rom. 1:16; Luke 6:27-28; Rom. 12:9-21
Gen. 4:7; Prov. 24:10; Prov. 21:22; Prov. 10:18; Eph. 4:29

Reflection

1. After reading today's devotion, I realize…
2. The key statements I need to remember and work on are…
3. The positive consequences of remembering and working on these
   statements will be…

DAY 338-42

PUTTING AWAY CHILDISH THINGS

*"Do not let your hearts be troubled. Trust in God; trust also in me. In my Father's house are many rooms; if it were not so, I would have told you. I am going there to prepare a place for you. And if I go and prepare a place for you, I will come back and take you to be with me that you also may be where I am.
(John 14:1-3)*

YOUR PAST DOESN'T DETERMINE YOUR FUTURE

Letting Go…

I realized long ago that if I wanted a new life I had to let go of the old one I was living. This wasn't easy for me. I had to stop fronting people and make a choice to get real. I always had to convince everyone that I was under control of my issues and my life. People knew I was fronting. I couldn't hide the fact that I was a mess. I was so stuck but I couldn't admit it. I felt so much guilt and shame for my actions and sins, yet I couldn't admit it or accept it.

I felt like a failure for a long time because I couldn't change no matter how much I tried. I was getting angry and bitter. My temper started to grow and I started to become violent and mean. All along I thought I was in control of my feelings and actions, but they had control of me.

I never felt sorry for myself like most people do, I just hated myself. I was in a cycle of self-sabotage and pain and I truly didn't know how to get out of it. I was fighting the fact that I had to admit and accept my weakness, my pain and my defects. That's hard for a person who thinks they have to be perfect. I realized that the choice to live in denial, pride and fear was only making my life miserable. I needed to go to Jesus and give Him my pain and burdens.

I love what Ed Cole said, "Maturity doesn't come with age; it comes with acceptance of responsibility." That's exactly what I needed to do... take responsibility. One of the marks of spiritual maturity is the quiet confidence that God is in control.

Ask yourself:

1. What emotions, weaknesses, hurts or defects are keeping me stuck? Could it be fear, anger, anxiety, worry or doubt?
2. How are my choices affecting my life?
3. Do I line my life up with God's Word? Do my words match my actions?
4. I needed to accept God's will for my life in order for it to change... do you accept God's will and purpose for your life? Do you accept how He's trying to change you to be the best you can be?
5. What hurts and weaknesses are the hardest to let go of? Why?
6. I need to let go of...

After you complete the questions above take some time and complete this checklist. It will help you to see where you stand when it comes to sanctification and brokenness.

UNDERSTANDING BROKENNESS

"Blessed are the poor in spirit, for theirs is the kingdom of heaven. (Matt. 5:3)

Instructions: Check off the statements that you can truly agree with. Complete the reflection questions after each section.

☐ I understand that God uses pain, hardships and adversity to change my self-will and to pull me closer to Him

☐Pain and suffering is used to build my character. It closes the gap between me and God

☐Brokenness leads me to surrender to God

☐I believe God uses my brokenness to conform me into His image and to make me more Christ-like

☐I can admit when I'm broken and confused

☐I can admit and accept when I'm stuck

☐I believe brokenness leads to repentance

☐Trials and adversity are used to prune my character and to bring about the fruit of the spirit in my life and relationships

☐I have the same attitude as Paul did when it comes to my thorns (2 Cor. 12:7)

☐I try not to resist what God is trying to do in my life. Sometimes I need to keep my habits in check, my relationships in check, fears and anger in check

☐Adversity has kept my spiritual life fresh

☐Storms increase my faith in God

☐Brokenness allows me to live a deeper life

☐Brokenness shows me what I need to change about my personality and character

☐When I'm broken I thirst for God

☐Adversity hasn't pulled me to my addictions, compulsions, hang-ups or bad habits

☐Adversity and hardships are God's way of pruning off my dead branches and when I work through my pride I start to bear fruit

☐Adversity, brokenness, hardships and loss have lead me to the cross and I am grateful

☐If I remain contrite I won't become a shallow person

☐I'm not bored with my spiritual life

☐I stay humble and welcome feedback from others

☐I ask God to show me my heart

☐I honestly believe in my heart that apart from Jesus I can do nothing. I'm incomplete without the Trinity

☐I confess my weakness, bad habits and sin to God and others

☐I need the Holy Spirit to guide me through change, healing and growth

Reflection

1. After reading today's checklist I realize…
2. The key statements I need to remember and work on are…
3. What can I do to change the areas I need to work on?
4. What kind of support and accountability do I need?

5. The positive consequences of remembering and working on these statements are…

Keep in mind:

1. You need to accept God's help and power.
2. Find out why it's hard to receive help.
3. Apart from Christ you can do nothing.
4. Remember….you're a new person now…. God wants to change you from the inside out.
5. "We must be willing to let go of the life we have planned, so as to accept the life that is waiting for us." – Joseph Campbell
6. The Tao Te Ching says, when I let go of what I am, I become what I might be. When I let go of what I have, I receive what I need. Have you ever struggled to find work or love, only to find them after you have given up? This is the paradox of letting go. Let go, in order to achieve. Letting go is God's law." – Mary Manin Morrissey

Take action…

1. Look up the following passages and paraphrase each one.
   ☐ John 16:8-11; Acts 2:37; 1 Thess. 1:5; Rom. 8:12-13
   Gal. 5:16-17; Eph. 5:18; John 15:10; 1 John 2:2-6; 1 John 5:2-3
   Luke 6:12; Mark 1:35; Acts 4:13

DAY 343

PUTTING AWAY CHILDISH THINGS

"Therefore whoever hears these sayings of Mine, and does them, I will liken him to a wise man who built his house on the rock: and the rain descended, the floods came, and the winds blew and beat on that house; and it did not fall, for it was founded on the rock. Now everyone who hears these sayings of Mine, and does not do them, will be like a foolish man who built his house on the sand: and the rain descended, the floods came, and the winds blew and beat on that house; and it fell. And great was its fall." (Matthew 7:24-27)

I never had a policy; I have just tried to do my very best each and every day.
~Abraham Lincoln

BUILD YOUR CHARACTER

Dwight Eisenhower describes character with this quote, *"The qualities of a great man are vision, integrity, courage, understanding, the power of articulation, and profundity of character."* Is this how you would describe yourself?

We need to work hard at not allowing adversity to compromise our character. In fact, adversity is designed to make us fight even harder. See yourself as the comeback kid. Life provides us with many obstacles that we have to overcome in order to be successful. Recovery and sanctification require *ambition and drive.*

I really believe in this saying, "When the going gets tough, the tough get going." We can't quit every time something doesn't go our way. When the world says, "Give up," Hope whispers, "Try it one more time." (Author Unknown)

Learn to be ambitious and envision yourself succeeding at whatever you set your mind and heart to. Work hard and keep moving up. We need to keep looking for ways to improve our lives so we can benefit someone else. Let's make our presence known today. Let people hear your voice when you shout it out loud.

How would you describe your character? How would the people who know you best describe you? Ask them.

Keep in mind:

1. Blessed are those who hunger and thirst for righteousness, for they will be filled. (Matthew 5:6)

2. But seek first his kingdom and his righteousness, and all these things will be given to you as well. (Matthew 6:33)

3. Not only that, but we rejoice in our sufferings, knowing that suffering produces endurance, and endurance produces character, and character produces hope. (Romans 5:3-4)

Ephesians 5:26-27 - That he might sanctify and cleanse it with the washing of water by the word, that he might present it to himself, a glorious church, not having spot, or wrinkle, or any such thing; but that it should be holy and without blemish.

I wrote a resolution to give you an idea of what we need to do to build our character so we can be more Christ-like in any given situation. (Col. 2:6-7) I suggest that you write your own as well.

Resolution to be more Christ-Like:

I will take the time to open up to love. Cynicism and feeling that I'm smarter than anyone else will block my ability to feel and express love. Being aware of this when my buttons are pushed will help me to let go of this behavior. I will try to be less pessimistic and see the good in people's motives. I will still trust my gut.... but I will not automatically assume the worst.

My character is important. I will make sure that my actions line up with my words and that my words line up with my beliefs and values. Character is formed when I continuously practice my beliefs. Abraham Lincoln once said, "Character is like a tree and reputation like its shadow. The shadow is what we think of it; the tree is the real thing. I desire so to conduct the affairs of this administration that if at the end, when I come to lay down the reins of power, I have lost every other friend on earth, I shall at least have one friend left, and that friend shall be down inside me."

If our character isn't solid who will follow us? Who will listen to what we have to say?

Ask yourself:

1. Am I working on my character?
2. What qualities am I lacking? Patience, kindness, follow through, honesty, commitment, ownership, adaptable, assertive, active, accountable, service, etc.
3. Every personality has positive qualities ....what are mine and do I focus on them?
4. Review the fruit of the spirit and decide which fruit you lack the most. Make a plan to work on it.

Take Action…

1. Look up the following passages and paraphrase each one.
   - ☐ Psalm 1:1-3; Matt. 13:23; John 15:2-3; John 15:4-5; Rom. 7:4
     Luke 6:43-44; Col. 1:10; Col. 3:12-15; 2 Tim. 2:22;
     2 Peter 1:5-8; Titus 3:14; 1 John 3:18; Phil. 3:12-14; Col. 3:12
     2 Tim. 1:7; Heb. 5:14; Heb. 12:1

Consider this...

In order to build and/or rebuild our character to be more Christ-like (Ephesians 4:13-15) we need to:

1. Practice confession: Reveal you faults, bad parts and successes.
2. Ask for help and accountability.
3. Do the opposite of the character flaw or defect you're trying to change and overcome. For instance: if you tend to lie, practice honesty.
4. Walk in God's grace and forgiveness because we're not perfect.
5. Practice forgiveness. Seventy times seven.
6. Don't keep secrets, this only breeds shame.
7. Have a support team that you trust and will point you to God's truth and principles.
8. Manage your negative emotions. Grieve and mourn if you need to.
9. Keep expectations realistic.
10. Try to be idealistic but still strive for excellence in Christ.
11. See both the good and bad in situations.
12. Role model after Christ.
13. Practice prayer daily.
14. Read and mediate on God's word daily.

Reflection

1. After reading today's devotion, I realize...
2. The key statements I need to remember and work on are...
3. The positive consequences of remembering and working on these statements will be...

DAY 344-346

PUTTING AWAY CHILDISH THINGS

The whole earth will acknowledge the LORD and return to him.
All the families of the nations will bow down before him. For royal power
belongs to the LORD. He rules all the nations. Let the rich of the earth feast and
worship. Bow before him, all who are mortal, all whose lives will end as dust.
Our children will also serve him. Future generations will hear about the
wonders of the Lord. (Psalm 22:27-30)

REBUILDING YOUR LEGACY~ REBUILDING YOUR FAMILY

Today I want you to take a look at your family and see if it needs some healing. I made a checklist of beliefs, behaviors and actions that will bring about reconciliation to your family. Read through the checklist and check what you need to work on and are willing to do.

Checklist for rebuilding my family

In order to have a healthy family, with God's help I will.....

- ☐ Be honest about what I want to change about my family
- ☐ Be honest about what I would like see changed in a family member (attitudes and behaviors)
- ☐ Take responsibility for my part to make my family healthy
- ☐ Take responsibility for my part in making my family unhealthy – this means changing certain behaviors that create conflict and tension in the family
- ☐ Figure out what is creating the distance between myself and my family members
- ☐ Be honest about why I might be hurt, frustrated, or angry
- ☐ Talk about how I was offended
- ☐ Find ways to connect and bond
- ☐ Learn how to trust my family with my feelings, mistakes and choices (good or bad)
- ☐ Admit my shortcomings
- ☐ Admit when I'm wrong
- ☐ Communicate needs, wants, likes, dislikes, etc.
- ☐ Learn how not to isolate or withdraw
- ☐ Problem solve with my family
- ☐ Spend time with my family
- ☐ Communicate what I feel and think in a loving way to my family
- ☐ Identify my strengths and weaknesses as a parent or child

☐ Discuss with my family members why certain negative behaviors are occurring and see what I can do to help or change if I need to
☐ Be tender, gentle, and soft toward my family members
☐ Find a way to earn back trust
☐ Hug my family members more
☐ Be more affectionate
☐ Watch my tones and body language when communicating – checking for a harsh critical tone
☐ Ask how I might be hurting a family member

I will commit to do the following things this week to rebuild my family relationships:

-
-

Reshaping exercise…

Family Relationships: What do I want to change?

Family Traits

1. What trait(s) do you want to work on the most? Share your reasons.
2. What traits do you think you already have has a family?
3. What are you willing to do to make these family traits a reality?

Rebuilding Relationships…

Instructions: Put the family member's name below and work through the following sentence stems. Do your best to finish the stems 6-10 times.

Family Member_____

1. I want to change the following things about our relationship…
2. I like it when…
3. I don't like it when…
4. I feel closer to you when…
5. I need …
6. Can we…
7. I want you to work on…
8. When you talk to me sometimes I feel…
9. I am going to do the following things to make our relationship better:
10. I know I hurt you when…

11. How do I make you angry?

Take action...

    1. Look up the following passages and paraphrase each one.
        ☐ Deut. 6:6-7; Deut. 32:7; Psalm 22:30; Psalm 71:18
            Psalm 78:1-8; Psalm 79:13; Exod. 20:12; Deut. 5:16

Reflection

    1. After reading today's devotion, I realize...
    2. The key statements I need to remember and work on are...
    3. The positive consequences of remembering and working on these statements will be...

DAY 347-349

PUTTING AWAY CHILDISH THINGS

When I was a child, I talked like a child; I thought like a child, I reasoned like a child. When I became a man, I put the ways of childhood behind me. For now we see only a reflection as in a mirror; then we shall see face to face. Now I know in part; then I shall know fully, even as I am fully known. (1 Cor. 13:11-12)

AM I AN ADULT?

For the next several days we're going to spend some time defining adulthood and common signs of maturing in the Lord.

Today I want you to see if you need to rebuild your adulthood. There are many reasons why we can get stuck in childlike mentality as an adult. When God saved you, one of His goals was to heal those holes in your soul that occurred during your developmental stages.

Read through the list and check off what you think you currently need to work on.

Ask yourself...

Do you:

- ☐ Still need approval
- ☐ Avoid disapproval
- ☐ Fear rejection
- ☐ Lack self-confidence
- ☐ Feel guilty about your past
- ☐ Have a problem sharing your opinions and ideas
- ☐ Feel shame about your past
- ☐ Have a problem believing that you deserve good things in life
- ☐ Avoid conflict at all costs
- ☐ Have the need to please others
- ☐ Have a problem affirming or saying nice things to, or about, yourself
- ☐ Have a hard time receiving God's forgiveness for real or perceived faults, past failures & mistakes
- ☐ Have pent up anger and rage against people in your past
- ☐ Lack clear direction and clarity of goals for your life
- ☐ Have a problem with pessimism
- ☐ Fear failure
- ☐ Allow mom or others to treat you like a child
- ☐ Act like a child
  - 1. In what situations?

Take action…

1. Look up the following passages and paraphrase each one.
   - ☐ Col. 2:19; 1 Cor. 3:6-7; 2 Cor. 9:10; Phil. 1:6; Heb. 5:11-14

2. Refer back to sanctification and healthy self-image.

Reflection

1. After reading today's devotion, I realize…
2. The key statements I need to remember and work on are…
3. The positive consequences of remembering and working on these statements will be…

DAY 350-352

PUTTING AWAY CHILDISH THINGS

Be imitators of me, as I am of Christ. (1 Cor. 11:1)

When I was a child, I talked like a child; I thought like a child, I reasoned like a child. When I became a man, I put the ways of childhood behind me.
(1 Cor. 13:11)

CHARACTERISTICS OF ADULTHOOD AND MATURITY

God wants us to be childlike but He also wants us to be mature and to put away childish behaviors. Today I want you to see just how grown up you are. Read through the checklist I have provided below and check off what applies to you.

If you consider yourself to be an adult, it's likely that you're able to do the following:

- ☐ Realize that maturity is an ongoing process, not a state, and am continuously striving for self-improvement.
- ☐ Manage personal jealousy and feelings of envy.
- ☐ Have the ability to listen to and evaluate the viewpoints of others.
- ☐ Maintain patience and flexibility on a daily basis.
- ☐ Accept the fact that you can't always win, and learn from mistakes instead of whining about the outcome.
- ☐ Does not overanalyze negative points, but instead looks for the positive points in the subject being analyzed.
- ☐ You realize that everyone has negative thoughts sometimes, but you choose not to dwell on them.
- ☐ Able to differentiate between rational decision making and emotional impulse.
- ☐ You never give up on your dreams.
- ☐ Understand that no skill or talent can overshadow the act of preparation.
- ☐ Capable of managing temper and anger.
- ☐ Keep other people's feelings in mind and limit selfishness.
- ☐ Being able to distinguish between 'needs' and 'wants'.
- ☐ Show confidence without being overly arrogant.
- ☐ Handle pressure with losing self-composure.
- ☐ Realize that some good comes out of every bad situation.

- ☐ You realize that worrying and feeling sorry for yourself is just a waste of time.
- ☐ Take ownership and responsibility of personal actions.
- ☐ You don't take it personal when someone hurts you. You just smile and take better precautions to protect yourself next time.
- ☐ Manages personal fears.
- ☐ Able to see the various shades of grey between the extremes of black and white in every situation.
- ☐ You can say you're sorry, admit you're wrong, and move on.
- ☐ Forgive yourself
- ☐ Accept negative feedback as a tool for self-improvement.
- ☐ Aware of personal insecurities and self-esteem.
- ☐ You are aware of what drives you to do the things that you do.
- ☐ Able to separate true love from transitory infatuation.
- ☐ Understanding that open communication is the key to healthy relationships and progression.
- ☐ You listen to others and try to understand their side of the story.
- ☐ Make their own choices and decisions
- ☐ Learn how to agree to disagree to preserve relationships and unity.
- ☐ Master God-given skills, talents and abilities to serve God and others.

Take action...

1. Look up the following passages and paraphrase each one.
   - ☐ 1 Cor. 3:1-2; 1 Cor. 13:11; 1 Cor. 14:20; Heb. 5:12-14
     1 Peter 2:2; 2 Cor. 13:9; 1 Cor. 14:20; Rom. 12:1; Rom. 4:18-21;
     Luke 17:5; Heb. 10:22; Psalm 131:2; 1 Cor. 3:1-3; Heb. 5:12-6:1

Reflection

1. After reading today's devotion, I realize...
2. The key statements I need to remember and work on are...
3. The positive consequences of remembering and working on these statements are...

DAY 353-356

PUTTING AWAY CHILDISH THINGS

"In the future, when you experience all these blessings and curses I have listed for you, and when you are living among the nations to which the LORD your God has exiled you, take to heart all these instructions. (Deut. 30:1)

SIGNS OF ADULTHOOD AND MATURITY

Today we're going to explore our basic human rights. I believe that when we practice these rights it's a sign of adulthood and maturity. In order to develop the ability to apply these to our lives we need to know who we are in Christ, and we need to be abiding in Him.

Take some time to read through the list and check off what you struggle with. The attitudes and behaviors that you check off are the things you need to focus on. Explore the underlying beliefs and thoughts and make sure you line them up with God's Word. Try to figure out with whom and when you have a hard time applying these personal rights. Share your answers with God and your support team.

As a Child of God:

- ☐ I have a right to all those good times that I have longed for all these years and didn't get. (Jer. 29:11-14)

- ☐ I have a right to joy in this life, right here, right now — not just a momentary rush of euphoria but something more substantive. (Neh. 12:43; Job 8:21; Ecc. 2:26; Rom. 15:13; Ecc. 5:19-20; John 15:9-11; Psalm 126:2; Luke 6:21)

- ☐ I have a right to relax and have fun in a nonalcoholic and nondestructive way. (Matt. 6:25; Phil. 4:6; Mark 6:31; John 4:6; Gen. 2:2; Exod. 20:8-10; Psalm 23:2; Prov. 10:5)

- ☐ I have a right to actively pursue people, places, and situations that will help me in achieving a good life. (Eph. 4:16; Col. 2:6-7; Acts 15:32; 1 Cor. 10:16-17; Eph. 4:15-16; Eph. 5:29-30; Col. 3:15)

- ☐ I have the right to say no whenever I feel something is not safe, or I am not ready. (Matt. 5:37; Prov. 4:23; 1 Peter 2:11; Rom. 6:19)

- I have a right to not participate in either the active or passive "crazy-making" behavior of parents, of siblings, and of others. (1 Peter 5:8; 2 Peter 3:17; 2 Cor. 10:4; Psalm 1:1; John 1:1-2; 1 Tim. 1:9-11)

- I have a right to take calculated risks and to experiment with new strategies. (Psalm 18:30; 2 Tim. 3:10; Prov. 4:18; James 1:2-4; 1 Peter 4:17; 2 Cor. 4:7-9)

- I have a right to change my tune, my strategy, and my funny equations. (Prov. 3:5-6; Psalm 25:4-5; Jer. 18:5-10; Jer. 26:3; John 3:10)

- I have a right to "mess up"; to make mistakes, to "blow it", to disappoint myself, and to fall short of the mark. (Rom. 3:23; Rom. 8:1; Job 25:4; Jer. 17:9; John 3:19; Rom. 7:24; Rom. 5:12; Rom. 8:10)

- I have a right to leave the company of people who deliberately or inadvertently put me down, lay a guilt trip on me, manipulate or humiliate me, including my alcoholic parent, my nonalcoholic parent, or any other member of my family. (John 15:18-19; John 17:14; 1 John 3:13; Prov. 4:23; 1 Peter 2:11; Psalm 1:1; 1 Peter 1:23; 1 John 3:6; 1 John 5:18; Psalm 34:14; Isaiah 1:16-17)

- I have a right to put an end to conversations with people who make me feel put down and humiliated. (Prov. 4:23; Psalm 1:1; 1 John 2:6; Rom. 8:6; Prov. 17:14; Prov. 20:3; Prov. 26:17,21; Rom. 16:17; 2 Tim. 2:23)

- I have a right to all my feelings and the right to express all my feelings in a nondestructive way, and at a safe time and place. (Prov. 14:13; Prov. 25:28; Eph. 4:25-27; Eph. 5:18; Col. 3:8; 1 Tim. 2:8; James 1:19-20; Prov. 16:32; Titus 2:1-14)

- I have a right to develop myself as a whole person emotionally, spiritually, mentally, physically, and psychologically. (Ephesians 4:24; Rev. 2:17; Rom. 6:4; Col. 3:10; 1 Peter 1:3)

- I have a right to as much time as I need to experiment with this new information and these new ideas, and to initiate changes in my life. (Phil. 1:6; Col. 2:6-7; Heb. 12:2; Phil. 3:13-15; Gal. 3:3; Heb. 10:14)

- I have a right to sort out the bill of goods my parents sold me — to take the acceptable and dump the unacceptable. (Rom. 12:1-2; Rom. 5:12-19; Eph. 2:3; Col. 1:10; 1 Thess. 4:3-6; Heb. 6:1-3)

☐ I have a right to a mentally healthy, sane way of existence, though it will deviate in part, or in whole, from my parents' prescribed philosophy of life. (John 15:1-10; Exod. 32:29; 1 Chron. 29:5; Prov. 23:26; Rom. 12:1; Acts 15:5-11; Titus 2:11-14; James 4:8; 1 Peter 1:22; 1 John 3:3; Zec. 13:8-9)

☐ I have a right to carve out my place in this world. (Jer. 29:11; Psalm 33:11; Prov. 16:9; Prov. 20:24; Prov. 21:1; Gen. 18:19; Rom. 11:5; 1 Cor. 1:1; Eph. 1:4-5; 2 Thess. 2:13)

☐ I have a right to follow any of the above rights, to live my life the way I want to. (Deut. 11:26-27; Gen. 18:17; 2 Sam. 7:20-21; 1 Cor. 2:9-10; Eph. 1:9; Josh. 24:15; 1 Chron. 28:9; Jer. 26:3; Ezek. 18:21-23; Rom. 10:11; James 4:15; Psalm 40:8; Psalm 143:10; Matt. 6:10)

After reading this list, what do you need to work on? Make a list and start today. Once you are clear about your boundaries, you must educate people as to how to act in your presence. If you find yourself getting angry, irritated or sad when a boundary is crossed make sure you don't hold back your thoughts or feelings. You're only hurting yourself by causing emotional and physical stress. The more we hold in our emotions the farther we get from God and others.

Consider this ...

1. As an adult, or as we approach adulthood, we have the responsibility to make sure our beliefs line up with God's truth. Also, we need to make sure our beliefs and values are our own. For us to grow spiritually and become Christ-like we need to make sure we know why we believe what we believe and value what we value.
2. Adulthood and spiritual maturity go hand in hand. We need to develop our spiritual understanding (Col. 2:2) and grow in our discernment of God's will so we can behave accordingly (Col. 1:9-10).
3. As we grow in stature (Luke 2:39-52) like Jesus did, we need to learn how to stand up for our rights, have self-respect and love ourselves (Matt. 22:39). Make sure you stand up for your values, and if you don't agree, say so (Eph. 4:15; Prov. 27:17).
4. Don't idealize anyone. If you've put people on a pedestal in your mind, take them off.

Take action...

1. Look up the following passages and paraphrase each one.

☐Gal. 6:5; 1 Cor. 12:21; Ecc. 4:10; Luke 7:47; Phil. 4:19; Luke 11:9;
2 Cor. 10:5

Reflection

1. After reading today's devotion, I realize…
2. The key statements I need to remember and work on are…
3. The positive consequences of remembering and working on these
   statements are…

DAY 357-359

PUTTING AWAY CHILDISH THINGS

*But when He heard this, He said, "It is not those who are healthy who need a
physician, but those who are sick. But go and learn what this means, I desire
compassion, and not sacrifice, for I did not come to call the righteous but
sinners." (Matt. 9:12-13)*

ADULTS TELL GOD WHERE IT HURTS

I believe that as adults we need be able to tell God where it hurts. As an adult I
need to have the courage to be open to God and others about what I need or want.
Today, let's look at some practical ways we can go about doing this.

Openness…

1. When you go to a doctor you tell him or her where it hurts. The same
   is true with God. He wants to open your soul – mind, will and
   emotions – so that you can see the truth about your life. Remember,
   He's the great physician and He came to help the sick.

2. Your life will not change if you're not willing to face the truth and the
   origin of your immaturities, brokenness and bad habits.

Resurrected…

"…For you died to this life, and your real life is hidden with Christ in God."
(Col. 3:3)

1. When you died to your old life you became spiritually resurrected. At that very point of receiving Jesus, God started to show you the truth about Himself, others and yourself.

2. There's a movie called "Limitless" and it was about this pill that helps you to access your entire brain. Everything becomes clear when you take it. The same is true with God. When you received His son your life became clear. You start to see things as they really are and everything gradually starts to make sense. You see the truth about life and why you are the way you are. You received this supernatural power to do the impossible with God. He tells us in Matthew 19:26 - Jesus looked at them and said, "With man this is impossible, but with God all things are possible."

3. Be willing to face the truth about your choices and behaviors. God will show you the ways behind your actions. (1 Cor. 13:11)

4. Admit to un-manageability and behaviors and attitudes that make you feel powerless.

5. Researching the truth about your actions, choices and attitudes will heal your life. Healing will occur when you go under God's knife.

6. Your past influences what you do today, especially when you don't understand it. In Christ, your past doesn't determine your future if you allow Him to show you what you need to see to heal.

The Past...

It's an erroneous belief to think that God doesn't want us to address our past. So many people that I come across think this because of what Paul said in Phil. 3:13-14.

"No, dear brothers and sisters, I have not achieved it, but I focus on this one thing: Forgetting the past and looking forward to what lies ahead, [14] I press on to reach the end of the race and receive the heavenly prize for which God, through Christ Jesus, is calling us."

1. In these verses Paul was referring to giving up his performance based love and acceptance attitude and beliefs. He was tired of trying to earn his righteousness. Paul was making a confession and a resolution. He realized that his way wasn't working and he needed to live out his faith in a new way. Actually, this verse is a great example of how we need to

expose and confess our past behaviors and attitudes so we can be transformed.

2. Think about what you're hiding. What's in the dark? What's hurting inside that you're keeping to yourself? Are you hiding anything from God?

3. To live your new life in Christ you need to be willing to ask God to search your heart (Psalm 139:23), why? Because God can, and will, show you what's making you anxious, angry, depressed, ashamed, guilt ridden, resentful, and fearful. "For [as far as this world is concerned] you have died, and your [new, real] life is hidden with Christ in God (Col. 3:3). You need to understand and mourn these issues (Matt. 5:3) so you can understand why you feel these things so you can live your new life in Christ likeness.

Take action...

1. Look up the following passages and paraphrase each one.

☐Rom. 5:3-5; Heb. 2:10; James 1:3-4; 1 Peter 5:10; Gal. 5:22-23; Eph. 4:22-23; Phil. 1:9-11; 2 Thess. 1:3; Col. 2:2

Reflection

1. After reading today's devotion, I realize...
2. The key statements I need to remember and work on are...
3. The positive consequences of remembering and working on these statements are...

DAY 360-362

PUTTING AWAY CHILDISH THINGS

And without faith it is impossible to please him, for whoever would draw near to God must believe that he exists and that he rewards those who seek him.
(Heb. 11:6)

ADULTS CONNECT TO GOD

The mature thing to do is stay connected to God. He's our Father. He loves us. We can't let our childishness interfere with our relationship with God. When we were children we might have pouted or held our breath because we didn't get our way.

Today I want you to read a declaration of faith pertaining to staying connected to God. I strongly suggest you write your own.

Declaration of Faith...

I need to let God love every part of me so I'm letting go. I want to be the best I can be and I know without Him I can't. I'm going to make what's important to God, important to me, so I'm surrendering my values. My values are my compass and they give me direction. If my values aren't based on God's ways I will be derailed.

I'm a very passionate person and I want to learn how to let God in. He gave me my desires.... my ambitions. God is the author of Passion. If I love Him and surrender to Him my life will be what I want it to be. Ben Franklin once said, "If passion drives you, let reason hold the reins." I'm going to renew my passions everyday as I renew my commitment to God each day.

Loving God with my whole heart will not only bring me *love, peace and joy,* it will also bring me success and answers when I don't know what to do. I'm staying close to the one who sees the big picture of my life. I'm not going to wander away. I've done the lost sheep thing and the prodigal thing. I'm going to learn from my mistakes.

Ask yourself:

1. Does God have my values? Are they based on God's ways?
2. Do I follow my values consistently?
3. What am I passionate about and do I talk with God about it?
4. Am I learning from my mistakes? Which ones am I repeating?

Take action...

1. Look up the following passages and paraphrase each one.

☐Rom. 12:2; 1 Cor. 3:1-3; Gal. 5:22-23; Eph. 4:22-23; Phil. 1:9-11;
2 Thess. 1:3; Matt. 6:33; Luke 12:31; Prov. 28:5; Dan. 2:17-23;
Psalm 119:20; Isaiah 26:9

Keep in mind…

God wants us to communicate with Him on a regular basis through prayer. As adults we see the importance of prayer. I want you to take a look at how you apply this spiritual discipline in your daily life so I provided a checklist for you to review.

PRAYER

"Be earnest and unwearied and steadfast in your prayer [life], being [both] alert and intent in [your praying] with thanksgiving." (Col. 4:2)

Instructions: Check off the statements that you can truly agree with. Complete the reflection questions after each section.

☐I pray for strength and guidance
☐I pray for adoration
☐I pray to confess
☐I pray to feel close to God
☐I pray to seek God's will
☐I pray daily
☐I don't pray enough
☐I pray to worship
☐I pray to supplicate
☐I pray often for others
☐I believe prayer changes things
☐Prayer is how I connect to God
☐I pray to offer thanksgiving
☐I share my gratitude through prayer
☐I'm humble when I pray
☐I share my needs, thoughts and feelings with God when I pray
☐I ask the Holy Spirit to lead me in prayer
☐I pray through tough times
☐My life has changed because of prayer
☐I understand the principles of prayer
☐I believe prayer brings forth healing
☐I pray the scriptures and God's promises
☐I pray for specific things

☐God says yes, no, and wait

☐I need prayer to make needed changes in my life

☐I need prayer to be Christ-like

☐Prayer brings me peace of mind and renews my mind

☐Prayer brings me joy and happiness

☐I attend prayer meetings regularly

☐I see God answering my prayers

☐I keep a prayer journal

☐My prayers are like the Lord's Prayer

Reflection

1. After reading today's checklist I realize…
2. The key statements I need to remember and work on are…
3. What can I do to change the areas I need to work on?
4. What kind of support and accountability do I need?
5. The positive consequences of remembering and working on these statements are…

Prayer:

1. Father help, me to.....

DAY 363

PUTTING AWAY CHILDISH THINGS

"Therefore, as God's chosen people, holy and dearly loved, clothe yourselves with compassion, kindness, humility, gentleness and patience." (Colossians 3:12)

ADULTS UNDERSTAND THE IMPORTANCE OF STAYING HUMBLE

Just for Today… I will keep my mind and heart open to learn from God and other people. If I make a mistake I will admit it and learn from it. If I need help or guidance I will ask for it. I will pray and lean on my support.

Humility... is at the heart of recovery and sanctification, without it you can't grow, heal or change. God wants His children to realize that their life was originally designed to be lived out through Him, not apart from Him (John 15).

Humility (is)...

      a. Essential to staying sober minded
      b. Needed to look realistically at the damage your addiction(s), bad habits and character defects have caused
      c. Allows you to look honestly at the problems you have and the concerns of others so you can take ownership and responsibility for your life. You no longer think you're right and they're wrong. You become open minded.
      d. The path to healing and change
      e. Breaks down denial and defenses that keep you sick and stuck
      f. What frees you from your sick secrets that keep you wrapped in shame and guilt.
      g. Admitting defeat
      h. Opens the door to all your core issues under the addiction and compulsions.
      i. Begins your transition into recovery and healing
      j. God's remedy to relapse and backsliding

Daily disciplines and practices of humble people...

      1. They ask for help
      2. They seek wisdom from people who are wiser and more experienced in recovery and their walk with God
      3. They seek answers and solutions to their problems
      4. The say "I don't know" without feeling inadequate
      5. They manage their emotions
      6. They are honest with themselves about their needs, ideas, feelings, wants and fears
      7. They admit brokenness and sin
      8. They make a right estimate of one's self ~ Charles Haddon Spurgeon
      9. Confess that they are in a season of famine or drought and
                  o Practice -James 5:16
                  o Practice -Deut. 32:1-2
                  o Practice -Psalm 1:2-3

Keep in mind:

      1. The only humility that is really ours is not that which we try to show before God in prayer, but that which we carry with us in our daily conduct. –Andrew Murray

2. Humility is the only true wisdom by which we prepare our minds for all the possible changes of life. –George Arliss

3. Humble yourselves before the Lord, and he will lift you up. (James 4:10)

4. All of you, clothe yourselves with humility toward one another, because, God opposes the proud, but gives grace to the humble. (1 Peter 5:5)

5. For everyone who exalts himself will be humbled, and he who humbles himself will be exalted. (Luke 14:11)

6. Humility and the fear of the LORD bring wealth and honor and life. (Proverbs 22:4)

Resolution…

- I will practice humility each and every day.

Reflection

1. After reading today's devotion, I realize…
2. The key statements I need to remember and work on are…
3. The positive consequences of remembering and working on these statements will be…

DAY 364

PUTTING AWAY CHILDISH THINGS

"A man should never be ashamed to own he has been in the wrong, which is but saying, in other words, that he is wiser today than he was yesterday."

~ Alexander Pope

Many plans are in a man's mind, but it is the Lord's purpose for him that will stand. (Proverbs 19:21)

CARRY ON

Q: What's your first reaction when things don't go the way you planned?

When things go wrong our first reaction or instinct is to blame our problems on someone or something. A lot of people spend more time placing the blame than rectifying the problem. Elmer Letterman said, "A man may fail many times but he won't be a failure until he says, someone pushed him."

Blame originated in the Garden of Eden. (Gen. 3:12) Like Jon said, "We all have the blood of Eden running through our veins." I think we're a lot like Adam and Eve. His first response to God was "It's your fault God; it was the woman you gave me." Then God confronted Eve and her response was "The Serpent deceived me." This is a classic example of blame shifting and it's still occurring thousands of years later. The point I want to make here is that we are accountable for our actions and problems, even if it's not your problem. We are responsible for our reactions and responses.

Remember, when you point the finger at someone, you have three more pointing back at you. I realize that blaming gets the problem off our shoulders, but how will our problems get resolved? How will our character grow? I think of Tommy when he got laid off. I'm sure he was upset for a while but eventually he and Gina took responsibility.

I want you to remember when things don't go your way, or you make a mistake, you need to draw near to God and the people you love and trust. When and if adversity occurs, always remember that God has your back. Take time to think about all the times God has provided for you.

Here's a list of attitudes and actions we can take when things don't go our way:

1. Take responsibility and ownership for the situation and problem. If you failed own it, don't hide it. If life sends you on a detour, own it and find your way out.

2. Stop expecting life to be fair, because it's not.

3. Face the situation and work hard at finding a solution. Work through the pain and own your part in the situation. Don't wait for others to fix you.

4. Realize that diversion prolongs our dreams and goals, as well as depletes our faith and confidence.

5. Henry Cloud and John Townsend once said, "Blame is comfort food for the soul."

a. People are always blaming their circumstances for what they are. I don't believe in circumstances. The people who get on in this world are the people who get up and look for the circumstances they want, and, if they can't find them, make them. (George Bernard Shaw)

6. See the opportunity to do something new

7. Stop complaining, there's a purpose for everything. Seek solutions.

8. Remember, trials are but lessons that you failed to learn, presented once again. So, where you made a faulty choice before, you can now make a better one, and thus escape all pain that what you chose before has brought to you (A Course in Miracles).

9. Always admit your wrongs

10. Take a look at how pride and blame are affecting your life. Do you like the results?

11. Stop blaming:
   a. The devil
   b. Your childhood
   c. God
   d. Your parents
   e. The economy
   f. The environment
   g. DNA

12. Difficulties are opportunities to better things; they are stepping stones to greater experiences. Perhaps someday you will be thankful for some temporary failure in a particular direction. "When one door closes, another always opens, as a natural law it has to be, to balance." (Bryan Adams)

Take action...

1. Look up the following passages and paraphrase each one.

   □Num. 23:19; 1 Sam. 15:29; Prov. 19:21; Jer. 44:29; Heb. 7:21; Psalm 110:4; Psalm 119:89; Matt. 5:18; 1 Peter 1:23-25; Psalm 33:11; 1 Cor. 15:58; Phil. 1:27; Rom. 8:37

Reflection

1. After reading today's devotion, I realize...

2. The key statements I need to remember and work on are...

3. The positive consequences of remembering and working on these statements are...

DAY 365

PUTTING AWAY CHILDISH THINGS

You know that only one person gets a crown for being in a race even if many people run. You must run so you will win the crown. Everyone who runs in a race does many things so his body will be strong. He does it to get a crown that will soon be worth nothing, but we work for a crown that will last forever. In the same way, I run straight for the place at the end of the race. I fight to win. I do not beat the air. I keep working over my body. I make it obey me. I do this because I am afraid that after I have preached the Good News to others, I myself might be put aside. (1 Cor. 9:24-27)

THE COURAGE TO ... KEEP TRYING

Just for today…..

Fight for what you want and don't give up. While God works in the background, keep your confidence. God tells us that our confidence in Him will be richly rewarded and that when I do His will I will receive what He has promised. (Hebrews 10:35-36) Remember, what you do today determines your tomorrow.

Happiness is a choice…

Your happiness isn't based on the circumstance it's based on what God can do. Happiness is an inside job and you need to do your part. Your relationship with God is collaborative. Pick up your cross or mat and move toward Jesus. Focus on the good things you have. (Phil. 4:8)

Be a winner…

Put on God's armor. You're in a spiritual battle every day. (Eph. 6:12) Satan doesn't rest. Each day, from the time you wake up, he will try to discourage and discredit you so God looks bad. He's the one who whispers "Quit" or "Give up." Rebuke those lies and keep running straight for the prize. When you abide in Christ He will bless you with what you need to succeed.

Keep your faith...

"Listen to and obey all the Laws I am telling you today. Love the Lord your God. Work for Him with all your heart and soul." (Deut. 11:13). So if you do this God will give the rain for your land at the right times, the early and late rain. So you may gather in your grain, your new wine and your oil. He will give grass in your fields for your cattle. And you will eat and be filled.

Take action...

1. Look up the following passages and paraphrase each one
   Deut. 11: 14-16; Matt. 5:6; Phil. 3:13-14; 2 Tim. 4:8; Heb. 10:35-36; Heb. 11:26; Col. 2:2; Psalm 119:35; Psalm 16:11; Matt. 5:3-10; 1 Peter 3:14: James 1:1-4

Reflection

1. After reading today's devotion, I realize…
2. The key statements I need to remember and work on are…
3. The positive consequences of remembering and working on these statements are…

REVIEW & REPAIR

Reshaping Your Soul

1. What did I learn this past month about myself, God and others?

2. What concepts or ideas stood out to me in the devotions? Why?

3. What adjustments do I need to make in my life?

4. What needs to change, if anything, about how I think, feel and act?

5. What changes have I made so far? What actions have I taken?

6. How are people reacting to my changes?

7. Steps I will continue to take are…

8. I'm committed to…

9. My victories this week were…

10. God please help me with…

SUMMARY OF VOLUME 1

Volume 1 laid the foundation for what you needed to do to work through God's sanctification process. For 243 days I focused on helping you identify and work through any distortions of God you might have had as a result of your childhood and poor teaching. I also taught you how to surrender to God and how to allow the Holy Spirit to help you live according to God's will and purpose. You learned how to put away childish things (1 Cor. 13:11) and how to identify your obstacles to spiritual and emotional maturity (sanctification- working out your salvation). You identified the inner conflict that prevents you from becoming the person God has designed you to be and the lies you believed that kept you stuck, and how to replace them with God's truth.

I spent several weeks on teaching and helping you to clarify and understand your identity and position in Christ. We also spent several days uncovering Satan's lies and how he distracts you from God's truth by finding a way to get you off God's Potter's wheel.

By addressing the importance of facing the truth you discovered how to change Biblically and how to receive the help you need to relinquish certain sins, bad habits, brokenness and immaturities so you can renew your mind. You explored and worked through the fears that kept you from healing and working out your salvation.

Finally, we spent 122 days addressing how God uses the sanctification process to develop our character, to heal childhood wounds and losses we incurred along the way. You did an extensive review of your life which helped you to connect with your immaturities, habitual sins, bad habits, brokenness and character issues, as well as identify things attributed to generational habits, generational curses and family upbringing.

VOLUME 2

INTRODUCTION

Volume 2 will pick up right where Volume 1 left off. Using the same format God's Healing Hand's Volume 2 will:

- Teach you how to manage damaged emotions by exploring the flawed beliefs behind them.
- Teach Christians (new or old) who struggle with habitual sin, bad habits, addictions /addictive behaviors how to live out their new life in Christ.
- Teach Christians how to have a Christ-like character
- Provide practical ways to live out the "New Life" in Christ.
- Teach Christians how to develop self-control so that they can face life's toughest challenges and to find hope in God.
- Teach Christian's how to live within God's economy, design and system of life and relationships.
- Help Christians see where they're heading in their new life
- Show Christians how and why they might stray away from God and their new life.
- Help Christians build healthy habits.
- Help Christians to see what they want out of their new life with Christ
- Help Christians see what they want and need to change and improve about their life and relationships.
- Help Christians to work through faulty beliefs that keep them stuck in habitual sin and immature behaviors and attitudes that prevent them from living up to their full potential.
- Teach Christians how to take responsibility and ownership of their soul: thoughts (beliefs), choices, feelings, values, behaviors, desires, attitudes and limits.

In Closing...

My hope and prayer is the same. Allow the Holy Spirit to free you from a broken heart and an under developed character so that you will receive a deep healing from the inside out so you can live a Victorious Christian Life. Stay on the potter's wheel no matter how hard life gets, and always remember, God is *reshaping you. Till the day you go home to be with Jesus.*

Made in the USA
Columbia, SC
08 July 2020